Jonathan and **Angela Scott** are award-winning authors and internationally renowned photographers based in Kenya. They have written and illustrated twenty-six books, including *Big Cat Diary,* based on their hugely popular BBC series. They are the only couple to have individually won the prestigious Wildlife Photographer of the Year Competition, Jonathan in 1987 and Angela in 2002. They divide their time between their beautiful home in a leafy suburb of Nairobi—with giraffes as their neighbours—and a cottage at Governers' Camp overlooking the wildlife-speckled plains of the Masai Mara. They can be found online at www.jonathanangelascott.com

Praise

'Jonathan Scott understands the animals he photographs so well that it is as though he has entered their minds and can see the world as they do.'

—David Attenborough

'Written with such heartfelt passion and intimate knowledge, and illustrated with some of the most evocative photographs of big cats ever taken, this is one of the greatest natural history books ever published. Jonathan and Angie know the Masai Mara's loveable leopards better than anyone else on the planet and, in this welcome new edition [...] bring their remarkable story up to date. Brilliant stuff.'

—Mark Carawadine, co-author of *Last Chance to See*

'Great naturalists are rare, but when they are superb storytellers and exceptional photographers they are unique... Jonathan and Angie Scott prove their extraordinary mettle here with an astonishing and tender tale.'

—Chris Packham

The Leopard's Tale

Jonathan and Angela Scott

SPEAKING TIGER

Speaking Tiger Publishing Pvt. Ltd
4381/4, Ansari Road, Daryaganj,
New Delhi 110002, India

First published in the UK by Elm Tree Books 1985
This edition first published by Bradt Travel Guides Ltd 2013
First published in India by Speaking Tiger 2017

Map by Trevor Vincent, adapted by David McCuthcheonFBCart.S

ISBN: 978-93-86702-25-8
eISBN:978-93-86702-26-5

For sale in South Asia only.

Typeset by

Printed at Thomson Press India Ltd.

Contents

'Now you *are* a beauty!' said the Ethiopian.

'You can lie out on the bare ground and look like a heap of pebbles. You can lie out on the naked rocks and look like a piece of pudding-stone. You can lie out on a leafy branch and look like sunshine sifting through the leaves; and you can lie right across the centre of a path and look like nothing in particular. Think of that and purr!'

RUDYARD KIPLING
How the Leopard got his Spots

Foreword

by Simon King

FEW CREATURES on earth can boast the charisma of the leopard. Whilst lions laze in the shade of a sprawling acacia, and cheetahs skip and cut blistering trails across open country, leopards watch, wait, drift and slip on the fringe of our consciousness. They have been referred to as a darkness in the grass, a shadow, a ghost. These evocative descriptions only hint at the astonishing capacity for the leopard to remain invisible, making it one of the most sought after and least seen features on the agenda of any African safari.

It takes remarkable people, with empathy, tenacity, patience, knowledge and, above all, a love for the subject, to consider producing a book about these capricious cats, and Jonathan and Angela Scott are just such beings. I have the good fortune to consider both my friends and we have spent many months together in the Masai Mara during the production of *Big Cat Diary*, and many hours together discussing the meaning of life over a glass of wine or three. To tackle a subject as elusive as the leopard also requires a dogged perseverance and the sanguinity to accommodate many hundreds of hours spent in fruitless waiting. Under such circumstances, a sense of humour must be coupled with a core of calm and these qualities abound in the authors of this book.

It is one thing to write about ghosts, quite another to capture images of them. And what images. Pouring over the stunning photographs held within these pages, one could be forgiven for thinking that these cats are easy to see. Such moments of intimacy, drama and beauty abound. These are the fruits of a labour that has drawn blood, mctaphorically and sometimes literally!

Only after many years of study, missed opportunity and sacrifice could such an astonishing gallery be collated.

But perhaps the single most engaging feature of this account of the most elusive of all big cats, is not its revelation of behaviour but rather that it is a story of individuals, of characters that fill out their two-dimensional fact sheets with feeling, hardship and achievement. Both Jonathan and Angie are as interested in the fortunes of the dynasty of cats that they have followed for so many years as they are in the conservation and future of the species as a whole and this empathy shines through their work. As you journey with them through their words and pictures you will be sharing a unique relationship between human beings and wild creatures. From the fortunes of Chui and Half-Tail to Zawadi and Bella, the real-life drama plays out with more danger, joy and hardship than any soap opera, and with far more gravitas for being true.

One word of warning, though; do not expect a trip to Kenya, or any other region where leopards still slink through the shadows, to offer up the same exposure to these glorious predators as you will witness within these pages. They are still the darkness in the grass, the eyes that watch you go by but remain for the most part unseen. Unless of course you are prepared to spend the next thirty years of your life setting about unravelling their secrets!

Preface to the 2013 Edition

SO HOW fares the leopard in 2013? Since I wrote *The Leopard's Tale* thirty years ago circumstances have deteriorated for big cats around the world. Tigers now number just a few thousand, due to the devastating effects of the trade in skins and body parts for Chinese traditional medicine. In Africa the lion is under intense pressure outside National Parks and Game Reserves as the scramble for land and resources intensifies. In a recent report, the African Lion Working Group warned that only '30,000 African lions remain in the wild, inhabiting less than 20 per cent of their former range'. They noted that the lions' survival 'is threatened primarily by conflict with people over depredation on livestock, bushmeat snaring, and the loss of prey and habitat.' Concerns persist about the thorny issue of trophy hunting, which has long been defended as a way of conserving large tracts of wild land where photographic tourism isn't viable and other sources of income for local communities are meagre. Distasteful as many of us find the idea of killing big cats for 'sport', there is a strong argument for science-based reform of trophy hunting to ensure that appropriate and sustainable quotas are set and implemented rather than trying to impose bans and trade restrictions.

Such issues are relevant to the leopard, too. Export of leopard skins and hunting trophies is currently permitted from thirteen African countries by the Convention on International Trade in Endangered Species (CITES). Tighter controls are needed to ensure that sustainable hunting quotas are set and abided by; that only older males are shot; and that female leopards are never hunted.

Though leopards across the world belong to one species, they show sufficient genetic variation for at least nine subspecies to be recognised. All

African leopards belong to the subspecies *Panthera pardus pardus*, with the other eight found in different parts of Asia. Some of these subspecies are highly endangered, such as the Amur leopard with just thirty to forty known individuals and the Arabian leopard with a population of less than 200.

The leopard is smaller, more adaptable and more elusive than its larger relatives and has proved itself capable of surviving in close proximity to humans. It has by far the greatest range of any of the world's big cats and is still locally common in parts of Africa and tropical Asia. But this is no reason for complacency. Despite their secretive habits leopards are easy to poison and trap and in some areas have been over-hunted as trophies. Leopard skins are still worn as adornments in traditional ceremonies and body parts are much sought after for use in traditional medicine in parts of Africa and beyond. Not surprisingly the leopard has disappeared from almost 40 per cent of its historic range. The IUCN Red List currently classifies it as Near Threatened and warns that it may soon warrant listing as Vulnerable, as was the case during the height of the trade in spotted skins in the 1960s and '70s when it was fashionable to wear a leopardskin coat. Nobody is sure how many leopards still prowl sub-Saharan Africa's forests and mountain ranges. But we do know that a report published in 1988 estimating 700,000 African leopards is as 'impossibly optimistic' now as it was then.

Today the Mara is one of the best places in the world to see a wild leopard and, while the sight of 'the spotted one' still evokes gasps of wonder and excitement from visitors, thankfully the general standard of behaviour around predators is better than when I first set out to watch leopards in the 1970s. Kenya now has a Professional Guides Association, and driver training is an established part of the operation of many of the camps and lodges. Visitors too are better informed about animal behaviour and the natural world, thanks to the deluge of wildlife programmes such as David Attenborough's many marvellous blue-chip series – and *Big Cat Diary*.

On our travels around the world Angie and I have come to realise that if conservation is to work it must embrace all interested parties. A good example of the way the tourist industry can do this is seen at Mfuwe Lodge, owned by the Bushcamp Company in the South Luangwa National Park in Zambia, where we host a safari each November. Every visitor wants to see leopards, but there is much else besides to enjoy and the guides make sure guests embrace the whole experience. The guides at Mfuwe are highly trained and motivated – they love their work and are proud of their status as some of the best in the business. Mfuwe works closely with the South Luangwa Conservation Society, a community-based project that does a sterling job with its anti-poaching and de-snaring programmes. It supports the scientists from the Zambian Carnivore Program, who monitor the lion, leopard, cheetah, hyena and wild dog populations across the country. Mfuwe also supports local schools and offers bursaries, along with the local textile and handicraft industry, through visits for their guests. This all-embracing approach builds capacity and encourages local communities to have a positive attitude towards both National Parks and the tourism industry.

We have also recently initiated a project called Leopard Guardians with conservation partners at the John Keells Group in Sri Lanka. The aim is to support leopard conservation through good tourism practice, including the initiation of drivers' training programmes, the collection of baseline scientific data, using camera traps to help identify individual leopards and their range, and working with local communities bordering the Park to provide them with predator-proof pens to help eradicate livestock losses.

The leopard has always been a special creature for Angie and me. If this extraordinarily beautiful and enigmatic big cat is to survive we have to be constantly vigilant on its behalf. Otherwise the leopard, along with the tiger and the lion, will slip into the recesses of our imagination forever.

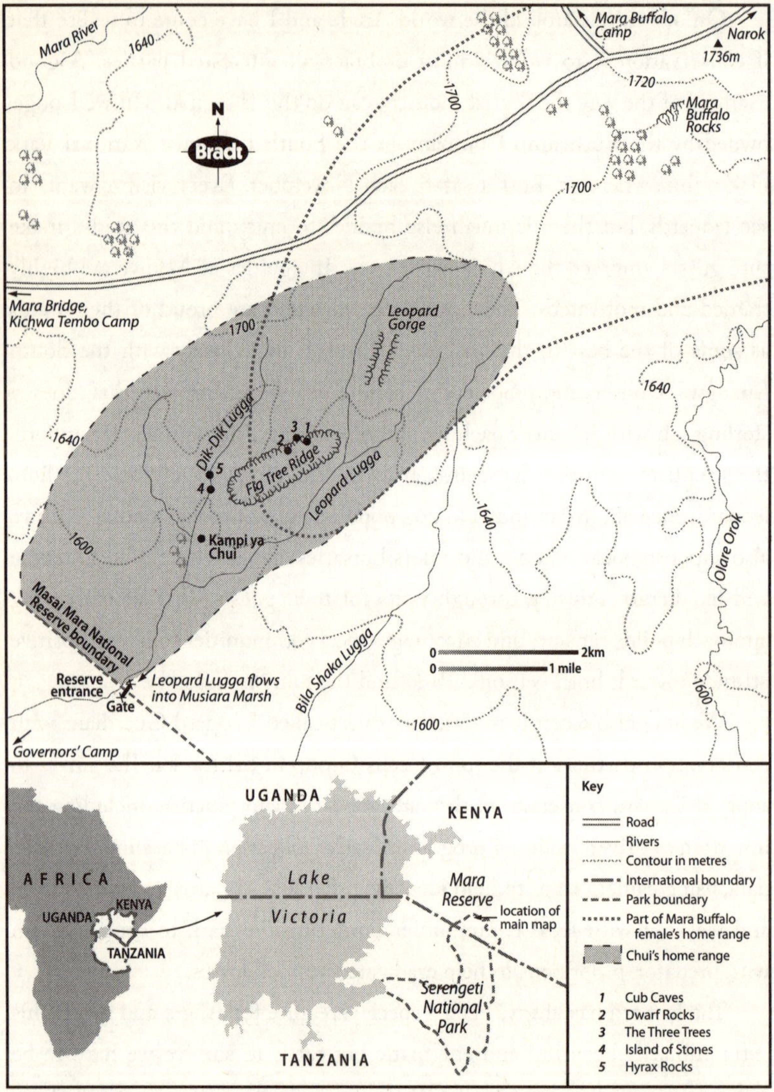
Mara River
1640
Mara Buffalo Camp
Narok
1736m
1720
1700
Mara Buffalo Rocks
N
Bradt
1700
Mara Bridge, Kichwa Tembo Camp
1700
Leopard Gorge
1640
Dik-Dik Lugga
1640
Fig Tree Ridge
Leopard Lugga
1640
Kampi ya Chui
1600
Masai Mara National Reserve boundary
Olare Orok
Bila Shaka Lugga
0 2km
0 1 mile
Reserve entrance
Gate
Leopard Lugga flows into Musiara Marsh
1600
1600
Governors' Camp
UGANDA
KENYA
AFRICA
KENYA
UGANDA
TANZANIA
Lake Victoria
Mara Reserve
location of main map
Serengeti National Park
TANZANIA
Key
Road
Rivers
Contour in metres
International boundary
Park boundary
Part of Mara Buffalo female's home range
Chui's home range
1 Cub Caves
2 Dwarf Rocks
3 The Three Trees
4 Island of Stones
5 Hyrax Rocks

Introduction

EVEN BEFORE I first set foot in Africa ten years ago, I knew which of the wild animals I most wanted to see. It was the leopard that embodied my idea of Africa: an animal of supreme grace and agility, a hunter of the dark concealed in a spotted coat.

When I was a small child on a Berkshire farm, the annual visit to Regent's Park Zoo was the highlight of my year. I still remember standing spellbound in front of a barren enclosure as a huge male leopard padded up and down. Occasionally it would pause and stare at me through pale green eyes before setting off again on its endless journey. Surely this must be 'the cat that walked by himself', I thought, equally convinced that Rudyard Kipling really did know the secret of 'How the Leopard got his spots'. But I knew if I wanted to learn more about that leopard, then I would have to journey to Africa.

I saw my first wild leopard in Tanzania's famous Serengeti National Park in 1975, while travelling overland from England. Four months later, I was still desperate for the chance to share more of Africa's beauty, and in particular the spectacular wildlife of East Africa. An onward boat ticket from Cape Town to Australia now seemed of little importance. Nothing figured in my plans but a life in the bush. How, I wondered, had it taken me so long to discover Africa!

After two years working among the wildlife of Botswana I returned to East Africa. Once more the Serengeti provided me with a brief glimpse of the elusive leopard as I continued across the Tanzanian border into Kenya's Masai Mara National Reserve.

The Mara is the jewel among Kenya's Parks and Reserves, a predator's paradise, renowned for its magnificent lions. There was even a time when it could boast the most visible leopard population in the whole of Kenya. But by the time I went to live at Mara River Camp in January 1977 to collect material for my work as a wildlife illustrator, leopard numbers had been drastically reduced. Even when a leopard was seen it invariably raced for cover, a jumble of spots vanishing into the long grass. And with good reason. Leopards were being poisoned, trapped and shot both inside and outside of the Reserve: shot and trapped by poachers for the price of their skins; shot by professional hunters as trophies; and poisoned by Masai herdsmen who were putting down meat laced with cattle-dip to rid the vicinity of their cattle bomas of predators and, latterly, to share in the financial rewards of poaching.

Ironically, the scarcer leopards became, the more visitors clamoured to see them. As well as being an animal of unquestioned beauty, the leopard is the most secretive of Africa's large carnivores. In consequence it became the icing on the safari cake, the most sought after and difficult to find of Africa's 'Big Five' game animals. The other four members of that illustrious club, the elephant, rhino, buffalo and lion, could all be guaranteed to a visitor on safari in the Mara, yet the mere mention of the word leopard sent the drivers and tour guides scuttling for cover.

The Masai Mara is the only one of Kenya's Parks and Reserves where you may drive 'off the road', free to create your own path through the bush and to explore wherever you desire. But this privilege extracts a price. When it is dry the Mara's gently undulating landscape is one of the easiest places in East Africa to drive across country, yet a single heavy downpour can turn the rutted tracks into a nightmare of slippery black-cotton soil that clings to tyres and obliterates even the heaviest of tread. Prolonged rain renders large portions of the Reserve impassable. Low-lying areas turn into shallow lakes, and intermittent watercourses or luggas swell with flood water, necessitating lengthy detours. Consequently the area is a maze of tracks that change from year to year.

Unfortunately my enthusiasm to explore this new world, together with my faith in four-wheel-drive vehicles, combined forcefully to keep me in constant trouble. I spent long hours learning about the underside of Jock Anderson's vehicle as I vainly attempted to extract myself from marsh or lugga, cursing my poor judgement and bracing myself for the inevitable embarrassment of being found hopelessly stranded.

Fortunately I had been entrusted to the care of Joseph Rotich, an enormously wise and kind guide of the Kipsigis tribe, who knew more about the ways of the Mara than anybody else I had met. It was he who invariably located my whereabouts, even though I sometimes managed to lose myself in the most unlikely places. He would arrive with a wry grin on his handsome face, wagging a finger and shaking his head in disbelief at my latest misadventure, yet far too much of a gentleman to berate me for my stupidity. Eventually, after many mishaps and considerable structural damage to the vehicle, I learned where and when one could safely cross that particular patch of black-cotton soil or ford a slippery lugga. Yet to this day, the Mara still has tricks to play on the unwary!

I soon realised that Joseph knew more than just the secret of circumventing a sticky patch of marsh, for Joseph, it transpired, was known to the other drivers as 'Bwana Chui': Mr Leopard. To me Joseph was, by now, 'Bwana Everything', seemingly able to locate lion kills, cheetahs and rhinos at will. Drivers from the other camps often went out of their way to find Joseph, always stopping him to ask if he had seen something unusual, and invariably he had. But Joseph's speciality was leopards. When I mentioned the dreaded word he smiled. 'Leopards are very difficult,' he replied. 'Experience and knowledge of an animal's habits count for everything, and you have very little of either. Be patient.'

Mercifully for leopard enthusiasts, they do leave unintentional clues to their whereabouts: a kill draped in the upper reaches of a tree, scratch marks clawed into bark and, if you are very lucky, the telltale sight of a spotted tail dangling invitingly among the foliage. But according to Joseph's wise counsel there is nothing quite like finding and watching leopards to impart experience, and for the first few months I managed very little of either.

Then one day Joseph took me to Leopard Gorge. I had heard tour drivers talk about this place and when I spoke of it to Joseph he promised to show me how to get there. It was, he said, where he always took visitors if they were anxious to see a leopard. The very thought that there was a particular place named for leopards, a place they were known to frequent, filled me with fresh enthusiasm. Joseph told me that up until 1973 he had often found leopards there, but that in recent years they had become very scarce. The reason he still visited the Gorge so regularly, he explained, was that if ever an area looked like home for a leopard it was Leopard Gorge, and that in itself seemed to make people feel better, even if they did not see one!

Once I had learned the way to the Gorge, barely a day passed without my paying it a visit. Yet try as I might I never saw a leopard's footprint, not even a glimmer of a long white whisker, or a fresh kill, let alone a real live leopard.

Reluctantly I was forced to accept that the returns from leopard spotting were meagre indeed. By now there were few individuals to be seen in the northern Mara and those that had survived adopted the most nocturnal of habits and knew how to conceal themselves from prying eyes. For the time being the leopard became a creature ascribed to luck, 'Shauri ya Mungu', as Joseph would say, the business of God.

When Tanzania decided to close its border with Kenya in February 1977 it was a mixed blessing for Kenya's tourist industry. Nairobi-based safari operators were no longer permitted to send their clients direct by road or air to Tanzania's famous Parks and Reserves, featuring Lake Manyara, Ngorongoro Crater and the Serengeti. Instead Kenya was forced to concentrate on developing its own wildlife resources.

Kenya's Masai Mara and Tanzania's Serengeti are one and the same: part of a vast ecosystem, covering an area of 9,600 square miles and containing the largest herds of grazing mammals in the world. Prior to the border closure the Mara had been little more than an overnight stop for tourists returning to Kenya from the Serengeti, just as it had been for me in 1975. But when Tanzania shut the door on Kenya's tourist industry, the Mara began to assume an importance that had previously only been hinted at.

In August and September each year the annual wildebeest and zebra migration arriving from the Serengeti plunges back and forth across the Mara River in a wave of spectacular crossings. This, together with the magnificent black-maned lions and an abundance of other predators, ensured that the Masai Mara finally received recognition as the finest 700 square miles of game country in the whole of Kenya.

In May 1977 the Kenya government announced a nationwide ban on the hunting of all wildlife, ending a system that had brought itself into disrepute. Sport hunting, like poaching, was by then completely out of hand. By the end of the year the government had made another historic decision, prohibiting the sale of wildlife products in curio shops, and giving their proprietors three months to dispose of existing stocks. These timely decisions would mean the difference between life and death for some of the Mara's leopards.

To the north of the Reserve those safari camps which had previously catered for the clients of professional hunters now expanded to accommodate the influx of tourists who could no longer visit Tanzania. With the proliferation of tented accommodation on Masai-owned land around the periphery of the Reserve, and the expansion of Governors' Camp within it, vehicles now crisscrossed every inch of game country in their search for animals. The narrow trail passing through Leopard Gorge, once the private pathway of Masai, cattle and wildlife, was obliterated beneath the tracks of four-wheel-drive vehicles.

One morning, in July 1978, as I sat in my vehicle photographing the Marsh Lions, I noticed another car flashing its headlights, a sure sign that the driver was either stuck or had seen something special and wanted to share it with me. It turned out to be Joseph and my heart missed a beat as he told me that a leopard had been sighted with two young cubs in the Leopard Gorge area. He smiled hugely, enjoying my delight at his good news. Apparently the female was very shy and almost impossible to observe, fleeing at the first sight or sound of a vehicle. But her cubs were bolder, sometimes appearing at the entrance to one of the many caves situated among the rocks in the Gorge.

Day after day I searched the area, scanning each tree and rocky outcrop with my binoculars until, late one evening, I found them. As I approached a large eleaodendron tree on the south side of the Gorge, I glimpsed a slight movement among the leaves. Before I could stop the vehicle a dark spotted shape dropped from the branches and slunk away to the rocky lip of Leopard Gorge.

It was the female at last. My heart pounded wildly. I inched the vehicle forward, hoping to catch a further glimpse of her, but she had gone. As I neared the tree I noticed the carcass of a six-month-old wildebeest calf sprawled in the grass. There, crouched over it, wide-eyed and bloody-faced, were the leopard's two cubs.

I sat motionless, spellbound at my first sight of the tiny leopards. For a long moment we stared at each other until I foolishly tried to reach for my camera. Careful as my movements had been, they were nevertheless too sudden for the wary cubs, who streaked across the open ground to the safety of the rocks.

I waited for a few minutes before starting the car and then drove down into the Gorge itself. Though I searched the area carefully I could find no further trace of mother or cubs. They had vanished, yet I knew they were close by. With so many cool, shady caves to hide themselves in, the leopards would not have travelled far.

During the next year I had reports from drivers and friends of the cubs' whereabouts, though I only saw them myself on a handful of occasions. Their mother remained a mystery animal, shy and intolerant of vehicles. I was told that the cubs were a male and a female, though I never got to know the young male and I received no further reports of his whereabouts once he was eighteen months old.

The female cub, or Chui, as the leopard is known in Swahili, grew into a magnificent animal. Sometimes months would pass during which I would see nothing of her. Then, as if by magic, she would suddenly reappear from her secret world: treed by the Marsh Lions along the lower reaches of Leopard Lugga, chased from her kill by hyenas of the Ridge Clan or just quietly resting on some comfortable rocky ledge.

Once Chui had proved herself capable of killing sufficient prey for her own needs, contact with her mother virtually ceased. The desire to feed by herself and lead a solitary existence seemed to outweigh any further benefits that a life with her mother might provide. When the two separated, towards the end of 1979, Chui was about eighteen months old. She had retained Leopard Gorge and its surrounds within her own home range, thereby overlapping the area used by her mother.

As Christmas 1980 approached Joseph once more brought good news. A leopard with two very small cubs had been seen at the entrance to a cave situated high up among an enormous rocky outcrop at the east end of Leopard Gorge. It was Chui, now almost three years old and accompanied by her first litter. Joseph and I slunk furtively around the vicinity of the Gorge, trying to avoid precipitating a torrent of vehicles from the other camps. News of leopards invariably spreads like wildfire in the Mara and would quickly have turned the area into a mad house, ensuring Chui's early departure with her cubs.

In the end our attempts at secrecy were to no avail. The lions of the Gorge Pride saw to that. Two weeks after I first set eyes on the cubs I found their rocky hide-out seething with lions. The pride had been hunting in the area for the last few days and their menacing presence had not gone unnoticed by Chui. There was no sign of the leopards, and for a while I feared that the cubs had disappeared for good.

I saw Chui's cubs together on only one occasion after that, perched atop a small euclea tree along the northern reaches of Leopard Lugga. They were by now six months old and seemingly safely on their way to adulthood.

It was not to be. A few weeks later one of the cubs was trapped and killed by a lioness from the Gorge Pride, among thick bush along Leopard Lugga.

Chui and her other cub could only watch from the safety of a nearby tree. The one remaining cub appeared every so often and was last seen in Chui's company in 1982.

I was told that a leopard who might have been Chui produced a litter of cubs in Leopard Gorge later that same year, though I personally never saw them and there was no sign of mother or cubs by the end of 1982. Theoretically a leopard can raise her cubs to the point of independence and produce a new litter at two-yearly intervals, so it may indeed have been Chui. It could even have been Chui's mother.

As fate would have it, I was forced to spend six months of 1983 in England, due to a back injury. Friends wrote to tell me that two adult female leopards had given birth to cubs within six months and four miles of each other, providing visitors with a rare spectacle. Suddenly the northern Mara was enjoying its best leopard viewing for more than ten years, even eclipsing that once offered by the Serengeti.

By the time I returned to the Mara in September 1983 one of the leopards, known as the Mara Buffalo Female, and her two eight-month-old cubs were located around a rocky bluff, three and a half miles northeast of Leopard Gorge. Though I knew the area well I had never seen this particular female before. To my great delight the other leopard turned out to be Chui, whose cubs were little more than two months old and as yet rarely seen.

1. The Birth of the Cubs

HIDDEN AMONG the thorn thickets of the northern Mara is the place called Leopard Gorge. Its bold rocky relief contrasts sharply with the gently undulating plains and scattered acacia bushes which are such a feature of Masailand. Out on the plains there is a feeling of the vastness that is Africa: wide open spaces stretching to the horizon with barely a tree or bush to disrupt the vistas. But Leopard Gorge is not like that. It is steep-sided and close-walled, in places shutting out the early morning light when the plains below are already bathed in a soft warming glow.

There are times when the Gorge can chill your heart: it is a nightmarish place to come face to face with a cantankerous old buffalo bull if you are on foot safari. As darkness closes in, the unearthly whoops and giggles of the local hyena clan echo against its walls, competing with the thunderous roars of the Gorge Pride who sometimes pass through on their nocturnal wanderings. Yet this area is also prime leopard country. With its massively comfortable fig trees to lie in, cool and secure caves to hide in, and access to the whole spectrum of prey species, the Gorge has everything a leopard could need.

In the mid-1970s a huge male leopard occupied the territory of which Leopard Gorge was but one small part. He was occasionally to be seen resting in one of the giant fig trees at the entrance to the Gorge where he could keep a watchful eye on the surrounding countryside. But he was shy of vehicles and never tarried long, quickly descending from his aerial perch to disappear among the jumble of rocks.

The male was big by leopard standards, the size of a half-grown lioness, weighing at least 140 pounds. Measured from nose to tail-tip he was well over seven feet long, more than one third of which was taken up by his beautiful spotted tail. His coat was short-haired and the fur along his back and within the rosettes was the colour of stained wood. When he stopped to look over his muscular shoulders or peer from behind a concealing boulder he would lower his broad head, with its torn and scabbed left ear, and stare warily. Only then did one notice his most distinguishing feature: an opaque cast clouded over his enlarged left eye, bestowing upon him an air of fierceness that once seen was never forgotten. The cause could have been a shotgun pellet, thorns, a porcupine quill or disease.

Somehow the old male survived the '70s. He finally disappeared from the area in 1980, but not before he had been seen mating with Chui's mother and had presumably sired the two cubs I had first watched that afternoon in July 1978. Chui was the first of a new generation of leopards whose parents had, through their natural wariness and ability to live undetected close to man, survived the poachers and professional hunters.

It was now 1983. As Chui stood among the protective canopy of the giant fig tree which guards the western entrance to the Gorge she could see far out on to the plains below. On either side the Gorge tumbles away amid a tangle of boulders and acacia bushes, bounded to north and south by shallow luggas. The more extensive of these is called Leopard Lugga, a tree-lined gully that acts as a reservoir for whatever rain the area might enjoy. This lugga cuts across the approach track to the west of Leopard Gorge and then winds its way down to just north of the new entrance gate which provides access to the popular Musiara Marsh area, within the Mara Reserve.

The vehicle track emerging from the west end of the Gorge fords Leopard Lugga and then continues through scattered acacia bush towards an area known as Fig Tree Ridge, a rock-strewn outcrop topped with a number of enormous fig trees. The ridge continues west for one and a half miles before reaching Kampi ya Chui, a diminishing patch of forest that acts as a private campsite for professional safari operators. Draining south past the campsite is another intermittent watercourse called Dik-Dik Lugga. The area to the north, south and west of Fig Tree Ridge is composed of extensive acacia thickets, interspersed with rocky hills and open grassy meadows, ideal leopard country and the core of Chui's home range.

Many other animals shared this area with Chui, each adapted in its own particular way to benefit from the abundance and variety of food sources. Giraffe browsed the thornbushes and taller trees along the lugga edges. Zebra clipped the heads and stems from the predominant red oat grass, while wildebeest grazed the greener, leafier portions. Kongoni, topi and gazelles each selected their own particular level of plant growth. Troops of olive baboons scoured the ground for edible plants and insects, even occasionally capturing a gazelle or impala calf that had lain motionless, seeking concealment. Families of warthogs clipped the sweet young grasses close to the ground and rooted on their knees for tubers and other underground sources of food. The area was alive with life forms which in turn provided sustenance for the ever-watchful predators that have made the Mara famous: animals that themselves do not have direct access to the primary food source, produced by green plants from inorganic material through the marvel of photosynthesis. They must therefore kill the herbivores – or even other carnivores – in order to survive.

The herbivores can co-exist harmoniously because they are adapted to utilise different portions of the vegetation. The carnivores, by being nocturnal or diurnal, social or solitary, large or small, have only partially solved the problems of competition. Lions kill a warthog and then must sometimes war for possession of it with the local hyena clan. The cheetah successfully stalks a Thomson's gazelle only to lose it to the more powerful lion. A jackal snatches up a dik-dik and is then itself killed and eaten by a watchful leopard. Yet, regardless of how they kill or what they look like, the predators and scavengers are all an integral and vital part of the ecosystem.

This abundance of animal life, be it carnivore, omnivore or herbivore, therefore depends on the ability of the Mara to produce an unending flow of vegetable matter and that in turn requires an adequate supply of moisture. Since the drought of 1976 the area had enjoyed exceptionally good rainfall. But in 1983 the long and short rains failed. Gradually the thickets and forested areas were stripped of foliage, the grasses and seedlings trampled and eaten back. When the annual migration of wildebeest and zebra once more departed for the Serengeti little vegetation remained. If ever there was a time to look for leopard this was it, for by now many of their favourite hiding places were exposed to view.

Except when they are mating or when a female is accompanied by her young, leopards seem to prefer to spend their lives alone. To locate and capture relatively small and scattered prey animals is a time-consuming business. Several leopards hunting together, or moving in the same area at the same time, would create more disturbance and tend to frighten the prey species away. It is therefore more efficient for leopards to hunt and feed by themselves.

Each adult leopard occupies an area known as its home range, a place it utilises in its normal day-to-day activity and which provides it with the essentials of life: food, water, shelter and a mate. Chui inhabited an area of about ten to fifteen square miles for much of the year, though there were times when she ranged even further afield.

Range size may fluctuate from time to time and from season to season, reflecting the minimum needs of the animal during lean periods. It varies from one area to another according to the type and quality of habitat, particularly with regard to the availability of food and the density of other, larger predators such as lions and spotted hyenas. It is therefore not a constant that can be rigidly pinpointed on a map. Its edges are blurred and there may be tracts of inhospitable land within the range that are virtually never used. There were times, for instance, when Chui concentrated her main activity for quite lengthy periods of time in an area of just a few square miles.

The home range of a male leopard is considerably larger than that of any one female and is shared freely with females but not usually with other adult males. It is impossible for an area this large to be readily surveyed by a single animal. To deter interlopers, active defence has to be supplemented by more indirect means such as scent-marking and the animal's characteristic, rasping call.

The great advantage of chemical signals for this primarily nocturnal and far-ranging creature is that scent messages are persistent – they may last for days or even weeks in certain circumstances – in a way that vocalisations and the animal's physical presence are unable to be. Spray marks tainted with the pungent odour of secretions from the two anal glands situated beneath the root of a leopard's tail may inform other leopards of the sex, age, sexual status and possibly even the specific identity of the animal that has deposited them. Such long-distance communication methods are highly economic in that little effort is required to mark the environment and the chances of unexpected and possibly hostile meetings with one's own kind are greatly reduced. However, adult males do sometimes fight with each other.

While mutual intolerance is the general rule, the home range of female leopards may partially or completely overlap. But violent physical confrontation is very unusual, and most females I have observed look remarkably unscarred. The mutual avoidance mechanism used by both sexes appears to have evolved as a highly effective and non-damaging means of spacing leopards and reducing the competition for food. Transients and potential settlers tend to avoid crowded areas, rather than be warned off by the aggressive behaviour of those in occupation.

The home ranges of male and female leopards form separate mosaics. Because a male's home range is considerably larger than that of a female, it may include within its boundary the whole of one female's home range as well as part of another's. Some males may be fortunate enough to occupy a range that overlaps with parts of a number of females' home ranges. Likewise a female may occupy a range that is overlapped by portions of the home ranges of two or even three males.

Though adult leopards avoid direct contact with each other they must, at times, forsake their solitary ways in order to breed. But it is probably only during the six- or seven-day oestrus period that the female readily accepts the close company of a male. It is also likely to be the only time that he seeks hers. Meetings are therefore mostly brief and infrequent.

When a female leopard comes into oestrus, which is at intervals of twenty to fifty days, there are changes in the hormonal composition of her urine and probably also an alteration in the volatile nature of the secretions from her anal glands. Consequently her spray marks act as a powerful advertisement of her condition to male leopards. By calling and travelling widely when she is in oestrus the female further increases the chances of finding a mate. Because resident male leopards patrol their own home range frequently and thoroughly, they soon pick up the signals emitted by an oestrus female.

Leopards have rarely been seen mating in the wild, though they appear to follow the same basic pattern adopted by all the large cats. Copulation itself is brief and repeated frequently over a period of a few days after which the leopards once more resume their solitary existence. Both males and females are promiscuous in their sexual activities and the males will try to mate with any oestrus females they encounter within their own home range. Similarly a female may mate with one resident male, the males from adjoining ranges through which she passes or even with a transient male who manages to slip through the territorial net. This means that a female's cubs may be sired by different males from one litter to the next. In the process the males are able to avoid a parental role, leaving the onus of raising the cubs on the female.

One day during July 1983, Chui searched carefully throughout the length and breadth of the Gorge. She moved cautiously with head bowed, pausing every few yards to sniff for signs of other creatures which might have been frequenting the area. As she wandered along a game trail she could smell the fresh signs of the Gorge Pride, the same lions that had killed one of her first litter of cubs in 1981.

Chui suddenly stopped in mid-stride and stared straight ahead, her ears pricked up alertly. The scent of one of the lionesses was particularly fresh, quite distinct in its odour from that of a cheetah or another leopard. It led towards a rocky shelf shrouded by the dense overhanging branches and shiny green leaves of a number of teclea bushes, common along the lip of the Gorge. This was where Chui herself sometimes lay, for hidden behind the comfortable ledge was a deep channel, just wide enough for a leopard to sleep or take refuge in.

Chui hesitated. All her previous experiences with lions had taught her how dangerous they were. She would have little chance of surviving in a battle with the lioness, who weighed three times Chui's compact eighty or ninety pounds. The lioness would certainly kill her if she could.

There had been many times when Chui was forced to spend uncomfortable hours in the highest reaches of the nearest tree when the Gorge Pride had surprised her. With her ears laid flat, long whiskers bristling and canines bared in a threatening gape, she would cough and rumble at the lions below her. Fortunately for her, though lions can climb trees, they do not possess the surefootedness of an agile leopard. Consequently, having once treed their victim, they tend to give up, although on one occasion two subadult lionesses actually tried to claw their way up in pursuit of the panic-stricken leopard. But lions can still make life very unpleasant for the smaller cat by lying in the shade of the tree for the rest of the day.

So instead of continuing towards the ledge, Chui retraced her steps along the rim of the Gorge before crossing to the north. She peered briefly around the base of a tree. From that position she could see the lioness lying a hundred yards away, unaware of her presence. Then she melted away, keeping close to the cover afforded by the acacia thickets to the west. Though her spotted coat protected her in the dappled shadows of a fig tree or among the lichen-covered rocks within the Gorge itself, she was highly visible in more open country during the daytime. There was no long grass left to conceal her now, so relying on all her feline stealth, Chui continued towards Fig Tree Ridge. Within a few days her latest litter of cubs would be born, though this time Leopard Gorge would not be their birthplace.

Near the east end of Fig Tree Ridge stands an enormous fig tree, nearly forty feet tall and bigger than any that now grows along Leopard Gorge. Chui had often sprawled among the large, comfortable branches of this particular tree. Below the base of the tree a large, flat rock known as Top Rock formed the roof over the vertical entrance to a large cave. The cave itself was cool and dark and, tunnelled out of sight deep between huge rocks, the ideal place for a pregnant leopard. Within a radius of thirty yards were half a dozen other caves of different shapes and sizes into which cub-sized leopards could safely squeeze. This rocky area was known as the Cub Caves.

Leopards have a gestation period of approximately ninety to a hundred days. While this is a relatively short time for a large animal, it is an advantage for a predator which must spend a considerable amount of time actively hunting for its food.

It is thought that during early July 1983 Chui gave birth to two male cubs in one of the Cub Caves beneath the fig tree. Two to three cubs seems to be the normal litter size for leopards in the Mara. As leopard cubs are rarely observed before they are at least two months old, however, it is quite possible that larger litters are born, but that all their members do not survive.

Mortality among leopard cubs is certainly high in the Mara, as it is unusual for a leopard to raise even two cubs to the point of complete independence and I have never seen three large cubs from the same litter. Because the female receives no assistance from the male who sires her cubs, she must feed and protect them by herself, a difficult task for a single parent. Smaller size litters have therefore probably evolved with such solitary behaviour.

At birth leopard cubs weigh one to one-and-a-half pounds. Their eyes remain closed for the first six to ten days, so their own odour and that of their mother plays a very important part in their orientation. During these early days the mother leopard spends much of her time close to her cubs and assists them in finding her teats, by lying on her side and adopting a suitable nourishing position. By licking the cubs' perineal region she stimulates them to defecate and urinate. Cleaning the young and keeping them warm help to create a specific bond between mother and cubs.

It is possible that Chui's cubs established their own teat order within days of birth, in the same way as domestic kittens do. The regular deposition of the kittens' personal scent through nuzzling around their own teat allows them to relocate their correct position quickly while their eyes are still closed.

Teat fixation makes feeding more efficient as its orderliness minimises time and effort. This proved to be the case with Chui's youngsters. Prolonged fighting between the leopard cubs would also have torn Chui's teats.

One afternoon in early September Chui lay resting on Top Rock, gently grooming the long, snowy white hair on her belly. Suddenly she disappeared into one of the nearby caves, reappearing a moment later with a small cub dangling passively from her jaws. Unceremoniously she deposited it on the flat rock and, before it could move away, she returned with a second cub. She then lay down again, curled up on her side, wedging the cubs within the protective enclosure of her legs.

The spots and rosettes of the cubs' fur were so closely packed together that little of the pale ground colour showed through, giving their coats a greyish hue. Their eyes displayed the bluey glaze that is common to all young cats.

Though at times Chui lay flat out, her cheek resting on the smooth rock surface, she remained alert to any sign of danger. Her sensitive ears constantly twisted to pick up the slightest change in pitch or volume of the jumble of noises surrounding her, sounds that could alert her to the possible danger of an approaching lion, hyena or baboon, long before it could pose a threat to herself or the vulnerable cubs.

The cubs quickly learned to orientate to the place where Chui had chosen to hide them by homing in on its characteristic odour. This provided them with a zone of emotional security, keeping them safely within the cave area while their mother was away hunting. When Chui was forced to leave the young leopards to go in search of prey, they remained patiently hidden. Even though their stomachs might ache for milk they still did not call out for their mother. If they had, some other predatory creature might have snuffed out their cries for good.

Exploratory behaviour became more evident once the young cubs could see their way around. This period of emergence from the safety of their birthplace was a time of great vulnerability, as the cubs were not yet familiar with the surrounding locality. They were still relatively small and weak and there was always the danger of attack from predators.

During the first eight weeks the cubs spent most of their time inside the caves or crouching motionless, camouflaged among the shadows of the rocky ledges. Chui would often return to them during the hours of darkness, unseen by man or beast. Sometimes, unbeknown to the young leopards, their mother would be close by, resting in the giant fig tree above the Cub Caves. But every few hours she would descend from the tree and allow her cubs to suckle.

Even before the cubs were eight weeks old they had tasted meat, for Chui was bringing the occasional small kill back to them. At first the youngsters were bemused by the strange-smelling objects that their mother deposited next to them, but they eventually started to maul and play with the kills, wrestling and squabbling between themselves for possession. Their teeth were needle sharp and though they obtained little sustenance from these early offerings they had begun their initiation into the carnivorous ways of their mother.

When I first saw them, the cubs were already distinguishable. One was a lighter coloured animal with whitish cheeks. It was the more nervous of the two, always the first to retreat at the slightest sign of danger. The darker cub had a mischievous, pinched face and just the tiniest suggestion of a squint. I knew them as Light and Dark.

The skin on Chui's belly was brown and cracked, the fur matted and darkly stained where the cubs had pawed and suckled at her teats. Light always occupied the position closer to his mother's head when suckling. In consequence he received more attention, as it was far easier for Chui to groom him than to stretch far enough round to reach Dark. If only one cub was suckling and the other decided to join him, there was quite often a brief squabble. In these circumstances it was difficult to see if it was because one of the cubs was trespassing, or if it was simply due to the newcomer's efforts to squeeze into his own position.

There were occasions when Chui seemed to be using her long, sensuous tail as a means of maintaining physical contact with her cubs, *aaou'ing* softly and actually encouraging them as they scrambled over one another in their efforts to grab hold of it. Each time one of the cubs secured it between his paws or in his jaws, Chui would flick it away. But there was none of the irritable hissing or grunting, the tail thumping, that occurred when Chui wished to be left alone. In fact she would quickly bring her tail within reach again, feeling the cubs with it and sliding it like a furry reptile over their bodies. It had the same effect as if she had dangled a piece of rope in front of Light and Dark and sent them into what I could only presume must be a leopard cub's equivalent of ecstasy. Eventually Chui would end their game by turning to mouth and nibble them as they squirmed to escape her outstretched paws.

When the cubs became too much for Chui she would simply get up and leave, effortlessly springing into the fig tree where they could not as yet follow. From her perch she had a perfect view of Leopard Lugga snaking south through the acacia thickets to the plains beyond. Away to the east she could see the entrance to Leopard Gorge and its rocky environs. She was surrounded by thornbush, rocks and trees: perfect leopard country.

Now that the cubs were bigger, Chui's sudden disappearance into the tree would cause an outburst of high-pitched miaows, particularly from Light. But before long one or other of the cubs would initiate a fresh bout of play, and then all thoughts of their mother would be forgotten as they rolled and wrestled among the rocks. At times Light and Dark sat entranced at the conflicting sounds and sights around them: the buzzing insects, the booming morning call of ground hornbills and the barking of zebras as they filed past, forty feet below the cubs, momentarily stifling their play. The young leopards would watch, ears cocked, quivering with excitement at the sight of the strange striped objects.

Every so often a vehicle would arrive from one of the tented camps, following the well-worn tyre tracks above or below the Cub Caves. The upper pathway ran along the lip of the ridge, passing within thirty feet of the giant fig tree where Chui often rested, while the lower track followed the line of the ridge fifty feet below the cubs' hiding place.

At first, the appearance of a vehicle would cause Light and Dark to slink away to the safety of one of the Cub Caves, whose thick-walled interiors softened the effect of the unfamiliar objects. The cubs were clearly frightened by the large, noisy contraptions with their chattering occupants. Chui also felt threatened, even though she had seen many vehicles during her six years of life. It was the presence of her young offspring that caused her to lower her head and hiss out a warning, until the cubs had safely disappeared from sight. Then she too would slip away to a more peaceful place among the rocks or high up in the fig tree. But for the time being the other female and her cubs at Mara Buffalo Rocks were providing most of the leopard viewing, and Chui, Light and Dark remained relatively undisturbed.

As the sun disappeared behind a wall of grey clouds, the unmistakable cry of a white-bellied bustard echoed through the still air. Impala males roared out nasal challenges as they herded the females in their territories or chased away rival males. Chui watched from the fig tree.

Light and Dark lay quietly at the entrance to their cave. Huddled against each other they drifted in half sleep. As darkness closed around them their spotted coats faded to the colour of the surrounding rocks, until it was impossible to distinguish which was Light and which was Dark.

Chui sat up and yawned, then stretched with her hindquarters raised and long tail arched, before climbing carefully down the thick trunk of the fig tree. Her landing was as quiet as falling snow, the impact absorbed and cushioned by her supple frame and thick-soled paws. The cubs did not stir as their mother drifted away into the enveloping darkness, a solitary hunter in her own very private world.

Early next morning, before the sun had appeared, a short-legged, slender shape glided tentatively towards the cubs' sleeping place. The young leopards lay side by side, their tummies fat and warm, for Chui had returned during the night, allowing them to suckle before continuing in her search for food.

The cubs' noses wrinkled inquiringly at the approach of the slender mongoose whose fiery brown eyes and pointed face now peered into their cave. Light and Dark awoke with a start, responding to the intruder with an impressive explosion of sounds. The inquisitive mongoose quickly retreated, carrying his distinctive, black-tipped tail curled high in the air.

This particular mongoose often moved around the Cub Caves which formed part of his home range. He spent many hours each day searching for food: insects, small mammals, small birds, eggs and reptiles. There were even times when he nimbly raced up a tree to feed on an unattended leopard kill. He was a solitary hunter like the leopard, except that he hunted mainly during the daylight hours or at dusk, resting in thickets, crevices or adopted burrows during the night. There had been many a time when he had spent the hours of darkness in the cave in which Light and Dark now sheltered.

An hour after sunrise Chui appeared from the north, moving cautiously to the base of the fig tree. She did not visit the cubs or attempt to call them to her. Instead she made her way noiselessly over the rocks to the east of the Cub Caves, until she came to a large boulder called Half-Way Rock, the very same rock that the slender mongoose now crouched under. The two predators were only five feet from each other, yet if either animal knew of the other's presence it did nothing to acknowledge the fact – though Chui was not averse to killing and eating a mongoose if given half a chance.

Chui seemed uneasy. She rose and stretched before moving across to the entrance to the cubs' hiding place. There she paused and uttered a most peculiar sniffing sound – *pfff, pfff* – by blowing air sharply through her nostrils, two or three times in succession. She repeated these short sharp puffs as she moved around in front of the cave. It was a noise I had originally heard while watching Chui with her first litter of cubs in Leopard Gorge.

The sound in question is known as prusten or chuffling, and it is a vocal greeting used by some of the large cats, though not by lions or cheetahs. Tigers make a similar sound and snow leopards are said to use an especially soft and quiet form. One cat raises it head slightly and chuffles while looking directly at another. The meaning of the sound is apparently 'All is well, I am feeling friendly towards you.'

Chuffling proved to be a highly effective means of contact between a mother leopard and her cubs. Light and Dark certainly recognised the sound, for they immediately responded by appearing at the entrance to their cave, just as Chui's previous litter had done. However, none of the young cubs made the sound themselves at this stage in their lives.

Later I was to hear the daughter of the Mara Buffalo leopard excitedly chuffling in response to the sight and sound of her mother appearing from a cave beneath the tree in which the young female had been resting. By that time she was already fifteen months old. Chuffling in this latter instance seems to function simply as a friendly greeting. Initially Chui used it primarily as a means of locating and calling her small cubs from their hiding place. She also chuffled and used other vocalisations as a method of attracting the cubs' attention to herself, particularly if they began to wander away too far, or if she wanted them to follow her.

Though the solitary cats are not particularly articulate, Chui used a range of calls when socialising with her cubs. The sounds were often of a low intensity, meant only for finely tuned leopard ears. But sometimes, when all was quiet and Chui felt relaxed enough to let me venture to within the range of human hearing, I could sit and listen to the subtleties of the leopard's language.

Light and Dark excitedly greeted Chui, pushing their foreheads up under her chin, arching their tails and pressing themselves sinuously against her side, throat and forelegs. Chui responded by licking the cubs with her long pink tongue as she led them over Top Rock and out on to the top of a huge rock which formed the east side of the vertical cave. I named it Suckling Rock West and it was ideal for Chui's purposes: protected high up on the ridge face and providing good visibility, yet close enough to the safety of the caves if danger threatened.

Though the young cubs often remained safely out of sight when Chui was away hunting, they played vigorously with each other when she was in attendance. To begin with they had kept to within a few yards of the Cub Caves, learning to cope with nearby aspects of their environment and then gradually to deal with more distant features. Before long, their playful footsteps wore a highly visible trail around the rocks bordering their sleeping place. Their experience was continually broadening. Every conceivable object was thoroughly investigated, especially if it happened to move. Things were smelled, scratched, pawed, patted, bitten, shaken and chewed.

A small dead tree situated close to the fig tree provided Light and Dark with a perfect climbing frame on which to strengthen their young muscles and refine their climbing skills. Whenever the cubs were playing together, sooner or later one of them would go scuttling over to the climbing tree and claw his way up, to be followed shortly by his brother. They could already clamber right to the top, some ten feet above ground, steadying themselves with their sharp claws. They knew no fear of heights whether in the tree or strutting to the edge of the tallest rocks to peer inquisitively towards the ground forty feet below. Sometimes they would wrestle perilously close to the ridge face, quite confident of their own ability to retain their balance. Such natural skills would be essential to their survival in the months ahead.

Not far from where the leopard cubs were playing, the baboons of the Fig Tree Troop were slowly making their way back to the east end of the ridge. They had foraged almost continuously since morning, occasionally stopping to rest in the shade of an acacia bush during the hottest part of the day.

Baboons live in a home range which is passed on from generation to generation and covers an area of a number of square miles. The Fig Tree Troop spent most of their waking hours roaming the country surrounding the ridge in their search for food and water, and they were as familiar with it as Chui. But their day always began and ended at one of several sleeping sites, special places well furnished with suitable trees which provided them with a refuge from predatory animals such as leopards. One such roost consisted of three large fig trees situated 120 yards east of the Cub Caves. It was towards this site that the Fig Tree Troop were now headed.

It was six o'clock by the time the baboons advanced to within sight of the boulders surrounding the Cub Caves. Chui had forsaken the comfort of her fig tree earlier in the afternoon, wandering off in the direction of Leopard Gorge and leaving her cubs asleep on Suckling Rock West. But Light and

Dark lay hidden inside one of the caves long before the baboons arrived, forewarned by the grunts and screams of the noisy primates.

The baboons already knew all about the leopard and her cubs, for they had seen them on a number of occasions since Chui took up residence so close to one of their favourite roosts. Some of the baboons were even older than Chui and had learned how best to deal with her mother and the wall-eyed male during the years that they had shared part of the same environment. Now some of the troop members strutted around the rocks surrounding the Cub Caves, occasionally jumping away in nervous anticipation of some form of retaliation. But as it got darker their confidence began to ebb and soon the last of the troop drifted further along the ridge to the trees where they would sleep for the night.

Not long after nightfall, Chui killed an impala fawn which she stored in a small tree half a mile from the Cub Caves. After partially eating the carcass, she returned to her waiting cubs sometime before sun-up. The cubs were hungry and she suckled them before retiring to the fig tree. Light and Dark occupied themselves in gambolling about in the climbing tree in a manner that would shame any lion cub of a similar age. But it was not without mishap.

At one point Light lost his footing and only just managed to hang on to the thin branch he had been standing on. Using his sharp claws and all his youthful vigour he hoisted his back legs up to grasp the branch. He hung there, sloth-like, desperately trying to right himself. But it was hopeless. Gradually the strength ebbed from his aching muscles until he dangled by a solitary paw. He miaowed pathetically as Dark pawed at him from above. But as Light fell he righted himself to land in true cat fashion. Hardly had his feet touched firm ground than he was hauling himself back into the branches to molest his brother.

During the next hour Chui paid two visits to her cubs. On each occasion the cubs suckled and played with their mother. Suddenly at midday, Chui stood up, depositing the cubs in an untidy huddle on the rocks. She moved away quickly, and neither Light nor Dark attempted to follow her or even to see where she was going.

Unfortunately the same bushes which provided Chui with shade and cover also seethed with tsetse flies. They swarmed from their resting places like tiny fighter planes, hounding Chui unmercifully. Her only defence was to lash her tail, twitch her skin, shake her paws and snap her teeth at the vicious insects. At times she plonked down on her bottom in a most undignified manner or rolled over onto her back in an attempt to deal with the problem. Then, for a moment, she would sit upright, as if unsure what to do next, gently licking the painful places where the flies had bitten her.

Chui broke into a fast trot, but it made little difference as more and more of the insects pursued her. Finally, after eight long minutes, she reached her destination. Growing among a dense croton thicket at the base of the ridge was a slender tree. Below it, a narrow cave extended between two huge boulders: a cool retreat usually occupied by one or two of the dozen or more hyenas that comprised the Fig Tree Clan. Chui crawled into the cave and flopped onto her side. At last she found relief from the tsetse flies.

The tree that Chui lay beneath had a sparse crown from which the leaves had recently fallen, so it provided little shade or cover for a leopard during daylight. But wedged between two branches were the remains of her impala kill. Typically, the contents of the body cavity and the rump had been eaten first.

During the next four hours Chui remained in her cool retreat. Then, just after four o'clock, as the heat began to ebb from the afternoon sun, she slipped cautiously from the cave. For forty-five minutes she picked and tugged at the kill. Using her powerful jaws she crunched through the skull of the young impala and soon there was little left to feed on. All that remained now was for Chui to complete the task of meticulously cleaning all traces of blood and meat from her face and paws.

At about the same time that Chui had started feeding on her kill, Light and Dark emerged from their cave. They had slept intermittently during the afternoon, entwined within the comfort of each other's paws. Their eyes were still sleepy as they stretched and yawned before beginning to groom.

Concealed by the foliage of a nearby tree a martial eagle watched the cubs' movements with interest. Africa's largest eagle is quite capable of killing and devouring an animal the size of a three-month-old leopard cub. I had watched the same bird attack a Thomson's gazelle fawn and then successfully fight off the desperate challenge of the adult gazelles who had rushed forward to defend the youngster. Their efforts were to no avail, for the predatory eagle had already crushed the life from the young gazelle. Its talons are so long and powerful that they can easily skewer a man's hand.

As Dark crept up to the top of the ridge the massive eagle tightened its bone-crushing grip on the branch, yellow eyes glinting in the dying sun. But just as it was preparing to launch itself on silent wings, it caught sight of another movement, though this one came from among the thornbushes close by. It was Chui returning from her kill. The presence of the adult leopard made the giant bird falter and the moment it had waited for so patiently passed unfulfilled.

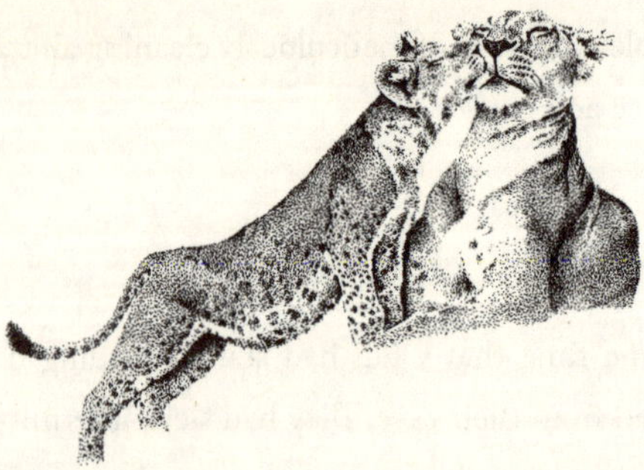

2. The Predators' Kingdom

NOT FAR from the Cub Caves a giraffe stared anxiously out over the thornbushes, dwarfing the newborn calf sprawled in an untidy heap at her feet. Awkwardly the mother spread her tent-pole legs to reach down and lick the baby. Her eighteen-inch tongue snaked over the calf, cleaning its wet, wrinkled coat.

The giraffe is Africa's tallest animal, towering over the other creatures with which it shares its home. A large male stands more than eighteen feet high and can weigh well over a ton. The ancient Greeks were so bemused by the sight of these extraordinary animals that they felt certain they were looking at the results of a pairing between a female camel and a male leopard, or pard as it was known. To this day the giraffe carries the species name of *camelopardalis*.

Adult giraffe have feet the size of dinner plates and a kick of such ferocity that they are capable of crushing the jaw or skull of an unwary predator. Occasionally a pride of lions is bold enough to attack a giraffe, though in the Mara it is usually only during the leanest period – between the short and long rains – when there is a paucity of easier prey for them to feed on.

Even though the giraffe mother had remained on her feet while giving birth, it was still a vulnerable time for her and the calf. So she had good reason to look nervously about her. Not far away a herd of frisky impala stormed through the thickets as hyenas cackled in the distance. The calf continued to sit on its knees oblivious of the dangers surrounding it in its new world, though it soon had other allies aside from its mother. Within minutes three yellow-billed oxpeckers arrived to perch on the calf's wavering neck. The birds' sharp, curved claws pricked and tickled the young giraffe's skin, causing it to shudder and twitch.

Oxpeckers regularly feed on blood-sucking ticks and flies that infest an animal's skin. But an open wound or scraps of afterbirth also supply welcome food. Besides a free meal, the giraffe provides the birds with a safe place to sunbathe, rest and even mate. And hair teased from the giraffe's coat can furnish the perfect soft lining for an oxpecker's nest. In return for this sustenance the host animal acquires alert sentinels who rise into the air shrieking their alarm calls at the slightest sign of approaching danger.

The disturbance made by the flight of the impalas seemed to unsettle the giraffe mother and caused her to move off a few yards, perhaps in an attempt to draw attention away from her calf or to encourage the youngster to get to its feet and follow her. Whatever the reason, the giraffe now glimpsed real danger in the form of two hyenas from the Ridge Clan, drawn by the sounds of other clan members feeding on the plains below.

Hyenas live by their finely tuned senses and a natural inquisitiveness that can often make a meal out of nothing. As they drew level with the giraffe they stopped. The larger of the two hyenas, a female, moved cautiously forward, her head bobbing up and down. Her sensitive nose searched the morning air, straining to pick out any interesting or encouraging smells. As soon as she saw the cause of the adult giraffe's concern the hyena closed in on the helpless calf, sending the oxpeckers screeching into the morning sky. Uttering a menacing grunt, the usually silent giraffe swung her great legs into action, lashing out at the oncoming predator. The sight of the giant animal advancing so determinedly towards her was too much for the hyena. She turned and fled, hurrying after her clan mate who had already continued on his way.

Once more the giraffe bent to lick her calf, periodically prodding the youngster with an enormous leg before moving away a few paces to encourage the calf to get to its feet. Responding, the calf rocked forward, raising its hind legs and then staggering on shaky limbs into an upright position. It wavered briefly before pitching headlong back to earth. But within a few minutes it found its feet again.

The mother giraffe's graceful neck gently embraced her calf, pressing it to her side and steadying the wobbly youngster as she licked and nuzzled it. The calf searched vainly for milk beneath the arch of its mother's front legs while the adult busied herself feeding on the nearest acacia bush. An hour and a half after giving birth the giraffe moved off with her calf tottering behind her.

Chui meanwhile had been watching from the fig tree. Her position high in the tree rivalled the aerial view enjoyed by the giraffe and provided a perfect view of the events unfolding less than a hundred yards from where she rested. Chui had returned briefly to her impala kill during the night before abandoning the fallen scraps of skin and bone to the Ridge Clan. Now the sight of the calf struggling to remain on its feet caused her to sit up. She leaned forward, following the giraffe's every move, her tail tip twitching from side to side with excitement. Even though the giraffe calf entered the world at a hefty 150 pounds, and stood over five feet tall, Chui was quite capable of killing it.

During the first few weeks a mother giraffe often leaves her young calf lying out while she forages up to a mile or more away for food. As it gets older the calf, together with others of a similar age, forms a crèche in the thornbush country, while the majority of the females go off to feed. Chui's father, the wall-eyed male, had himself killed an unguarded calf near to the northern end of Leopard Lugga. After eating from the carcass he had stored the remains fifteen feet up in the fork of a slender olive tree. Months later the giraffe's long leg bones still dangled in the wind, witness to the leopard's legendary strength.

It was not the size of the calf that now prevented Chui from attacking, it was the formidable presence of its mother. Chui had watched the hyena's approach and seen for herself the giraffe's flailing hooves: quite enough to banish any further thoughts of a meal from this particular source. If she had been a social creature, living and hunting with others of her own kind, like the lions, she would have acted differently. But she was a solitary killer whose survival depended on caution. Who would provide for the two small cubs peacefully sleeping in the caves below her if she injured herself?

So Chui soon lost interest in the arrival of a new life among the thorn thickets. Instead she looked out over the dry plains where all traces of green had now vanished. Columns of wildebeest drifted south, leaving a spiral of dust in their wake. The land cried out for rain.

Shortly after the giraffe gave birth to her calf a sounder or family of warthogs emerged from their burrow, situated 150 yards east of the Cub Caves, close to the base of the ridge. This particular sounder was composed of an adult female, two subadult females from the previous litter and three small piglets that had been born only a few weeks earlier, five and a half months after the female had conceived in May. An adult male who sometimes occupied a nearby burrow also accompanied the sounder at times, though usually only for brief periods.

The warthogs in the Mara farrow during the early part of the short rains, in October/November, the most favourable period for the lactating female and her new brood, as green grass is normally freely available.

The sow's two to four piglets are born in the warmth of a grass-lined burrow and when the tiny warthogs are barely a week old they emerge for their first look at life above ground and begin to graze. Though they may continue to suckle until they are four or five months old, milk is only a secondary form of nourishment after the second month.

Unlike most members of the pig family warthogs are grazers as well as rooters, preferring to feed on the fresh green grasses. They are typically to be seen rummaging around on the calluses of their densely haired knees, compensating for their stumpy necks. Now, as the dry season dragged interminably on, the warthogs were forced to wander further and further from the safety of their burrows, fanning out to scour the ground for rhizomes, sedges, herbs, shrubs and wild fruits – in fact anything that was edible, and that included carrion.

On this particular morning the warthogs gradually moved towards an open plain at the edge of the acacia thicket, concentrating on the thicker tussocks of grass, using their leathery, disc-shaped snouts to burst through to the more succulent bases of the stems. Every so often a pig would look up, thrusting its nose into the wind, testing for the ever-present threat of predators before returning to the task of feeding itself. The piglets already scrummaged around on their knees, perfect grey miniatures of their parents. Sometimes they would lie down to rest near the adults or cavort about, playfully snuffling and bumping against each other. When they tried to suckle from their mother's four long teats they had to compete with their two older sisters who, though driven away just before the sow had given birth to her latest litter, had since been reunited with their mother and were determined to share in the supply of nutritious milk during these harsh conditions.

The sound of an approaching vehicle caused the sow to look up. Visitors loved to see warthogs and were always anxious to photograph them. The pigs' comical faces and jaunty stride presented a compelling image. But what really tickled people's imaginations were those tails, which helped the tiny piglets to maintain visual contact with their larger relatives.

The vehicle hurried towards the pigs, who immediately turned tail and headed back towards Fig Tree Ridge. Briefly the sow paused at the entrance to her burrow as the three smallest piglets disappeared below ground, then she continued on her way through a gap in the ridge. But before she had gone more than a dozen yards the piglets popped like so many peas out of a pod back up to the surface and dashed after their mother. The car continued on its way, but other events had already been set in motion.

Chui had first noticed the warthogs when she had lost interest in the giraffe calf and cast her eyes to the south. In fact she had plundered this welcome source of food only days earlier, when there had been four piglets in the family. Once more the leopard's ears were pricked and her mouth tense.

The moment the piglets reappeared from their burrow Chui shot down the tree and ran off in a loose-limbed trot, head held high, following the warthogs' progress. With the advantage afforded by her elevated position on the ridge it was unnecessary for her to stalk or conceal herself at this stage. But on reaching a small acacia bush she paused, chin out, ears flat. Now she crouched, moulding her body to the contours of the ground, her spotted coat matching perfectly with the shadowy vegetation beneath the thornbush. She waited patiently, her breathing slowing to an imperceptible rhythm.

The place the warthogs had chosen to cross the ridge was a low point where the large rocks thinned out enough to provide easy passage to the feeding grounds above. The pigs proceeded cautiously, stopping every so often to listen to the sounds around them. The raucous call of a bare-faced go-away bird and the mewling cry of a young Verreaux's eagle owl intermingled, floating down from the nearby fig tree where the baboons slept at night.

Chui tensed, the powerful muscles of her hindquarters bunched beneath her loose, dappled skin, anticipating the moment when the family of warthogs would appear from over the horizon. She could already hear the sounds of their snuffling as they searched for underground sources of food. They moved slowly, still hidden from her view, feeding wherever a patch of succulent growth tempted them. But the sow was wary: perhaps she already sensed danger, had caught the scent of the hidden predator. Suddenly she broke into a trot and wheeled away, her youngsters falling into single file behind her, all holding their tufted tails aloft like tiny antennae.

As the last piglet hurried to keep in contact with its family Chui burst from cover. Uncoiling like a spring she bounded forward and bowled the young pig over, hooking it towards her with an outstretched paw and biting it – just once – before it had time to escape. It was all over in the blink of an eyelid.

As Chui charged, the mother and the other piglets scattered, running for their lives. Before the sow could even turn to see what had happened, Chui had carried the piglet off by its neck. She did not stop to try to feed. Instead she ran with her catch along the top of the ridge to where her cubs lay waiting.

Barely ten minutes after she had first left the fig tree Chui dropped the dead piglet on Top Rock. Then she called Light and Dark from their hiding place. But the cubs ignored the fresh kill and immediately started to suckle from their mother while a pair of eagle-eyed bateleurs circled overhead, ever alert to the presence of a free meal.

Bateleur eagles are the acrobats of the African sky, cartwheeling their displays on distinctive long wings. The sight of the scavenging birds brought an immediate reaction from Chui for they, like the watchful vultures, were a scourge to any leopard and would steal from Chui's kill if she let them. So she quickly ran back to where the carcass lay and picked it up. With a graceful spring she leapt into the fig tree, moving into the densest part of the foliage before draping the piglet over a thick fork, safely out of sight of the eagles.

Satisfied, Chui descended to lie on her favourite branch, which stretched for twenty-five feet from the west side of the tree. In the cool mornings she would recline along this smooth limb, resting her bottom comfortably on the ample support provided by the junction of two branches which formed a perfect armchair. Here she could rest in typical leopard style with her cheek pressed against her forearm. But as the sun's rays exposed Chui's resting place she would surrender her position to the stifling heat and climb higher into the shade of the dense leaf cover provided by the other side of the tree, where her kill now lay.

Within a few minutes the cubs started to protest at the disappearance of their mother and the source of their food. They moved about restlessly on the rocks below her, miaowing their distinctive high-pitched contact calls, *iau*, *iau*. Chui sat up and yawned, then reached forward, sway-backed, to rake her claws along the bark of the fig tree. Looking down she called softly, causing the cubs to squeal excitedly in response. Bounding easily into the top of the tree Chui picked up the piglet and descended. The cubs ran towards their mother, jostling each other in their efforts to reach her. Chui quickly pushed past them and dropped the carcass in a grassy depression behind Top Rock. But instead of starting to feed on the meat, the cubs again followed Chui, miaowing incessantly, content to ignore the bounty of food that lay only yards from them. Soon both lay suckling as Chui reclined in the shade. Though they were now more than three months old they still demanded the easy access of their mother's milk. But shortly afterwards Dark left the warmth of his mother's belly and cautiously approached the piglet.

At first the little cub dabbed and pranced around the kill, movements that soon attracted his brother's attention. As he did so a tawny eagle sailed across the blue sky and landed on a tree stump, less than forty yards from the cubs. Chui saw the bird arrive and immediately got up and moved protectively closer to her food while the cubs tugged and wrestled with the carcass.

All was amicable enough until the young leopards tasted meat, then, as they tore at the coarse hairy skin, their mood changed. The carcass was no longer just a plaything to be shared, it was food. Dark quickly straddled the kill, partially covering it, as if it was his alone. Light retaliated by biting his brother, clawing him on the head and provoking an all-out fight. Shapes dissolved into a jumble of spots as the cubs rolled and clawed at each other, limbs flailing and sharp white teeth bared in ugly threats.

Chui ran forward grunting, forcing her cubs apart by pressing down hard on them with open mouth, holding and nipping the youngsters while they squealed in protest. It seemed that the cubs were already reluctant to share food with each other. Only the close attention of their mother now tempered their hostility.

Shortly after midday Chui retired to her tree, submerging herself among the cool green leaves. She was invisible, just another part of the sunlight and shadows that filtered through the leaves. The piglet lay below her, half-eaten and neglected by the sleepy cubs whose stomachs now bulged, fuller with meat than ever before during their short lives. For the moment everything was peaceful in the leopards' world and Chui and her cubs could sleep, safely ensconced in their hiding places.

Once more the tawny eagle returned to see if its patience had been rewarded. It is Africa's commonest eagle, sometimes ungraciously referred to as the poor man's golden eagle. In reality, like all birds of prey, it is a master of the skies blessed with a visual acuity that can pinpoint the movement of a tiny mouse at over a hundred yards.

The eagle turned sharply and floated quietly towards the fig tree. It landed with a noisy flapping of outspread wings. Chui opened her eyes instantly, but did not move, confident that on this occasion her presence was sufficient to deter the eagle from swooping down to plunder her kill.

As the oppressive heat subsided Chui left her cool retreat and called the sleeping cubs from their cave to join her on the kill. It was nearly five o'clock and cars had already begun to gather on the track along the top of the ridge. The clouds once more performed their daily routine, massing from the east and storming along the distant Siria Escarpment to obliterate the afternoon sun. Columns of thick grey smoke from fires set by the Masai funnelled skywards, beckoning to the rains as large black herds of wildebeest filed back into the Reserve from the dry plains to the east.

These animals were not part of the great Serengeti migration, whose participants had retreated south of the border a month earlier. They belonged to a much smaller population from Kenya's own Loita Plains, to the east of the Reserve. But regardless of where the wildebeest or zebra originated, they all moved into the Reserve for the same reason: their lives depended on their ability to find adequate food and water. For as long as the herds remained free to migrate during the long dry season, they could sustain themselves. That is why the Mara was so important to them.

Chui was so busy feeding on the warthog, keeping a watchful eye on the vehicles and dealing with her squabbling twins that she failed to detect the Fig Tree Troop advancing silently from the west. As the first baboon appeared over the rocks, the cubs turned and fled for the safety of the Cub Caves.

If she had been threatened by lions Chui would probably have taken refuge in the fig tree. But that would be the last place to seek shelter when trying to avoid a troop of sure-footed baboons, who could perform aerial feats that even a leopard might find hard to match. She could have fled for the safety of the nearby caves, but instead Chui stood her ground, crouching over her hard-won food and lunging towards the nearest baboon. She was not about to desert her kill even in the face of the formidable mob that now confronted her. She growled and snarled, wavering between aggression and defence, the urge to attack and to flee. For a while the ferocity of her lunges and her threatening growls kept the baboons at bay. But this was a confrontation Chui could not hope to win, for the troop numbered more than seventy individuals, many of whom seemed quite ready to join in the affray.

As the seconds ticked by, more and more baboons arrived, barking and screaming at Chui. By now a number of large males had gathered, adding a menacing presence to the black wall of animals. Then, as if responding to some hidden signal, a dozen baboons advanced on Chui, like hyenas forcing a lion from its kill. The leopard's resistance crumpled and she fled, drawing the ugly mob with her like a howling gale.

It was in circumstances such as these that an intimate knowledge of her environment paid dividends for Chui. No time now to be looking for a suitable place to hide. She raced straight to a narrow, horizontal cave situated near the top of the ridge. But the baboons were not finished with her yet. They were everywhere, sitting on the boulder roofing the cave and prancing excitedly around it. Chui hissed and snarled, defying the mob to come any closer, confident that she was now safe from real harm.

By six o'clock the majority of the baboons had tired of the confrontation, particularly the larger males who, though present when most needed, did not waste further energy once Chui had retreated. The younger troop members, however, seemed less inclined to leave. Some of these smaller baboons climbed into the fig tree and walked out onto a willowy branch overhanging the place where Chui now lay, just visible at the mouth of the cave. They shook the branches and bounced stiff-legged in front of her, but it made little difference. Chui was staying where she was.

The young baboons exhibited a boldness in challenging the predator that had undoubtedly developed through previous experience. Just as the two frightened cubs, cowering in the caves, were acquiring another valuable lesson in survival, so too were the youngest members of the baboon troop.

Because baboons share their habitat with a variety of potentially harmful predators they have evolved a highly organised and effective group response to the presence of leopards. Both species have fearsome canines that are more like daggers than teeth. While leopards – particularly the males – have a size advantage, possess razor-sharp claws and an astonishing litheness and speed of reaction, they do not live in groups. The baboons' well co-ordinated communal response is their way of neutralising the threat of a leopard.

The baboons' behaviour was reminiscent of the mobbing of birds of prey by smaller birds. Mobbing is a form of harassment directed at predators by potential prey, characterised by the conflict between aggression and fear. The survival value of baboons' mobbing behaviour lies partly in the effectiveness of the loud bisyllabic alarm barks which the large males use as a means of warning other troop members of the presence and location of a dangerous predator. Mobbing often proves successful in driving a predator away and therefore increases the probability that it will eventually hunt elsewhere, for a leopard that is mobbed has lost all chance of a surprise attack.

The baboons made no attempt to steal the remains of Chui's kill. The lump of red meat still lay on the rock where she had defended it, clearly visible to the keen-eyed primates with their well-developed colour vision. Yet male baboons in the Mara regularly kill and eat young gazelles, impala fawns and even African hares. Perhaps the reek of leopard scent deterred them, or was it simply that they, like cheetahs, did not wish to feed on meat that they had not actually killed for themselves?

Later that night, while the baboons slept in the safety of their own fig trees, Chui and the cubs hurriedly finished the remains of their kill. As they fed, the familiar roars of the Gorge Pride drifted down from Leopard Gorge, half a mile away. Briefly Chui stopped feeding and listened. For some time now the Gorge had reverberated to the sounds of these lions, and Chui had wisely avoided the area. She would not overcome the menace of the baboons by moving with her cubs to Leopard Gorge.

It was early November and the short rains, which usually arrive in mid-October, had not yet materialised. Now the signs were more promising, and each afternoon the heat built up along with the dense cloud cover. In the west rain was already cascading down, drawing the plains game from drier areas in expectation of the new grass which would sprout within hours. The wind gusted through the ancient fig trees along the ridge, shaking free the dried leaves and sending them swirling and tumbling to the rocky ground. At last the rain blew in.

Chui sat up to scrutinise the country around her which was shrouded in a fine mist. Satisfied that there was no easy prey or danger nearby, she descended and called softly. When the cubs failed to appear Chui circled around the rocks, sniffing to pick up their scent. She called again and this time two excited cubs ran from the cave where they had been sleeping. Dark nipped at his mother's heels, while Light wandered up and down under her belly and between the arch of her forelegs.

Ignoring the drizzle, Chui sat at the base of the rocks and allowed the cubs to suckle, reaching down every so often to groom their wet fur. When she looked east again she noticed the warthogs feeding close to the place where she had killed before. Chui had been watching them earlier and now she responded quickly, hurrying away along the top of the ridge.

But this time a male impala caught sight of her and immediately blasted out a nasal snort of alarm. The pigs looked up, recognising the antelope's distinctive warning, and turned towards the direction in which the impala was looking. For a moment the crouching predator and her intended prey stared at each other, then the warthogs turned and raced away. Chui sat up, signalling her loss of interest in the pigs, for she was still too far away to give chase. Once all the prey species had been alerted to her presence there was nothing for Chui to do but return to where the cubs sat waiting.

Chui was an excellent mother, reacting with care if her cubs ventured into a potentially dangerous situation. When she had her first litter in Leopard Gorge, I had watched her quickly descend from a fig tree so as to lead them back to safety when they had exposed themselves in the open as they attempted to join her.

With each new day Light and Dark were reacting more confidently to the various elements in their environment: the twittering of birds, the movements of game animals and the presence of possible danger. Previously they had tended to flee from any unfamiliar object that moved towards them. Now they were learning to deal with life in a more discerning manner.

Chui responded to her cubs' development by no longer confining them to the rocks immediately surrounding the fig tree. She now encouraged them to accompany her on walkabouts, chuffling to them as she smelt and investigated her way along the ridge. There were still times when the cubs showed just how vulnerable they were without her protective presence. When Light became stranded below the rock on which Chui and Dark rested, he miaowed in distress, his usual reaction when feeling unsure of himself. Chui answered him with a throaty call, encouraging the cub to join her. But the steep sides of the rocks surrounding the Cub Caves were too tall for Light to negotiate and he seemed uncertain what to do next. Eventually Chui and Dark solved his problem by moving down to join him. Light ran to his mother, who rolled on to her back, clutching the cub to her chest and enveloping him in a playful embrace.

It has been reported that leopards transfer their young cubs to a new hiding place every few days. The longer a leopard maintains her cubs in one particular place the greater the chances that a marauding lion, hyena or even male leopard might find and kill them. Jackals, baboons, pythons and large eagles are also known to be capable of killing small leopards if they find them unprotected. Though the mother leopard keeps her cubs clean when they are very small, telltale scents and scraps from kills eventually provide clues to their whereabouts.

All young cubs, be they leopard, lion or cheetah, face a difficult period when they first start to follow their mother, and the mortality rate is considerable. A lioness does not bring food back to where she has hidden her cubs in the way that both Chui and the Mara Buffalo leopard did. Instead lion cubs are kept in seclusion until, at six to eight weeks, they are sufficiently mobile to be led to a kill, and can gradually be integrated into the sociable existence of their mother's pride. Despite the powerful protective presence of the mother and the added security offered by the pride system, lion cubs are still vulnerable. There are times when a lioness miscalculates the safety of a situation and finds herself confronted by strange lions or a group of aggressive hyenas. It is a pathetic sight to see a frightened mother forced to hurry to a safer place, a baby dangling from her mouth and two or three frantic cubs trailing behind her as they try desperately to keep up. By the time cheetah cubs are eight weeks old they no longer require a permanent abode, leading a nomadic existence as they follow their mother from feeding site to feeding site, bedding down wherever evening finds them.

The fact that the long rains had failed earlier in the year and the short rains were proving to be little more than thunderous showers posed as great a problem for Chui as the resulting lack of vegetation did for the herbivores. Now that the grass and bushes had been stripped bare there was little cover to shield the movements of a leopard with cubs. The hours of darkness would undoubtedly provide some protection, but there were few places that could offer the security that the caves of Fig Tree Ridge afforded – at least until the young leopards were capable of disappearing quickly up the nearest tree.

To make matters worse, the lioness that Chui had so carefully avoided four months earlier had herself given birth to two cubs in a cave close to the place where Chui had seen her. Sometimes I would encounter the lioness lying in the grass suckling her tiny cubs, or pause to photograph the two pride males posing statuesque and sphinx-like on a rocky outcrop in the glorious early morning light. On another occasion I found the whole pride feeding on the fresh carcass of a huge bull buffalo that they had killed during the night. There could be little doubt that, for as long as the lions chose to remain in Leopard Gorge, Fig Tree Ridge would be a far safer refuge for Chui and her cubs.

When I first started to try to follow the development of Chui's cubs there had been long periods when the wary young leopards remained hidden in the Cub Caves. If Chui was not in attendance I could not be certain that she had not moved the cubs elsewhere during the night. There were even days when Chui did not appear at all – possibly to avoid unnecessary conflict with the diurnal baboons – only returning during the hours of darkness to suckle the cubs or to bring them a small prey animal or a portion of a carcass that she had already partially consumed.

On the days when Light and Dark slept in later than usual or when Chui was absent, I would continue on my way and try to catch up on events at Mara Buffalo Rocks: the location of the other female leopard and her two ten-month-old cubs. This entailed a five-mile drive further east through beautiful scenery, most of which was also good leopard country. En route I searched the surrounding luggas and thickets in the hope that I might find a male leopard or even Chui while she was away from her cubs.

The quickest way to the Mara Buffalo Rocks was to follow the narrow, rock-strewn vehicle track that wound its way up over Fig Tree Ridge, and then continued east across Leopard Lugga towards the Gorge. From there the track continued amid dense acacia thickets which eventually opened out into a gently undulating plain. To the north of the track a stony ridge ran from west to east, covered with thornbush and euphorbia trees. Cloaking the base of this low ridge were patches of forest which provided any leopard in the area with excellent cover for hunting sorties along the edge of the plain. It was along this ridge that the Mara Buffalo Female and her two cubs were now to be found.

Once the drivers from the various tented camps learned that leopards were to be seen with some degree of regularity they, like myself, were only too happy to make the long drive to Mara Buffalo Rocks. They knew that they were unlikely to find a better opportunity than this to show their clients a leopard. Word soon reached Nairobi that the Mara was once again a good place to view leopards. People started to arrive at the camps and lodges announcing, 'We've come to see the leopards.' Tour vehicles from other parts of the Reserve made special game drives from as far afield as Serena Lodge, Fig Tree Camp and even Keekorok Lodge, fifty miles away by road. I even received a letter from a fellow leopard enthusiast in Australia asking when would be a good time to come and photograph the leopards!

There was now a better chance of finding a leopard than of seeing a cheetah. The page reserved for leopard sightings in the visitors' game record book no longer looked so bare. For the more fortunate visitors there was now the unique possibility of seeing both leopard families during the course of a single game drive – six leopards! All of this was marvellous for the visitors. But not necessarily for the leopards.

The Mara Buffalo Female had first come to people's attention when she was seen mating in the vicinity of the Mara Buffalo Rocks during the latter part of September 1982. Three months later she gave birth to her cubs in a deep crevice, fifty feet from the main cave which she and her cubs now favoured as a daytime resting place.

The leopards were by no means alone in their use of this particularly secure environment, forced to share it with hyraxes, mongooses and agamid lizards. Close to the base of one of the two enormous rocks bordering the leopards' cave was a hyena den, which sometimes reverberated to the growls and giggles of its occupants. But the vertical gap providing access to the cave had to be reached by an athletic leap up from the ground, something that the hyenas were unable to accomplish – though they did sometimes try.

The Mara Buffalo Female was not like Chui. Her journeys to and from the cave were much more furtive and if people tried to get too close, which was invariably the case, she would simply disappear from view. Usually she would be safely hidden by seven o'clock in the morning, though there were times when she tarried a while longer, sniffing and marking around the bushes and rocks, or secreting herself in a dark passageway among the dense croton thicket at the westerly edge of the rocks. It was unusual for her to emerge before six o'clock in the evening, often later, though invariably she responded to the urge to be moving as it got dark, a vulnerable time for diurnal prey species. Very occasionally, when not unduly disturbed, she graced us with her elegant presence, venturing from the cave to lie quietly among the bushes or on top of the rocks where she could observe the activities of the other animals around her. And what moments those would be. When the opportunity arose she, like Chui, hunted during the daylight hours.

Thirty yards from the cave was a narrow patch of forest which extended east for half a mile, following the line of the ridge. The trees were the same as those found in Kampi ya Chui, predominantly *Euclea divinorum* and *Diospyros abyssinica*. A large troop of baboons often slept among these trees. On the mornings when the baboons were present they would leave their roosting place and spread out from the forest to scour the countryside for food. Often two or three of the larger males would swagger over to the rocks and investigate the area for signs of the leopards. They, like the Fig Tree Troop, knew only too well the places in their home range which were most likely to harbour danger, and they took every opportunity to harass the leopard and her cubs. But once having satisfied themselves that there was no chance of a confrontation they would continue on their way.

Occasionally members of the troop would spot one of the leopard cubs among the rocks or lying under a bush. Then the alarm barks would echo menacingly forth and the leopards would hurry back to the safety of the main cave, at times pursued by one or more of the males. They had learned long ago that baboons were one of their most formidable enemies, capable of tearing the cubs to pieces given the chance.

Another less natural problem confronting both leopard families was that the areas surrounding their rocky hideouts were easily accessible to vehicles approaching from above as well as from below. In other, less drought-stricken years grass-shrouded boulders would have crunched a few oil sumps and gear boxes in retaliation for the intrusion. Instead, well-defined tracks soon developed, creating a most unsatisfactory situation for the leopards, who could now be virtually encircled. There were times when more than twenty vehicles together packed the surrounds of Mara Buffalo Rocks. As Chui's cubs became more visible in their activities, they too were subjected to the same kind of pressure.

The concentration of vehicles around predators is not a new problem facing Kenya's Parks and Reserves. The authorities at Amboseli National Park, nestled at the foot of Mount Kilimanjaro, have struggled for many years to deal with it. It is by no means an easy task and requires a high degree of co-operation between tour drivers and their clients, and those who seek to control the situation. But people do not always respond well to being 'regulated', and the drivers and couriers are understandably anxious to make clients happy.

Predators are the key visitor attraction in places like Amboseli and the Masai Mara. The 75,000 people who now annually visit the Mara naturally want to make the most of the limited time they are able to spend on safari: a journey that for many will be the trip of a lifetime. Yet unregulated visitor use can at its worst have the most undesirable effects, as the following two incidents, involving Mara leopards, illustrate.

On 3 August 1983, seven visitors were on an early-morning game drive out on the plains to the north of the Mara Reserve boundary. The tourists were in convoy with another vehicle from one of the tented camps, enjoying watching the plentiful plains game: families of zebra, herds of wildebeest, small groups of topi and a multitude of dainty gazelles. But it was the chance of seeing some of the Mara's many predators that added an extra element of excitement to their game viewing.

No other animal generates more unparalleled excitement among both visitors and drivers than a leopard. So it was, on this particular morning when the two vehicles unexpectedly came across a large male wandering out in the open. As the cars approached the leopard fled for the nearest patch of bush, an isolated thicket among a sea of open plain.

Unmolested and in good health, the leopard is a shy, retiring creature showing a marked fear of man. If confronted it will usually flee for the nearest available cover. But when injured or forced into a position where escape seems impossible, it becomes a formidable adversary with a reputation to rival that of the Cape buffalo. An angry leopard is the very incarnation of ferocity, a perfectly designed killing machine, capable of concentrating all its considerable energy into a short-range attack of lightning speed.

The vehicles pressed forward, with their occupants desperately straining to catch a glimpse of the frightened cat. Suddenly the leopard burst from cover and charged towards the nearest car, leaping upwards and hooking its claws on to the open sides of the Toyota Landcruiser. Fortunately the driver reacted quickly, and effectively, by taking off his rubber sandal and forcing the animal's claws free.

The leopard tumbled to the ground and soon moved further out into the open. Instead of immediately leaving the disturbed leopard to retreat to a place where it felt more secure, the vehicle tarried a little longer. The driver warned the visitors to keep down as the leopard was by now threatening to repeat its attack.

Among the passengers was a middle-aged woman on her first visit to Africa. She was sitting in the row of seats behind the driver, wedged between her sister and a young boy who crouched next to the open window space on the side of the vehicle towards which the leopard now charged. Incautiously the woman leant towards the window to try to take pictures of the furious animal. The driver accelerated in a desperate attempt to outdistance the charging leopard. But it was too late.

It was perhaps fortunate that the woman had her camera raised to her face, for it undoubtedly saved her from more serious injury. The leopard sprang towards the car, focusing his full attention on the woman, biting her elbow and clutching her in his forepaws. One paw ripped into the underside of her wrist, exposing the tendons. The other paw clawed into her back and shoulder, leaving deep scratch marks, though her clothes helped protect her from greater damage. As the leopard was mauling the woman he stood on the young boy, whose only injury was a scratch on the leg.

The leopard now shifted position and tried to drag the woman with him. The men sitting behind her tried vainly to kick the leopard away, while hanging on to the woman's legs to prevent her from being pulled further towards the far window. After what must have seemed an eternity the horrific situation was brought to an end by the driver bravely putting his beret over the leopard's eyes, causing him to release his vice-like grip on the woman. A final shove and the leopard was back in the wild again.

Back at camp, the woman was patched up by a doctor and the manager, before being flown to Nairobi by the Flying Doctor Service. After a number of days in hospital she was discharged and continued her recuperation at the coast. She was already planning her next trip to Kenya for the end of the same year!

A more recent incident was to have a more harrowing ending, this time for the leopard. One morning in an area to the south of Governors' Camp some vehicles sighted a male leopard. It was not an animal that the drivers knew and he was obviously unfamiliar with the close attentions of vehicles. Under normal circumstances young male leopards disappear from their mother's home range to seek a territory of their own, probably in an area far away from their birthplace. Consequently, many of the Mara's male leopards originate from areas where they have never learned to tolerate vehicles as Chui had done. As secretive adults, they are far less likely to be conditioned to the situation in the way that inquisitive, tolerant and home-bound cubs tend to be. Nor are they ever shackled to one place for long periods of time as Chui and the Mara Buffalo Female now were.

Excitedly the drivers pursued the animal as he ran off along the bank of the lugga. Unfortunately, a group of lions from the Paradise Pride had also seen the leopard, and they too pursued him. When confronted by humans or vehicles, the last place a leopard usually seeks shelter is in a tree. But as two of the Paradise lions ran towards him, the leopard had no alternative but to flee up the nearest tree. Vehicles quickly closed in around the agitated leopard, which was visibly distressed by the experience, hissing and snarling at the occupants.

With the leopard out of their reach in the tree the lions soon lost interest and moved away fifty yards to rest in the shade of some bushes. A little while later the frightened leopard fled from the vehicles and ran in the direction of the lions. They were waiting. Two of the males closed in as the leopard ran headlong towards one of them. The lions attacked the leopard in the same way they would an alien lion. The leopard clawed desperately at the lion's face as the larger predator's jaws clamped around his throat. The second male quickly closed in behind the leopard and bit into his lower spine. It was all over in a matter of seconds.

A third male now ran over and sniffed at the dead leopard, grimacing with teeth bared in a 'flehmen' face, a typical response to a significant odour. He in turn was joined by a lioness and her ten-month-old cub. The female opened a patch of skin on the leopard's belly, exposing the flesh which the cub licked. But as was usually the case, the lions disdained the flesh of a fellow predator.

So, a leopard who had endured to adulthood in an area that supports one of the densest lion populations in the whole of Africa, learning through experience how best to avoid the dangerous larger predator, had been forced into a situation that he could not hope to survive and which he would normally have avoided at all costs.

Predators maintain an uneasy relationship with each other under the best of circumstances, for they share a harsh competitive existence. Lions have always killed leopards, irrespective of their age or size. Conversely leopards kill and eat lion cubs that they find unprotected. But this was an unnecessary death which did not follow the natural laws. For the tourists, the thrill of seeing a leopard had been replaced by the knowledge that their presence had directly contributed to the savage killing they had just witnessed.

Whether these incidents are the result of lack of experience or inadequate training, over-excitement or a misplaced loyalty to their clients and the tips that they might earn, there is a need for stricter control of drivers' activities, particularly in the Mara, where off-the-road driving is the norm and vehicles are able to encircle animals. After all, the wildlife is meant to have absolute protection and visitors are but privileged spectators.

Some people argue that it is the constant presence of vehicles that ultimately conditions the game, making it approachable and allowing visitors to obtain good photographs. But if only people would be a little more patient, approach the animals with greater caution and keep as quiet as possible, life would be far more tolerable for the animals.

Of the three large African cats, the lion is the least adversely affected by the presence of vehicles, and the cheetah the most. Unlike the cheetah, the leopard, if unduly disturbed, can survive as an entirely nocturnal creature. However, matters become more complicated when leopards have cubs and the cover in their area is depleted. Then a leopard may find itself shackled to one place, as in the case of Chui and the Mara Buffalo Female.

Ultimately, as man and leopard come into greater conflict, the leopard's survival will depend on the protection of areas such as the Mara. The laudable steps that the Kenya government has taken to preserve its wildlife have without doubt resulted in an increase in the leopard population in many parts of Kenya in recent years. The Masai Mara is, as a result, one of the most complete game-viewing areas in Africa. It would be a pity if this were in any way diminished.

A number of the older and more experienced rangers and drivers such as Sigera, the head driver at Governors' Camp, who had known the lean years when leopards were rarely seen, did what they could to influence the less responsible people. Joseph would just shake his head and hold up his hands in despair when he came to visit. I felt sick at heart to see the leopard mothers hissing and snarling at vehicles, at times being provoked into charging the cars. I soon found myself wishing that the leopards would just vanish.

3. Chui's Competitors

AFTER BRIEFLY attending to the needs of her cubs, Chui had left them and headed west along the ridge, immediately attracting the attention of the blood-sucking tsetse flies. A hundred yards to the south, a group of vervet monkeys stopped feeding in the acacia bushes and set up a distinctive chorus of stuttering alarm calls as the leopard came into view. As they did so a lone hyena appeared from over the ridge, a giraffe thigh bone clamped between its jaws.

The giraffe's brave efforts to save her youngster had been to no avail. Time and again she had charged the hyenas as they gathered around her injured calf. But their far-carrying whoops and cackles had quickly summoned more and more clan members. They had poured in from every direction, forsaking their resting places among the rocky caves of Fig Tree Ridge and the orange-leaved croton thickets at the edge of a nearby hill. As the giraffe confronted one hyena, others moved in to bite and pull at the helpless youngster whose hind leg had been left trailing from some mishap during the first days of its life.

The end was inevitable. Screams, growls, giggles, cackles and whoops mingled into a hideous cacophony of sound, emanating from the mass of seething bodies which wrenched and tore at the bloody carcass. Periodically a hyena would pause from the frenzied activity and jerk its head upright, large ears cocked, mouth parted to reveal powerful, bone-crushing premolars as it searched nervously for approaching danger. Before waiting vultures could plummet from the sky the carcass had been dismembered.

Hyenas are creatures of dubious ancestry most closely related to the cats and mongooses, though they have adopted the lifestyle of the dog family. They do not kill their prey in the manner of cats, who bite, strangle or suffocate the life from their victim. Hyenas have not perfected a single killing bite, though they have the most powerful jaws of any of Africa's carnivorous mammals. Instead they eat while killing, which in its own way is a highly efficient means of despatching prey, however unpleasant it may be to look at. They compete with other clan members by eating as fast as possible, ripping hunks of flesh out and swallowing them whole, rather than by fighting over the kill as lions do. Hyenas can consume the equivalent of a third of their body weight, and their large neck muscles and well-developed forequarters are ideally suited to their style of killing and to carrying off pieces of carcass to be devoured in a quieter place.

Chui had heard the sounds of the Ridge Clan's kill, but she was more interested in searching for her own prey. The hyena checked its stride as it caught sight of the leopard, then quickly galloped off, pursued not by Chui, but by two other clan members eager to steal the meaty bone for themselves.

During their cautious wanderings around the Cub Caves, Light and Dark had discovered a maze of hiding places among the massive boulders close to their birthplace. There was always a safe haven for them within a few yards of wherever they happened to be playing and they could already move with surprising speed when the need arose.

Once more the slender mongoose wandered on his daily rounds, though on this occasion he was free to investigate the inner recesses of the Cub Caves. For the time being at least they had been abandoned by the leopard cubs and it was safe to enter. Having satisfied himself that there were no scraps of food to be scavenged, the mongoose paused for a moment to watch the playful cubs before departing.

It was yet another uncomfortably blowy day and by the afternoon the clouds were piled up in great layers, blanketing the hot air and forcing it back to earth. Shortly after four o'clock the cubs emerged, sleepy and ruffle-coated. Their latest resting site was a deep furrow, situated between the edges of a pile of flat rocks, which opened out among a patch of tall grass. A small tunnel ran beneath one of the rocks, providing just enough space for two small cubs to lie undetected. Now they lay on their sides in the grass, gently wrestling and biting each other, quietly cocooned in their secret green world.

By five o'clock a few shards of light had managed to pierce the grey cloud cover and filtered through onto the cubs. Gradually their play became more vigorous, even though Chui had not yet returned. The cubs transferred their attentions to a patch of secondary growth that spread like a protective fence of branches and leaves around the base of the fig tree. It rose ten feet into the air and acted like a ladder that would one day take the young leopards into their mother's aerial domain. It would not be long now before Light or Dark clawed their way up the swollen trunk of Chui's fig tree.

After nightfall Chui returned to the cubs, having unsuccessfully hunted for prey along Dik-Dik Lugga at the west end of the ridge. Next morning, as darkness receded into a grey gloom, she dozed on Top Rock.

Moving into the fig tree, Chui sat and studied a herd of impala feeding among the thornbushes to the north. It was a miserable, overcast day: iron-grey skies and a chilly wind that rustled noisily through the leaves of the fig tree.

Chui descended and sat for a moment on Top Rock, gazing out over the countryside like an enormous ornamental cat. Suddenly she was on her feet, reacting immediately to the irresistible sight of yet another party of warthogs. The pigs were trotting nonchalantly from the bushes on their way back towards Fig Tree Ridge. Chui slunk off in pursuit, accompanied almost immediately by two minibuses that had been watching her. The vehicles scrambled noisily over the rocks to keep pace with the elegantly stealthy feline, in the process routing a herd of Cape buffalo which stampeded away, leaving Chui looking somewhat confused at the sudden disappearance of her intended meal. For lack of alternative cover Chui quickly retreated to the protective canopy of a nearby tree which fortunately grew among a maze of rocks of sufficient size to keep the minibuses at bay.

The tree Chui had chosen was one of three that formed a distinctive triangle, each growing fifty yards from the other; a pappea, a euphorbia and the one that she now rested in, an eleaodendron. All three were quite different in shape and size yet each had on occasion been all things to Chui and other leopards: a resting place, a secure refuge and a larder for kills executed at the edge of the nearby thornbush country.

Hyenas often skulked around the rocky margins of the area where the Three Trees stood, resting under the reclining cradles formed by the gardenia trees, or beneath a convenient patch of croton bush. And there was always the chance of finding a lion in the area.

Chui lay exposed to view, straddled along a broad limb just beneath the base of the tree's thick foliage. Like the figs, it was a species of tree much favoured by the Mara leopards, providing thick limbs and good leaf cover. Below Chui the buffalo herd settled down again to chew the cud in a black semicircle. As the wind shifted restlessly the scent of leopard created a fresh ripple of movement among the recumbent herd.

In ones and twos the buffalo got to their feet, bulbous wet noses pushed pugnaciously into the air. Some of the more curious individuals moved forward a few paces, perplexed by the cat's smell. Their noses pointed directly to where the leopard lay facing them, yet their bovine eyes seemed unable to distinguish the cause of their alarm.

Eventually, one of the massive bulls lunged sideways in jittery response to some sound or movement. The result would have been no less dramatic if somebody had prodded each and every buffalo with a red-hot branding iron, galvanising the entire herd into collective action. Like a smartly drilled squad of soldiers they wheeled as one and made good their escape, snorting with fear.

Clouds of oxpeckers rose twittering as the buffalo stormed away. After a few thunderous yards the herd juddered to a halt and swung round to face the tree, momentarily hidden from view in the dust of their own departure. Once more the oxpeckers descended to probe and peck among the thick folds of skin, delving into ears and nostrils, and any other part of the tick-infested beasts that they could reach.

Although her scent had caused such panic, Chui offered no threat to the buffalo. A single leopard is incapable of endangering an adult buffalo, which can weigh as much as three quarters of a ton. They are equipped with vicious horns and have the power and willingness to protect themselves and their calves: there were far easier prey animals for Chui to concentrate on. She might attack a sick or very small calf in exceptional circumstances; the only way a leopard is really likely to gain a meal from a buffalo is as a scavenger, feeding on the remains of another predator's kill or on an animal that has died from disease.

Chui's attention was already directed elsewhere. She watched as wildebeest fed in a wide arc along the rocky hill to the west of Dik-Dik Lugga. But once again she was attracted by the presence of warthogs: two adults and a single piglet which were busy feeding, facing away from Chui, under a small clump of whistling thorn. She came down from the tree and peered furtively around its base.

In broad daylight, without the help of any cover, Chui compressed her ninety pounds in the way only a leopard can, rippling towards a solitary tree stump seventy yards away. She was a fluid arrangement of loosely articulated flesh and bone, capable of moulding herself perfectly to the demands of concealment. Then, quite inexplicably, she stopped and sniffed the ground, rolling and squirming on her back. Had she found a pile of dung or a smell to roll in, a smell that perhaps resembled a sexual odour? Whatever her reason, it was peculiar behaviour in the midst of a careful hunt.

Though Chui stalked very close to the warthogs it was not close enough. From where I was it looked as if Chui was only a few yards from the pigs and I was sure that at any moment she would rush forward and pounce on the piglet. In the end the warthogs seemed to sense the predator's presence and drifted away with their one surviving youngster trotting ahead of them.

Chui started to make her way back to the cubs. Briefly she paused to look around from atop a huge, grassless termite mound. But there was nothing to interest Chui here, so she bellied carefully down its smooth side and headed back towards one of the Three Trees.

She gathered herself and then leapt easily upwards, hanging momentarily by her razor-sharp claws, before bounding into the lowest fork of the euphorbia. She lowered her head and investigated the grooved bark, sniffing carefully. Before she came down again she reached upwards and raked the bark with the sharp claws of her forepaws. The resulting odour-tainted claw marks produce a visual and olfactory signal which probably helps establish the leopard's whereabouts to members of its own species. This action also stretches muscles and keeps the animal's claws sharp by peeling off any loose strips from the surface of the claws that are ready to flake off. Certainly Chui did this with great regularity.

Shortly after two o'clock Chui arrived back at the Cub Caves. She passed the hiding place in the long grass where her cubs now slept and climbed noiselessly into the fig tree. For almost an hour she rested, untroubled by her cubs or by flies, until her relaxed demeanour suddenly changed and she shot into the dense foliage on the east side of the tree. There she sat staring into the distance as the wind gushed into her face, bringing with it the unmistakable high-pitched sounds of Masai voices.

To begin with, the tribesmen were hidden from sight among the thorn thickets, causing Chui to bob and weave in her attempts to see them. Soon three red-cloaked figures came into view. They were tall and lithe, each carrying a slender spear, a short sword and a variety of sticks. Their easy, relaxed stride reflected their attitude to the situation: they had no shoes, no guns, no vehicles, but were armed with their courage and an understanding of wild places born of a lifetime of experience in the bush.

Less than half a mile away members of the Gorge Pride sprawled only yards from a fresh zebra kill. Buffalo lay concealed among the black shadows, peering from beneath dense acacia thickets, while Chui crouched nervously in her tree, watchful as the Masai passed nearly 200 yards to the north. She did not for one moment take her eyes from the humans, staring after them until they had vanished over the distant horizon.

The Masai, named for their unwritten tongue, *Maa*, have clung tenaciously to their distinctive life style for thousands of years. Once the most feared and warlike tribe roaming the high plains country of East Africa, they are now faced with the difficult problem of assimilating and adjusting to the needs of their country, and the demands of a cash economy.

Traditionally the Masai have occupied areas unrivalled in beauty and rich in soil, unselfishly sharing their land with the wild herds. Because their culture dictated the central role of cattle as food and sustenance, wild animals could in most cases be ignored, either as a source of meat or as direct competitors for grazing. But today the Masai's nomadic ways are being restricted to an ever-decreasing area as land is sold off to other tribes, leased for the cultivation of crops, fenced for intensive ranching and developed for the growing demands of tourism. And always there are more people, more cattle and more sheep and goats to feed.

Though a leopard might steal a sheep or a goat, an occasional calf or a dog, they pose little threat to the Masai or their stock in this particular area. With such an abundance of their natural prey there is little need for leopards to risk confrontation with Masai. True, a leopard might still fall foul of a piece of meat laced with cattle dip. But that would be unusual.

The Masai boys and herdsmen certainly took an interest in all the activity that the presence of the leopards generated among the tour vehicles. But they were as much intrigued by the tourists as they were by the leopards, and theirs was a casual and benign involvement.

Chui often rested during the hotter part of the day – from nine in the morning until five or six in the evening – though she usually remained alert to hunting opportunities, particularly if she was lying in a tree or on some vantage point that allowed her to keep a watchful eye on the prey species.

Though Chui nearly always moved off to search for prey each evening, her daytime activity pattern was modified by the needs of her growing cubs as much as by her own hunger. Light and Dark's increasing begging for access to her diminishing supply of milk undoubtedly helped encourage Chui to adjust to their need for more and more meat.

The majority of her kills during this period were drawn from the seasonal glut of young animals, particularly impala fawns and warthog piglets. These were certainly the easiest prey for Chui to catch, as well as being the most suitable for her to carry back to the cubs. The short rains were therefore an ideal time to be weaning young leopard cubs onto a meat diet. Chui also killed adult impalas and Thomson's gazelles, which she usually stored in the nearest tree. She could then feed on the carcass at leisure, though she did not yet risk trying to bring the cubs to feed with her.

Chui was far more likely to lose a large kill to the ever-vigilant hyenas. A male impala weighs considerably more than a female leopard and invariably proved too heavy or awkward for Chui to carry into a tree, unless she had time to remove the abdominal contents or eat some of the meat. If she was lucky she could drag the kill into bushes or down the concealing banks of a lugga. But there were so many little clues as to what she was doing that a hyena or lion might easily be alerted.

For some days now Chui had been taking a particular interest in the topi: large, elegant creatures which belong to the hartebeest family. They are one of Africa's swiftest antelopes, possessing excellent vision and responding to the slightest sign of danger. By now many of the females were accompanied by calves: drab, fawn-coloured youngsters who at this stage in their lives looked almost identical to their close relatives the Coke's hartebeest or kongoni. But within a few months the topi calves' dark thigh patches would become visible and then there would be no mistaking them.

The males of both species could often be seen standing motionless atop a termite mound, issuing by their presence a territorial warning to others of their kind, while at the same time keeping a wary eye out for predators.

Topi, like warthogs, give birth between October and November each year, at the time of the short rains. The welcome showers create a flush of new growth that provides rich milk for the youngsters and tender, protein-rich, green shoots for the time when they are old enough to feed themselves. Because the topi females give birth within a few weeks of each other it also helps lessen the impact of predation. The calves are highly visible to a watchful predator and losses would be greater if they were born in ones or twos throughout the year.

The females do not retreat to a secluded place to calve, preferring the security of the herds. Within a few minutes of birth the calves struggle to their feet and wobble away after their mothers on rapidly strengthening legs – if a lion, hyena, cheetah or hunting dog is not already running towards them.

Recently the topi had been cautiously picking their way through the rocks of Fig Tree Ridge, leaving the bare plains to the south to search for better grazing among the thornbushes and along the edges of Dik-Dik Lugga. From her position high in the fig tree Chui waited for the opportunity that would spur her into activity.

Perhaps 200 yards east from where Chui rested, a minibus pulled to a halt on the track running below Fig Tree Ridge. As the dust settled half-a-dozen occupants clambered from the vehicle. The object of their curiosity was a wildebeest skull: a solitary remnant from an old lion kill, now covered with a multitude of tube-like projections that erupted from the dry surface of the horns. The driver explained that these were the abandoned horn-fragment housings of a caterpillar; a stage in the life cycle of a slim-winged moth called *Tinea deperdella*, a relative of the clothes moth. The caterpillars hatch from eggs laid on the surface of the horns after the death of the original owner, be it wildebeest, buffalo or impala. Through their ability to digest keratin, the basic ingredient of horn, the caterpillars are able to provide themselves with enough food to metamorphose into fully fledged moths. The death of one animal thereby provides life for other creatures besides the more highly visible predator that has done the killing. The Reserve regulation that forbids visitors to carry such trophies home with them does far more than prevent the use of a potential loophole for the possession of wildlife products – it also ensures that natural cycles continue uninterrupted.

The sudden appearance of humans outside the shielding presence of their vehicle caught Chui by surprise. Though she tolerated the close proximity of people inside their vehicles, the sight, sound and smell of human beings on foot, be they Masai or visitors, prompted an immediate response.

Initially she sped into the topmost branches of the fig tree, then bolted down the tree and ran for seventy-five yards along the ridge in the opposite direction. Only then did she pause long enough to look back over her shoulder. On this occasion Chui's enforced departure from her resting place worked to her own advantage. From her new vantage point among the thornbushes she was even closer to the unsuspecting topi and their calves, some of which were lying down only eighty yards away.

The baboon troop had departed from their roost among the fig trees later than usual. Most mornings they were on their way by seven o'clock, but today they remained for some time at the base of the trees, sitting among the rocks in small groups, each consisting of a few favourite grooming partners.

By ten o'clock the troop began to move off, making their way towards another large tree that grew at the base of the ridge, only sixty yards from where the leopard cubs lay hidden.

The tree was distinguished at its base by a neatly cut hole which, over many years, had become smooth-edged by the forces of wind and dust, giving it an almost natural appearance. It was the place where, many years ago, a Masai honey hunter had located the nest of wild bees and hacked into the trunk to gain access to the honey. Having smoked the bees out he had scraped the honeycomb free and stuffed it into an old Kimbo tin, scavenged from one of the tented camps. A number of trees, marked in a similar manner, could be found deep within the Reserve itself, testimony to the days when the Masai were free to wander wherever they chose. The honey so collected would sometimes be sold or traded, or used to make a potent honey beer to be consumed in large quantities at special festivities.

Even now the gaping wound still harboured bees and other insects which provided food for a voracious female agamid lizard that waited as motionless as a chameleon. She was camouflaged the same colour as the bark, and scuttled in and around the hole, using precision timing and lightning reactions to snap up the insects.

The majority of the baboons passed the tree and continued into an open patch of ground beneath the ridge. Chui watched, motionless, hidden from their view high in her tree. One of the males paused beneath her, deftly plucking tender shoots of grass with his versatile primate hand, the same hand that could peel a ripe fruit or firmly grasp the gazelle fawns that he sometimes killed and ate.

Soon he continued east, unaware of or ignoring the leopard above him. Groups of zebra and wildebeest stood listlessly under scattered trees, like zombies in the brain-numbing heat, while others lay huddled in dark clusters beneath the thornbushes. Two subadult lions, a male and a female, lay in the shadows of a croton thicket, forty yards from the tree where Chui had looked down on the buffalo herd, and hyenas sought shade in the caves further along the ridge. But for the moment predators and prey waged an uneasy peace.

Out of the grey heat a wind suddenly picked up, tinged with a cold dampness. At last, just after three o'clock, it started to rain. Slowly the baboons moved further west, feeding on whatever they could scour from the drought-stricken land. One of the larger males, trailing behind the troop, paused to climb into Chui's fig tree, but by that time the leopard had departed.

The rain fell as fine drizzle, neither increasing in intensity nor stopping for more than a few minutes at a time. A little light filtered through, though it made scant difference to the overall effect, which was dull and drab. Colours faded into a lifeless uniformity of greys and browns.

By five o'clock the majority of the baboon troop were scattered along the narrow strip of open country between the base of the ridge and the acacia thickets to its south, barely a hundred yards from the Cub Caves.

Chui had watched the topi for more than an hour before deciding to stalk towards them. Then inexplicably one of the antelope and its day-old calf left the security of the herd and moved towards the edge of the ridge. As was so often the case, it was a prey animal unwittingly making itself vulnerable that initiated Chui's hunting effort. As the leopard knocked the calf to the ground its mother fled through the rocks. Though the frantic sounds of the topi mother could do nothing to save her calf, they carried to the sensitive ears of one of the Ridge Clan hyenas slumbering amid the croton thicket only a dozen yards away. At the same moment one of the baboons looked up, alerted by an alarm call that he too recognised. On seeing the leopard struggling with the calf, the baboon barked out his own alarm cry.

Responding instantly to the urgency of the call, two of the male baboons stopped feeding and raced straight towards Chui, galloping seventy yards to confront her. The animal that led the charge was a huge male, weighing sixty or seventy pounds, not much less than Chui herself. His thick fur bristled in an impressive mantle around his neck, making him look even larger and fiercer.

Chui had only one option as the hyena and the baboons closed in on her. She dropped the calf and streaked back towards the Cub Caves as fast as her legs could carry her. She was literally running for her life.

As she fled she was forced to run the gauntlet of the whole troop. The angry mob of males, females and juveniles converged from every direction, screaming and barking as the leopard jinked and weaved among them. The largest male which had led the attack stormed after Chui, now looking twice her size, and oh so nearly reached her as other baboons bumped and jostled her from the side. For a moment Chui almost slipped over as one of the primates grabbed at her fur. Then she whipped over the steep sides of the vertical cave and vanished into the darkness, where even the largest baboon would not dare to follow.

An hour later Chui crept back to where she had been forced to abandon her kill. But all she found was blood-stained grass.

4. Waiting for the Rains

DURING THE night a dark-maned lion from the Gorge Pride left the seclusion of Leopard Gorge and moved quickly towards the edge of the ridge. He was drawn by the sounds of the Fig Tree Clan feeding on a topi kill. The lion was hungry, eager to supplement the food that he plundered from the kills of the Gorge Pride lionesses.

As daylight beckoned Chui watched the feeding lion from the safety of Top Rock, 200 yards away. A number of hyenas still lurked at the edges of the thicket, sniffing and exploring for scraps, and one might easily have been misled into thinking that it was the lion that had made the kill and that the hyenas were waiting to scavenge the remains of his meal. Situations such as this have helped to create a woefully inaccurate picture of the lifestyle of the spotted hyena. Meticulous study in the Serengeti, including nocturnal observation, has partially redressed the balance, though to this day the adaptable hyena unfortunately still remains the most despised of Africa's commonly seen game animals.

Nearby, the Fig Tree Troop moved about in their sleeping trees and on the rocks below, little more than a hundred yards from the feeding lion.

Yet they made no attempt to harass the predator in the forceful way that they had reacted to Chui. Instead, they maintained a respectful distance, and it would be the baboons, not the lion, that sought the shelter of the trees if he approached.

Chui watched the lion with an intensity that she reserved for few other animals. Her every move reflected the dangerous presence of the male, and even Light and Dark remained fairly quiet, by their own boisterous standards. When Dark tried to bite Chui's tail she hissed a warning which, for once, was quickly heeded. Eventually the lion tired of chewing on the bones of the kill and abandoned the remains to the patient hyenas, who wasted no time in reclaiming what was rightfully theirs.

Chui moved carefully through the rocks to the base of the fig tree. When she could no longer see the lion, she climbed into the first fork of the tree and proceeded cautiously onto the west limb to sit and wait.

The lion plodded slowly along the ridge, his great head lolling from side to side, black lips parted to expose worn, yellowing canines. Chui could have remained silent and let the lion pass her by. Instead, as the male approached the Cub Caves where Light and Dark lay hidden, she rasped out an expressive cough of warning. The lion looked up in surprise at the sound of the leopard, then almost nonchalantly gave a deep grunt of his own as he continued on his journey.

A little sunshine arrived to brighten up the gloom, though not for Chui. On two occasions she returned to her cubs, but within minutes she was back in the fig tree again. To add to her problems a bee now flew into her tense, open mouth. Chui shook her head violently, drooling her long tongue and frantically dragging its rough surface against the roof of her mouth, salivating copiously. But it made no difference and eventually she was forced to swallow the bee.

Dark decided that this was an appropriate moment to try to clamber into the fig tree. Chui watched anxiously from Top Rock, though fortunately

Dark abandoned his attempt after only a few feet. His efforts seemed to unsettle Chui even more and she began to lead the cubs away to the east, but soon changed her mind and hurried with them back to the caves.

Chui returned to her vantage point in the fig tree and before long she tensed and began to growl. It was the lion. Chui had seen him moving beneath the croton bush where he now lay resting, some 200 yards to the west. Her warning growl could not be heard by the lion from that distance, though it served to send the startled cubs fleeing back to the safety of the caves.

A little while later Dark reappeared, moving around carefully on the rocks. He called, staring up at his mother, but still she chose to ignore him. So, ever so slowly, Dark clambered into the secondary growth around the tree's base and started to claw his way up the steep central limb that grew beside the main trunk. He did not bound up in the effortless style used by his mother – he was too small and unsure of himself to do that – instead he spread his paws wide and pressed his rounded tummy against the smooth bark, hoisting himself further and further into the air, until he reached a small junction twenty feet above the rocks. It did not look very stylish or elegant, but it was effective.

Though all cats have a remarkable ability to twist in mid-air and land on their feet, a fall from this kind of height could mean serious injury for the three-and-a-half-month-old cub. Despite all Dark's efforts, the route he had chosen failed to take him to a position where he could reach his mother. Chui ignored her son's strident miaows of distress and soon descended to where Light stood waiting on the rocks below. Perhaps that was her way of encouraging Dark to return to the ground. If so, it worked. Instead of backing down, Dark quickly clambered to a position where he could turn round and then came down head first, in a most untidy scurry. It was the end of a new venture for the tiny leopard and a significant landmark in his development.

Light and Dark soon ran off together to play in the climbing tree. Chui followed them, though moving far more cautiously than either of her cubs. She reached up and raked at the dead tree with her claws, receiving a playful swat on the nose from Dark. Chui briefly licked the cub and then leapt right over him into the topmost branches; in the process she almost completely dismantled the climbing tree. She stared into the distance, looking for signs of the lion, but there were none.

This pattern of activity continued throughout the afternoon: the cubs playing and Chui moving around nervously, the lion never far from her thoughts. Whenever Light or Dark ventured too far down the ridge Chui chuffled, attempting to draw them back to where she could keep sight of them. For a while she rested with her back against a protective wall of stone while the cubs dozed and suckled intermittently on her teats.

The wind began to build, bringing with it the first spots of rain. Chui finally succumbed to the waves of sleepiness that she had fought all day, drooping her heavy eyelids closed for thirty seconds at a time. But as the rain continued she retreated to the vertical cave at the base of Suckling Rock West. The cubs joined her, emerging from a ledge situated on the inner wall of the vertical cave. They sat side by side, licking the sweet rainwater from each other's fur. Then for a brief moment all three leopards groomed each other: Chui licked Light and, while he returned the gesture, Dark licked both of them.

Chui left the cubs and in a single fluid movement bounded up the steep west face of the cave spanning the ten foot wall. But as her head reached the horizon she tensed, hunching low before creeping onwards over the top. Satisfied that no immediate danger threatened, Chui chuffled to her cubs, who had been left stranded at the base of the vertical cave. Light and Dark struggled to find a way up the slope, eventually succeeding only by clutching onto the patchy vegetation and clawing their way to the place where their mother waited.

As the light began to fade, Chui watched a male Thomson's gazelle move across the ridge to her east, taking the same fateful route that the warthogs had used. The leopard quickly followed in stealthy pursuit but after only fifteen yards she stopped, looking nervously back over her shoulder to where the cubs sat waiting. Nothing, it seemed, not even food, was worth the risk of leaving her cubs or drawing attention to herself while the lion was still in the vicinity. So she returned to sit on Top Rock, staring to the west as it continued to drizzle.

Storm clouds loomed, the setting sun infusing them with a blood-red stain, painting colours that deepened to a still warmer concentration before fading into darkness. As it did so a distant grunting sound started to build, climaxing in a series of thunderous roars, amplified further by the wall of black rocks.

For a brief moment Chui sat bolt upright, her ears twisting towards the familiar sound, and the cubs stopped playing. Before the roars could die away they were answered by the voices of other members of Dark Mane's pride, calling from Leopard Gorge. Chui needed no more powerful reminder of who was king among the big cats. For Dark Mane the confrontation had been an inconsequential moment in a long hot day, an episode which had ended the minute he had passed the fig tree. But for Chui it had resulted in many hours of anxiety.

Chui failed to kill during the night but remained in the vicinity of Dik-Dik Lugga, the bush-infested gully that snaked south between acacia thickets towards Kampi ya Chui. As the dry season dragged on, the lugga edges attracted topi, impala and Thomson's gazelles, all seeking the last strongholds of food and water. Dik-Dik Lugga was therefore an ideal spot for a leopard to ambush an unwary prey animal.

Having at last discovered the secret of their mother's other life in the fig tree above them, Light and Dark would now pause periodically to stare expectantly into the tree, though there were many occasions when they saw nothing but blue sky and green leaves. The cubs had long since abandoned the sleeping place originally chosen for them by Chui. Now they often rested on Suckling Rock West, close to a narrow space leading into the side of the deep vertical cave. It was like a high window ledge protected within the confines of the cave itself. Light was still slightly wary of vehicles, though Dark seemed to realise that they meant him no harm and had quickly learned to ignore them, continuing with whatever activity occupied his attention at the time.

When they were lying on the rocks the cubs' coats blended perfectly with the mottled greys and browns of the boulders. The only thing that revealed their presence was the startlingly white underside of the tip of their tails which continued to flicker even when the cubs were otherwise motionless, like a tiny white tongue of light blinking in the darkness.

For their size, the cubs had enormous floppy forepaws which they used with varying degrees of dexterity to swat, grasp, dab and trip a brother. Round and round the cubs would strut, biting and pawing at their own and each other's tail. When they tired of playing with each other, they often occupied their time by biting and chewing leaves, grass, twigs and stones.

One of their favourite games was to find a suitably sized stone to dab at in typical cat fashion: leaping backwards as if the object were alive and moving of its own free will. Sometimes it would be mouthed and chewed and then dropped to revitalise the whole process. The other cub would usually watch in fascination, occasionally trying to get in on the act, though it was basically a non-team sport. When in the climbing tree they often hung upside down by their claws, behaving like young monkeys, frantically stretching to try to reach and pull at each other. Their balance was quite remarkable, allowing them to perch their oversized paws on branches of little more than an inch in diameter.

The skills that the young leopards gradually refined through experience were built on a solid foundation of inborn responses – behaviour patterns that did not have to be learned and which occurred naturally in response to cues from their environment. The crouch, stealthy approach and pounce are part of a sequence of instinctive behaviour patterns common to all members of the cat family. From the time they were first seen, the cubs would flatten themselves against the ground before rushing forward to pounce on a brother or their mother. Fortunately the *coup de grace*, actually administering a killing bite, was not so easily released; instead they only bit lightly into the neck or throat while holding each other down, though the victim did not always respond playfully.

The fact that something is instinctive does not mean that it cannot be improved. Play served as a means for the cubs to use these innate behaviour patterns long before they were able or required to hunt for themselves. Play may even help to keep such instincts from atrophying.

The beauty of play, as zoologist R. F. Ewer wrote, was that it allowed the cubs to participate in a form of substitute hunting and fighting, without any of the normal risks. They could fight without anger, stalk without hunger or greed, and flee without fear. Their play sessions were a jumble of fragmented responses repeated in all manner of combinations, for there was no culminating act – no eating of prey, no flight of a defeated rival.

The cubs' play was always exuberant; their actions earnest, eager, even joyful. It provided them with a means of expending excess energy – of which they had an abundance – helped strengthen muscles and maintained general fitness. It also served to reinforce the bonds with their mother and keep the young cubs together during the early, most vulnerable months while Chui was away hunting.

The majority of cats kill their prey by a well-aimed bite through the nape of the neck or the base of the skull. A precise death stroke is necessary for a solitary hunter that must overpower its prey quickly. But those members of the cat family that kill larger animals usually do so by grasping them by the throat and strangling them, though lions often also try to suffocate an animal the size of a buffalo.

By biting into the throat the lion, leopard or cheetah grasps the most vulnerable part of a large animal's body, and at the same time avoids its prey's horns. Likewise, thrashing hooves cannot reach the predator as long as it remains near to the prey's head, and it becomes relatively easy to prevent the animal from regaining its feet. The throat-hold may therefore be a special adaptation for dealing successfully with larger prey. The Mara Buffalo Female killed zebra foals and young wildebeest by this method and Chui strangled adult impala males and Thomson's gazelles, though both leopards sometimes bit smaller animals in the neck. But occasionally the prey manages to fight back or struggles so violently that the predator is injured and that can spell disaster for a leopard's cubs, as well as for the leopard itself.

On 9 November I arrived at the Cub Caves to find Chui lying among the rocks with a huge swelling masking the right side of her face. Otherwise she seemed to be in good health and her belly looked full and rounded, so she had undoubtedly killed and eaten during the night.

The nature of the injury suggested a blow of some sort or even an abscess. Perhaps she had caught the full force of a flying hoof as she lunged forward to grasp the rump of her prey. Possibly an adult warthog had sent her sprawling, as I had seen one do in the past when she had snatched up yet another piglet; or a topi mother may have turned and rushed in to defend her young calf, using her horns to rebuff the predator.

Light and Dark milled around Chui, rubbing up against her swollen face and forcing her to abandon them for the solitude of the fig tree. At first the cubs were content to play together, scampering up and down in the climbing tree. Before long Dark became absorbed by the activities of the agamid lizards, lying fascinated at the sight of the skittish reptiles. Suddenly he seemed to remember his mother. He looked skyward and called to Chui, who was sitting above him on the west limb of the fig. But she disregarded his miaows.

But Dark was now able to do more than just grizzle when he wanted to get his mother's attention. The tiny leopard clambered upwards, only to find that once again his route did not take him to where he wanted to be. Dark was still far too small to bridge the five-foot gap that separated him from his mother, even though she could leap four times that distance.

Chui did not approve of her son's intrusion into her previously sacrosanct environs, and she rasped and hissed at the young cub, sending him scuttling back down to the ground. But the days when the fig tree could provide Chui with a peaceful refuge from the unwanted attentions of her cubs were drawing to a close.

It was almost midday and no sooner had Dark descended than Chui caught sight of the baboon troop moving slowly along the top of the ridge and heading in her direction. She climbed higher up the tree while the cubs hurriedly disappeared and crouched safely on the ledge inside the vertical cave.

Two of the male baboons shinned up the tree and sat on Chui's favourite west limb. After a spate of vigorous branch-shaking they moved even higher and closer to Chui. She crouched along a slender branch just below the roof of the tree, protectively tucking her feet up underneath her, while rumbling and hissing.

Five baboons now flanked round Chui, antagonising her as best they could. One baboon stood up and aggressively lunged to within a few feet of the leopard, provoking Chui into a threatening teeth-bared snarl, though she still refused to flee. For the moment her intransigence seemed sufficient to make the baboons abandon their efforts and they quickly climbed down to the lower branches. Two adults and a female with a tiny black baby clasped tightly to the hair of her chest ambled along the base of the ridge, glancing almost nonchalantly up at Chui. As they moved off they crossed paths with a group of subadults and juveniles that were on their way back to confront the leopard again.

Despite all the baboons' efforts Chui remained calm, doing nothing to reinforce their aggressive behaviour. By keeping herself so close to the top of the tree she ensured that the baboons could not surround her or force her to descend. There seemed to be a certain ritual involved in the confrontation, as if each species operated by some unwritten code of conduct, based partly on past experience, which prevented an all-out clash that could have uncertain consequences for any of the participants. So, for the time being, Chui was forced to make her compromise and suffer the hot sun that beat down on her unprotected head and shoulders until the last baboon had moved away to join the rest of the troop feeding at the edge of the acacia thicket, near to their sleeping trees. Then she could relax once more and move to a shadier spot.

Just before six o'clock Chui sat up and gently scratched under her swollen face with her hind foot. She descended to the lowest fork of the fig tree for a final look round before dropping to the ground, then chuffled and *aaouuu'ed*, provoking an outburst of miaows from her cubs.

Having satisfied the cubs' hunger, Chui carefully washed her face by licking the edge of her forepaw and, in the same movement, wiping it down over her cheek and nose. She then squatted to defecate, briefly bent to smell the ground and diligently scraped grass and earth towards her droppings. Dark stood and watched, so fascinated by his mother's movements that he stalked forward and launched himself on to Chui's hindquarters, though she hardly seemed to notice.

Chui did not wait until darkness before departing from the Cub Caves. She proceeded slowly east along the ridge, leaving the sounds of the squabbling baboons behind her. She called repeatedly to her cubs, occasionally reinforcing her chuffling with a strangled, drawn-out miaow. As it got darker, Chui padded onwards – calling and moving, calling and moving – leading Light and Dark away on the longest journey of their short lives.

For some time Chui had wandered around the vicinity of Dik-Dik Lugga, an area with which she had become thoroughly familiar over the years, and somewhere where she often hunted or rested up during the daytime. It was situated more than a mile from the Cub Caves and was the place that she had chosen as her cubs' new home.

Initially Chui located the cubs around a bastion of rocks, inlaid into the west bank of the lugga and situated 400 yards north of Kampi ya Chui. The rocks were partially shrouded by a green curtain of croton bush, and were already home to a colony of rock hyrax which lent them their name.

At last it seemed that the short rains had arrived and it became temporarily impossible to drive along Dik-Dik Lugga close enough to be able to see past the shrouds of croton bushes that lined its edges. Cars that tried invariably got stuck in the slick, black cotton soil and in the process risked slipping into the lugga itself.

I had almost forgotten what it was like to search for leopards. During the next week I saw very little of Chui or her cubs and I thought that she would probably disappear again, keeping more permanently on the move. Worse was to follow, for I was told that sometime during this period Dark had fallen out of a tree, badly wrenching and spraining his right back leg. This was a devastating injury and at times Chui was forced to carry the crippled cub in her mouth.

For all their marvellous climbing ability, even adult leopards occasionally tumble from trees. Normally they land safely on their padded paws. But sometimes they sustain injuries, though probably more often to their face and jaw than to their shock-absorbent limbs.

It was a pathetic sight to see Dark. The bedraggled, forlorn-looking animal that I now saw was a mere shadow of his former self. Gone was the bright-eyed, extrovert cub that I had been so fortunate to watch during the last few weeks. There was an almost haunted look about him and his beautiful spotted coat had lost its healthy lustre.

Even when Chui rested quite close to her cubs it was often impossible to locate her among the rocks and croton bushes that choked the lower portion of Dik-Dik Lugga. Fortunately for me there were times when Light unwittingly revealed Chui's presence due to his penchant for trailing around after her if she got up from where she was resting. On this particular morning Light did just that, though Dark remained motionless, lying in the shade of the bushes. When he did get up and try to limp after his mother he was unable to catch up, so he reluctantly turned and hobbled back to the safety of Hyrax Rocks. Later Light joined him and for a while they sat together, side by side, framed by the green and orange leaves of the croton bushes, while their mother moved further down the lugga to rest by herself.

The cubs had by now lost the greyish tinge of their coats and the rosettes had expanded to make them look more like adult leopards, though they were still very much a Light and a Dark. Strangely, Chui's previous litter of cubs had also been a light and a dark cub, and the dark one had also had a pinched, squint-eyed face – just like Dark.

Though Chui had moved well away from the Cub Caves she could never hope to rid herself of baboons. The Fig Tree Troop counted Dik-Dik Lugga well within their own home range; they sometimes slept in the trees of Kampi ya Chui and often foraged in the area. But it would have been the same wherever Chui had moved because these adaptable primates have successfully colonised nearly every part of the Mara and they too need places with trees, rocks and bushes.

During the afternoon Chui ignored everything, wedging herself in the angle formed by three overhanging rocks, sheltering from the sun. Her cubs were 400 yards away, nestling safely among the bushes surrounding Hyrax Rocks.

There was nothing to announce the coming of the rain: it just arrived. Chui sat up with a start as a vicious clap of thunder burst from the sky, but by that time it was already pouring down. Though Chui usually ignored a light shower, she was now forced to shelter beneath a bush and crouch with her head bowed and eyes half-closed against the blinding rain. The lugga that had only recently been a dry, comfortable resting place was quickly transformed into a brown, raging torrent.

As the rain began to ease birds broke into varied song, once more rejoicing at the end of the drought. Chui shook herself repeatedly, setting free a fine spray of water that sparkled in the first rays of sunlight. But before she could set to work grooming the moisture from her wet fur, hyenas started to whoop close to Kampi ya Chui. It was the Fig Tree Clan, disputing ownership of a wildebeest kill which their neighbours the Marsh Clan had made on the common boundary of their territories. The hungry mobs stormed back and forth, creating a bloodcurdling assortment of battle cries. The sudden outburst of noise made Chui nervous and she immediately hastened back to where she had left her cubs.

On arrival at Hyrax Rocks Chui was confronted by a picture of abject misery. Two very wet and bedraggled leopard cubs sat huddled in a tree at the lugga's edge, mesmerised by the sight and sound of the rushing brook that had flooded their resting place. They greeted the appearance of their mother with a volley of high-pitched miaows. Hurriedly the cubs slithered down the tree, to rumble and squawk around Chui's legs, desperate for warmth and milk. Chui, however, seemed more interested in licking the moisture from their wet fur than providing them with succour.

Eventually Chui lay down on the muddy ground, cradling the cubs between her limbs. But it was not long before Light stopped suckling and began to groom his wet fur vigorously, leaving Chui to lick Dark, who had missed out on most of the grooming and was still soaked to the skin. Using her rough tongue Chui methodically drew the water from his sodden coat until Dark's fur bristled like freshly towelled hair.

The moment Chui transferred her attention back to Light, Dark quickly burrowed, like an insistent mole, under his mother's belly. The little cub looked painfully thin and gaunt, hunched up awkwardly in the manner of an arthritic old man, his back leg wasted and stiff. Even though he had earlier managed to clamber into the tree, he moved about as little as possible and when Light tried to trip him he ignored the invitation to play. All he was interested in was food.

Next morning I was surprised to find that the cubs were still located at their flooded retreat. I had expected that Chui might attempt to move them to a more suitable spot, but perhaps Dark's injury was still too much of a hindrance for her to be able to travel very far with the cubs.

Light was resting on top of Hyrax Rocks when I arrived, though there was no sign of his brother. Before long Chui appeared from further down the lugga, picking her way carefully over the slippery rocks now that the water had subsided to reasonable proportions. Light rushed towards his mother, who bent to lick him before moving away into the shade of the croton bushes. A few minutes later Dark appeared from the small cave where he had lain hidden within Hyrax Rocks.

Dark stretched and then set about grooming himself, pausing to watch Light wrestling with Chui. For a while he played with his tail, hooking it towards him and biting it. But when Chui moved even further away, Dark found it impossible to ignore her presence any longer. With a considerable effort he got to his feet and hopped on his three good legs as fast as they would carry him. As he did so he miaowed to Chui, who responded by chuffling at him. Eagerly he clambered over his mother's back as she reached round to lick his face.

It was pathetic to watch as Dark tried to follow his mother. Every step seemed to cause him pain and Light just would not leave him alone. He pounced on his helpless brother and wrestled him to the ground, holding him down by biting him in the neck and throat. Weakened by his injury Dark's only defence was to lie as still as possible, waiting for his brother to tire of the game. But the moment he tried to crawl forward to reach Chui's teats, the movements stimulated Light even further – just like a cat playing with an injured mouse.

It was noticeable that Light had at last started to lose some of his shyness. He was full of playfulness, chasing up and down in the croton bushes and pestering Dark. Light seemed instilled with a new source of energy, leaping and exploding into the air like a jack-in-the-box. It was difficult to know if this new-found confidence and vigour was a consequence of Dark's injury or just the natural process of Light's own development. Whichever it was, Light exploited to the full the opportunity to dominate Dark while his brother was less than a hundred per cent fit.

One morning, during the second week of the cubs' stay at Hyrax Rocks, Chui returned to them with the hindquarters of a freshly killed impala fawn. She had ambushed the mother impala and her youngster on the low hill just to the west of Dik-Dik Lugga, not far from Kampi ya Chui. Having already consumed part of the kill, Chui found it easy to transport the remains back to her cubs.

At the sound of their mother's call the cubs emerged from their hiding place beneath the rocks and ran to where Chui stood waiting. She pushed past them and carried the kill to Hyrax Rocks. Even though he still had a noticeable limp Dark somehow managed to keep up with Chui and the moment she dropped the kill he grabbed it and carried it into the bushes.

Light was forced to content himself with a suckle and a lick from his mother as she carefully nit-picked his fur, reaching places that he was unable to deal with. The moment Light tried to approach, Dark turned on his brother and attacked him savagely, chasing after him and bowling him over. Chui immediately got up to intervene, but the cubs rolled away from her before she could do so. Over and over they tumbled, biting and clawing, falling like two spotted rocks down onto the floor of the lugga. When they finally broke apart Dark rushed back to the kill, protectively straddling it with his belly and in the process even shielding it from himself.

Light crept back to Chui and soon lay wrestling with his mother while Dark spent most of the time threatening both his relatives rather than feeding. But eventually the hungry cub started to chew at the meat with his sharp cheek teeth.

The Fig Tree Troop had appeared earlier in the morning along the stony ridge to the east, eighty yards from the leopards. Slowly they moved closer to where Dark crouched. Sensing the danger, Chui edged towards Dark, as if about to try to move the meat to a more concealed position. But he was in no mood to relinquish anything now. There was a look of wildness about the skinny cub, who had not tasted meat for some days and had been unable to reach his mother's teats as often as he would have liked. So Dark faced his mother with all manner of vocal threats, forcing her to lie down again.

Chui called Light to her, repositioning herself between the two cubs and keeping watch to the west where the sounds of baboons could still be heard. Dark meanwhile decided to move his kill, dragging it tantalisingly closer to Chui and Light, before pulling it behind another rock. At the same moment

Chui lowered her head, twisted round and bellied back through the gap. She stopped briefly to peer over her shoulder before disappearing from view. The baboons were returning.

Surprisingly Dark limped over to Light and in a friendly gesture rubbed against his brother's head. But Light was hungry and interested only in the food, surreptitiously trying to slide past his brother. Seeing this, Dark quickly moved back to the meat, then just as quickly moved away again. Light took his chance and this time when Dark tried to return he had lost the initiative. Now the food was Light's possession and he quickly leapt forward to defend it. The cubs fought fiercely for nearly a minute in a manner that I had never observed among lion cubs, whose quarrels were usually resolved as soon as they started, or cheetahs, who never behaved in this manner at a kill.

It was almost ten o'clock and the cubs remained with Chui in the lugga, somewhat subdued by their violent encounter. The Fig Tree Troop now reappeared in force, stopping briefly to drink at the large pool of water further up the lugga. Shortly afterwards an impressive-looking group of large males moved to within thirty yards of where the leopards lay hidden. They paused to feed beneath a patch of acacia bush as if carefully weighing up the situation.

Light was so hungry that he decided to ignore the baboons and return to where the kill had been abandoned. As soon as he did so one of the keen-eyed males spotted his movements and strutted aggressively towards the croton bush. Light crouched over the food until the baboon lunged towards him and then he fled for the safety of a cave among Hyrax Rocks.

At this Chui erupted in a wave of deep growls and rumbles from a position of concealment in the floor of the lugga. The male grunted and yawned his own response to Chui while three more baboons galloped over and added their voices to a fearful chorus of barks and screams. The boldest of the males jumped forward again and postured with lowered head towards Chui, seemingly determined to drive the leopards from cover, but without success.

The moment the baboons dispersed, Light quickly scrambled back to the kill which had been left untouched. The hungry cub carried the food into the lower branches of one of the croton bushes, attempting to store it safely out of reach. When it fell to the ground Light immediately picked it up and returned with it into the bush. But when one of the leg bones dropped in front of Chui, she leapt forward and, quick as a flash, snatched it away. Light continued to try to store his portion of the kill among the branches of the croton bush, but each time he went to feed from the meat it fell to the ground again. Only after the eighth attempt did he give up.

Chui moved away, *aau'ing* and chuffling to her cubs. Dark quickly followed and shortly afterwards Light left the scraps and joined them. Later Chui thoroughly investigated the place where they had fed. First she paused to rake her claws along the slender trunk of a croton bush. Twice she stopped to defecate, once near the bush where the cubs had fed, and once at the place where she had first dropped the kill. Both times she scraped grass and soil towards her droppings, though it was difficult to see if this had the effect of covering them or simply left a visible scrape near to them. Covering might even extend the aromatic life of faeces by keeping them moist and encouraging bacterial activity, though initially it would reduce the smell.

Shortly after midday, Chui led the cubs away, choosing as their resting place the same part of Dik-Dik Lugga in which they had spent the previous afternoon. It was a hundred yards south of Hyrax Rocks and an ideal spot. There were nice flat rocks in the floor of the lugga to sprawl on, and Chui and the cubs could lie concealed beneath the shroud of overhanging vegetation, changing position from one side of the gully to the other as the sun rolled across the sky. Most important of all, a euclea tree sloped gently from the east bank, providing a means of escaping from lions or hyenas and hoisting Chui above the steep-walled lugga if she wanted to see what was happening in the world surrounding her.

It was hot and oppressive. The cubs lay flat on their backs, fat white tummies reflecting the afternoon light skywards again. Fifteen feet above them Chui reclined comfortably in the tree. When the cubs realised where their mother had gone they called to her. Chui ignored them, enjoying the solitude of her perch, but eventually she relented and climbed down to let them feed.

Later Chui climbed back into the tree and clawed at the bark. Light accompanied his mother and added his own small contribution of scratch marks to the same spot. As it started to rain Chui began to trek north again, leaving Light and Dark at Hyrax Rocks to pick over the pieces of skin and bone which were all that remained of their mother's kill.

As Light wandered aimlessly around in the lugga, he accidentally disturbed a small boulder. The stone clattered down the side of the embankment, causing him to jump back in mock alarm. The cub pawed and batted at the stones as if they were alive, causing a minor landslide as a whole pile of rocks tumbled to the lugga floor. This was something that even the injured Dark could not ignore. He hobbled determinedly into the bottom of the gully to join his brother, and for a while both cubs tried without success to recreate the initial excitement generated by the rock fall.

Chui continued her trek until she came to a thick island of croton bush at the lugga's edge. A dik-dik stood rigidly to attention, flexing his nose downwards and blowing air through it to produce a far-carrying and distinctive whistle of alarm. Other dik-diks heard him and stopped to listen, straining with their sharp antelope eyes to locate the predator. Chui turned and walked back down the lugga, ignoring the dainty creatures that watched her pass. She paused only once, reaching up a few feet on bent hind legs to claw another message on the bark of an acacia bush. Then she continued towards Kampi ya Chui, leaving Light and Dark safely involved with each other among the bushes of Hyrax Rocks.

5. The Leopard Family

CHUI'S CAREFUL hunt during the night provided her with a fully grown Thomson's gazelle buck. She had watched the dainty antelope for a long time as he marked his territory and fed among the short grass, not far from Kampi ya Chui. Once darkness had concealed her, Chui stalked along the east side of the forest and waited. Eventually the gazelle lay down to rest and the leopard crept forward, unseen. By morning the kill hung, half-eaten, in a slender tree overhanging the west bank of Dik-Dik Lugga, some 150 yards north of Kampi ya Chui.

The thud of small feet and the rustle of leaves betrayed the leopard cubs' position as they chased and wrestled with each other in the lugga floor. Even at this young age, theirs was a world of shadows and concealment, providing only a fleeting glimpse of a spotted coat to identify them by. Sometimes they paused to groom themselves diligently or bite and clutch at trees and bushes.

Two Masai appeared, chattering in high-pitched voices as they made their way along the east side of the lugga. Light and Dark must have heard the voices, though if they did they took scant notice. So perhaps they did not differentiate the voices from those of the tourists with whom they had become so familiar. The Masai often travelled to Dik-Dik Lugga, bringing their herds to drink at the large muddy pools that formed important reservoirs of water for them during the dry season.

Just before midday another Masai appeared. He walked casually towards my car, resplendent in his blood-red shuka. After exchanging greetings the man asked me where my 'manyatta' was and if he could have some water. When I told him that I had only a little tea he replied that tea was fine. I offered him a ginger biscuit, which he inspected carefully before eating it. It obviously tasted good, for he asked for another. I gave him the rest of the packet and wondered what the leopard cubs were making of all this. Before saying goodbye he invited me to visit him at his manyatta on the Talek River, just outside the eastern boundary of the Reserve, insisting that I must share meat with him at his own home. Then he continued on his journey, crossing the lugga barely forty yards north of where Chui had stored her kill. I had warned him of the leopard and her cubs, but he just nodded, acknowledging something that he already knew. He shrugged his shoulders and walked away.

I sat and watched him as he strode out into the plain. The game drifted apart to let him pass, then closed in behind him until he was just another tiny speck among many others.

I thought of the two of us. Me with my notebooks and my cameras taking it all so seriously, cocooned in my noisy tin box. He striding off, much more a part of the natural world that he shared with Chui than I would ever be.

Chui's steps were imprinted in the dark mud in the bottom of the lugga, plotting her early morning path to and from the kill. She rested now, hidden in the undergrowth near Kampi ya Chui, 400 yards from where she had left her cubs.

It was hot and muggy with big white clouds bubbling into the sky. Light and Dark lay curled up, wedged head to tail between two large rocks embedded in the lugga floor. Dark reclined with his paws pushed out against Light, as if trying to fend him off, while Light positioned his back feet up against his brother's nose and forehead. It looked most uncomfortable, yet the cubs dozed peacefully.

Bird song once more heralded the arrival of rain. Briefly it soothed the oppressive heat, though the few drops that fell dried quickly, evaporating to nothing. Meanwhile Chui remained alert to the presence of game.

At 3.30, she arrived back at the place where she had left her cubs. They rushed to their mother, pressing against her in greeting before settling down by her side, enabling her to groom the dampness from their fur as they lay suckling. A few minutes later, after the cubs had satisfied themselves, Chui climbed into the slender euclea tree. She looked about her carefully before calling to the two cubs. The young leopards looked enquiringly up at their mother and Light called in response. Chui chuffled, encouraging him to join her above ground, though Dark was less eager to ascend.

The tree was ideal for young leopards, for they could even climb up the first part of it without using their claws. But Dark had yet to recover his confidence fully since his fall and it still seemed to be causing him pain to flex his claws, as if he were wrenching on sore muscles. So he confined himself to the lower, thicker branches where he could move more easily. Light had no such inhibitions, moving expertly above his brother to explore the very highest reaches and narrowest of branches.

Just before five o'clock Chui left her cubs and headed south down the lugga again. Light started to follow her, but stopped when he received no signal of encouragement. Chui crept forward, concealing herself as she moved towards the kill tree. She was hungry and did not care to wait until darkness had settled around her. Instead she moved as cautiously as if she were stalking prey. Easing herself into the tree, she squeezed past the dangling carcass until she lay above it, facing down the incline of the limb. Hungrily she tore at the tender flesh, pulling out pieces of meat with her incisors and using her cheek teeth to break up the smaller bones and sheer off the rib ends.

When she had finished feeding, Chui gripped the remains of the gazelle by the neck, braced her back legs and attempted to wrench it free. But it was like trying to dislodge a grappling hook, for the harder she pulled, the tighter the gazelle's curved horns wedged into the fork. In the end Chui had no alternative but to leave the kill where it was, instead of carrying it with her.

During the night Chui led her cubs from their resting place and brought them to the kill. The cubs were eager to follow, for they had tasted and smelt the traces of blood and meat on their mother's face when they had greeted her. Until now Chui had always brought food to her cubs, rather than leading them to a kill and risking a confrontation with another predator, adopting the same pattern of behaviour as had been observed with the Mara Buffalo Female.

Now, as Chui fed, Light crept up the branch and tunnelled beneath his mother's sleek belly to get at the succulent red meat. He crouched, plucking small pieces of flesh with his sharp incisor teeth while Chui held the kill down with her dew claw. With most of the carcass already consumed, Chui stripped the flesh from the neck and sides of the gazelle's face, leaving a ghoulish mask suspended by a sliver of skin. Dark climbed up to join the others, pushing past Light on the narrow beam just as Chui stepped down from the tree.

Though all three leopards had well-rounded stomachs Dark was determined to continue feeding. He hissed and bared his teeth at the meat that swung so tantalisingly close to him, struggling mightily in his efforts as he dangled precariously over the limb, trying to hook the head of the gazelle up and over the branch. But to have succeeded would have sent him careering fifteen feet to the ground.

Chui suddenly appeared on the east bank of the lugga accompanied by Light. She chuffled, looking back over her shoulder to where Dark continued to feed, urging him to follow her. But the little cub was far too involved with the kill to heed his mother's call, so Chui reluctantly disappeared back into the lugga.

Later Chui climbed into the tree again and with one violent movement tore the head of the carcass free. Then she descended, while Dark busied himself with the gazelle's three remaining legs left dangling in the tree. He had even tried to prevent his mother from taking the carcass away from him. But on this occasion Chui had quickly taken possession of the kill by forcefully clubbing down on Dark's head with one large forepaw.

Chui sniffed around the base of the tree, pausing to eat any small pieces of meat that had been missed on previous searches of the area. Then she called to the cubs and crept cautiously to the edge of the lugga. Chui stared hard towards the west where Masai herdsmen and their cattle were making their daily journey to fresh pastures. Then, with a final furtive glance towards the tribesmen, Chui hurried across a loop of open ground and back into the safety of the bushes higher up the lugga. The cubs trotted quickly after their mother with their rounded ears twisted back against their heads.

Once she had reached the shade of the cool lugga floor Chui stopped and lay down, allowing the cubs the chance to suckle. When they had finished she moved slowly northwards, pausing every so often to flop down in the shade of the leafy bushes. Eventually, by this slow progression, the leopards arrived back at the cubs' original resting place, close to the euclea tree. When the cubs had settled down, Chui left them and continued on her way.

All through the afternoon the heat continued to build into a stifling, muggy swelter. No breeze, only a wall of cloud throwing the heat back to earth. Light was particularly restless, getting up and walking a few paces before flopping back down to the ground again. He groomed, stretched and rolled on to his back, clutching pawfuls of the ticklish grass that surrounded him. Then he was off again, stalking towards a nearby tree, fascinated by the sounds of the birds calling from their leafy domain above him.

Quietly, but all too visibly, Light crept into the tree. The birds watched him as he approached, fluttering out of harm's way long before the cub could reach them. He paused and lay as any leopard would: straddled over a cub-sized limb, arms and legs lazily dangling, chin and belly flattened along the branch. There he remained, hidden just above the base of the leaves, only his white tail tip flicking within view.

When the first fat drops of rain slapped against the leaves, Light sat up and looked around him. A cool breeze rustled the foliage above his head as the gentle pitter-patter of refreshing rainfall beat a tattoo on the rocks below. Light did not move, simply closed his eyes and slumbered beneath the umbrella of green leaves.

Shortly after five o'clock Chui reappeared from over the west bank of the lugga, not far from the tree where Light lay. For a moment she shone golden in the soft afternoon light, looking first east then west before continuing towards her cubs.

Light saw his mother approaching and rushed from the tree, almost treading on Dark's head, which protruded from among the hollowed-out tree roots where he had been resting. White-browed coucals bubbled their unique song to one another as the two cubs wheeled around their mother, rubbing themselves sinuously against her, their pointed fluffy tails flexing under her chin and across her chest and forelegs. Chui did not actually greet the cubs in response; her reply was simply to lick them.

For the next twenty minutes Chui and the cubs groomed and played. The cubs wrestled with each other while Chui pawed and mouthed her frisky youngsters. Every so often the cubs settled down to suckle again, sometimes for as little as two or three minutes and rarely for more than ten, though they often dozed for longer at Chui's breasts. Though Dark seemed slightly less inclined than Light to play with Chui, it was perhaps he who more closely resembled man's stereotype of what a leopard is like: aloof, self-possessed and enigmatic.

Chui and Light mouth-wrestled, sparring gently with open jaws until Chui managed to grasp the cub's head firmly between her forepaws. With Light wedged tightly in position she licked her great rasping tongue over his nose, eyes, ears and forehead while the cub remained motionless. But the moment she released him from her grasp again, Light leapt into the air and smothered his mother in all manner of playfulness and affection.

Chui groomed herself more frequently than I had seen either lions or cheetahs do. Sometimes it was no more than a few casual licks of a paw or her throat, but other times it developed into a more elaborate effort. The pattern varied according to the circumstances and which particular part of her anatomy needed attention. She would often nibble herself, using her incisors to 'nit-pick' for ticks and other parasites, loosening and removing patches of skin encrustations from her fur.

The same suppleness that allows a leopard to stalk its prey so effectively and charge with such explosive speed also permitted Chui to bend double, forepaws flopped by her sides, while grooming her belly. If she wanted to reach her genital region she simply cocked a back leg up over her shoulder and stretched down gently to lick herself clean, and in the process spread her individual scent over a greater area of fur.

When Chui found it particularly difficult to keep her balance while trying to reach one of her extremities she would sometimes hook her sharp claws into her rump or the root of her tail, pulling the desired portion of her body within range of her all-embracing tongue.

A cat's tongue is covered with recurved, hair-like papillae. These make the tongue so rough that it is not only a highly efficient toilet implement but can also be used to rasp particles of meat from bone. But all this grooming had other functions besides keeping the leopards clean. By grooming her cubs, Chui helped to reinforce the bond between herself and her sons. It also promoted cooling by allowing the evaporation of saliva from the leopard's fur and provided an additional source of vitamin D, produced on the animal's coat by exposure to sunlight.

Next morning the cubs were in the same area and once they had settled down for the morning I drove off in search of Chui. Finding no sign of her I returned to where I had left Light and Dark. To my horror, instead of relocating the young leopards I found a very bloated hyena lying contentedly on its side at the same place where I had last seen the cubs. For a moment I had visions of what might lie inside that grotesquely swollen stomach.

I searched for over an hour but there was no sign of the cubs and once more I looked accusingly at the hyena's fat belly. Just then birds began to twitter in a nearby tree, creating a characteristic alarm sound that I had often heard when the cubs were in view. The tree grew for some twenty feet above the ground and there, at the very top, lay Dark. He peered warily from his perch, never taking his eyes from the hyena. Eventually the arrival of more cars induced the hyena to move further down the lugga, leaving Dark to doze, a small, lonely shape framed against the dull grey sky. But where was Light?

Shortly after six o'clock the hyena sat up and scratched himself before ambling back to where Dark still perched in the tree. But first he paused at the spot where Chui and the cubs had rested early in the morning, sniffing and licking at the ground, then rolling where the leopards had lain. The hyena seemed intrigued by the leopards' scent, smacking his lips and greedily devouring any droppings he could find. When the hyena let out a noisy sneeze Dark opened his sleepy eyes in alarm, craning his neck to locate the predator's position.

Slowly the hyena continued towards Dark, sniffing and investigating the scent trail that led him unerringly back to the cub. The hyena climbed up the steep bank of the lugga, which brought him to a position directly below Dark. Dark watched, making no sound, ears pricked and eyes firmly fixed on the hyena below him. But once he had inspected the area carefully the hyena turned and headed south once more.

Dik-diks reappeared among the sparse cover of the acacia thickets, though they did not see the leopard cub curled up in the fork of the tree opposite them. The terrier-sized antelope moved carefully, selecting fruit, seeds, buds and leaves from a variety of shrub and herb species. The male – distinguished by the possession of horns – marked the communal dung midden at the edge of his territory while his lifelong mate and their youngster waited to do likewise.

It was a relief to find Light and Dark together again next morning. They had concealed themselves at the base of the euclea tree, where creepers, stems and leaves meshed across the tree's roots, covering a hollow that had eroded behind them. It was almost impossible to see the cubs and even the most alert and determined predator would have found it difficult to extract the young leopards from their retreat.

Chui walked quickly along Fig Tree Ridge, anxious to rejoin her cubs and rid herself of the flies and vehicles that pursued her. She broke into a trot as she neared the junction of ridge and lugga, then vanished into the coolness of green shade and moist earth. It was just after 8 a.m.

The cubs eagerly responded to their mother's call and soon their spotted heads bobbed in unison as they drew hungrily on her teats. Though she had brought no meat for them and made no kill for herself, she could still provide a modicum of nourishment for her four-month-old cubs.

Now that Dark's leg was thoroughly healed he and his brother could once more indulge in their complete routine of play, all of it negotiated at full speed. Sooner or later these vigorous sessions would result in a cub becoming just a little bit over-boisterous or being bitten a little harder than he liked. At times it even seemed that having a brother was a disadvantage and could inadvertently cause serious injury, particularly when they played together in trees.

Shortly after ten o'clock Chui moved with the cubs towards Hyrax Rocks, pausing to drink at one of the small pools of water that had collected in the wake of the welcome showers. It was hot and Chui seemed unusually intolerant of the cubs. When they first arrived at Hyrax Rocks she allowed them both to suckle. But after a few minutes she got up and continued north, rumbling and hissing at her youngsters as they tried to play with her tail. When Light returned to his mother and tried to suckle he was vociferously repulsed.

The more Chui continued to deny them, the more frantic her cubs became as they wandered around, miaowing plaintively. Dark tried once more to get near his mother, flattening his ears and hissing back at her when she grunted at him. In doing so he provoked an even harsher retort. Chui lunged at him and chopped down, open-mouthed, over Dark's neck. The young cub squawked with surprise and alarm at his mother's violent rebuke, though in fact he was physically unhurt. Temporarily Dark retreated from the conflict and lay on a rock in the half shade of a croton bush. Weaning Light and Dark was not going to be easy for Chui, for they were still eager to suckle if given the slightest sign of encouragement, even when well-filled with meat.

Wisely, perhaps, Light was far more cautious about trying to suckle than Dark. The fact that taking up his suckling position brought him well within range of his mother's hostile front end may have persuaded him to be less insistent. Chui tucked her legs up beneath her, making it impossible for him to squeeze in. When he did try the more direct approach he received the same treatment as Dark. Chui simply grasped him by the back of the neck and sent him tumbling over the rocks. Eventually, having denied her milk to both cubs for forty minutes, Chui relented. By rolling onto her side she signalled that she was finally prepared to accommodate them.

As the day progressed a pleasing feel of dampness was borne on the breeze. All three leopards were by now forced to pant rapidly to keep themselves cool. This always gave them a look of considerable distress, though in fact it is a highly efficient and essential process. Sweating is of negligible importance as a means of regulating the leopard's body temperature. Panting helps promote cooling, allowing evaporation of moisture from the surface of the nasal passages, the tongue and the mouth. Chui would sometimes pant at over 150 beats a minute, synchronising it to the frequency of her breathing. The energy expenditure is therefore minimal, even though it looks exhausting.

Chui generally took great care not to overstress herself, refraining from resting for lengthy periods in direct sunshine and avoiding unnecessary exertion during the hottest part of the day. Though she drank quite regularly, particularly after a long journey during daylight and sometimes after eating, she was capable of going for lengthy periods without water. A leopard's water requirement can, when necessary, be satisfied from the blood and body fluids of its kills: this allows them to survive in some very arid parts of Africa, but only if they avoid heat stress.

Chui was hungry and the cubs' constant begging for food made her restless. She had failed to kill during her nightly wanderings, so now that it was cooler she left the cubs and moved south along the lugga, stopping occasionally to observe the surrounding countryside. But there was nothing to arouse her interest, only adult wildebeest and some zebra, both of which were too big for her to attempt to kill.

In the end, it was the ubiquitous warthogs which provided the leopard with another meal. Shortly after two o'clock Chui arrived back at Dik-Dik

Lugga carrying a piglet in her mouth. She leapt with it into a willowy tree that arched across the lugga like an enormous gallows. Without pausing to feed, she simply dropped the young warthog across a suitable fork and descended.

Dark was the first to respond, climbing nimbly past his mother and continuing to where the piglet lay. The wind gusted, swaying the cub precariously from side to side as he perched twenty feet above the ground. Dark quickly lay flat out along the branch and started to pull and chew through the coarse hairy skin. But there were no tusks or horns to help hold the kill securely in position. Very soon the inevitable happened.

Dark struggled valiantly to prevent the carcass falling to the ground, hooking his sharp claws into the hefty piglet as it slipped further off the branch. But it was just too heavy for the young leopard.

Surprisingly neither Light nor Chui moved to appropriate the kill as it fell. The young leopards had already established an efficient feeding regime. Whoever reached a fresh kill first not only took possession of it but also acquired temporary dominance and fed until sated. Only then would he peacefully leave the kill and allow his brother to feed. This system worked to both of the cubs' advantage, reducing to a minimum the time spent on bickering over food. Even though at this stage the kills made available to Light and Dark were often small, they still provided ample meat for both of them, though not for their mother.

Once more Chui seemed relaxed in the presence of her cubs, in sharp contrast to her obvious irritation earlier in the day. It was cooler and at last the cubs had meat to help satisfy their hunger. Chui lay on her back in a blanket of grass and shadow, with Dark sprawled comfortably across her throat. The smaller cub had gorged himself for nearly an hour and a half before abandoning the kill to Light.

When Light had finished feeding he carried the remains of the piglet towards where Chui and Dark were playing. Depositing it thirty feet away, he walked to his mother and received a cursory lick on his bloody face before continuing past to lie in the shade. The moment he had gone Chui got up and walked to the kill. At last she could satisfy herself with more than just the tantalising taste of blood and meat from her youngsters' sticky faces.

Chui fed slowly and methodically, stopping every so often to look about her, conscious that feeding on the ground made her and the cubs vulnerable to attack. She quickly chomped up and swallowed a leg bone, including the tiny trotter, though it would shortly reappear in her faeces as an indigestible clue to her diet. Little from the small kill would be wasted, for Chui was still hungry, slicing through the stomach wall and shaking it free from its contents before eating it.

Dark joined his mother, sliding his tail like a soft, furry arm alongside Chui's back. She sat up like a giant house cat – and more than any lion or cheetah that was what she reminded me of – lifting a forepaw to wash her face carefully, thereby signifying that she had finished her meal.

During the night, Chui left the cubs in the lugga and went off in search of more food. Early next morning Light and Dark were to be seen wandering around an island of stones in the lugga floor, somewhere destined to become a favoured resting place for the cubs when they were in the area.

It was a clear sunny day so I decided to visit the Mara Buffalo Caves in the hope of watching the other leopard family. I had been told that they were still in the area, though by the time I arrived mother and cubs had sought the shade and security of the main cave.

Driving back along Fig Tree Ridge during the late afternoon I was surprised to find Light sitting alone on a distinctive rock formation much utilised by a troop of dwarf mongooses. I was told that Chui had returned to Dik-Dik Lugga after I had departed and collected her cubs. She had then moved with them to Dwarf Rocks, a mile away to the east. But there was no sign of Chui or Dark, though I searched the surrounding area carefully.

Eventually Light curled up on the smooth-surfaced rocks, looking small and very vulnerable. He watched with head cushioned between his paws as an eighteen-month-old hyena raced out on to the plains where other members of the Ridge Clan were already feeding. The sight of the hyena sent Light slinking away in real leopard fashion, keeping close to the ground and using the greatest of stealth. He could not have picked a more uncomfortable-looking refuge for his new resting place – a euphorbia tree growing close to the rocks. He stared above him through the maze of finger-like branches that erupted, cactus-like, into the sky. But comfort was not the priority and he quickly clawed his way to safety.

By early next morning the clouds had spread a blue shadow over the distant Siria Escarpment. The Fig Tree Troop were just descending from their sleeping places as I passed on my way to Dwarf Rocks, while an elephant and its young calf fed busily on the bushes further along the ridge. A small group of impala females and their young fawns watched as a solitary jackal hurried past with the head and shoulders of a luckless gazelle baby wedged firmly between his jaws. Everything seemed to be here except for Light: today there was no sign of him. Instead I found Dark. What was going on, I wondered?

Dark was alone at the Cub Caves, grooming, biting roots and stems, and generally keeping busy. A short while later he began to move west along Fig Tree Ridge, weaving his way among the rock piles, smelling carefully, searching for signs of his brother. Sensibly he proceeded with a degree of uncertainty, as if nervous of what he might find among the caves and crevices. He laid his ears flat and bared his teeth as he slouched and hissed at the dark interiors that he confronted on his chosen path.

Finally Dark abandoned his lonely search. He was moving no further: a wise decision, for hyenas regularly rested in the area and there was always the menacing possibility of walking into one of the Gorge Pride lions. So the young leopard remained where he felt most secure, not far from the Cub Caves.

A few minutes before six o'clock hyrax started to screech, causing Dark to look up. I wondered if the young cub had learned that the sounds might signify the arrival of his mother, for it was Chui. Dark trotted a few yards in her direction, stopping briefly to look around nervously before galloping onwards towards her. They met sixty yards from the Cub Caves. Dark greeted the return of his mother with a display of great excitement.

Chui became noticeably restless once it became apparent that Light was missing. She kept getting up, moving away a few yards and then returning. Each time she lay down again Dark tried to suckle and she in turn gave the cub a thorough head wash as he rolled and flanked against her throat. Chui sat up, looking around for signs of the missing cub, who had not been seen with his mother or Dark since the previous morning.

Half an hour later Chui hurried away in the direction of Dwarf Rocks, a sense of urgency in her movements. Dark miaowed and squawked, reaching up to grasp at his mother's teats whenever she stopped. But Chui pressed forward, leaving her son scrambling between her legs, like a train passing through a tunnel. She received his message clearly enough, but for the time being she was ignoring it.

Chui stopped every so often and smelt along the ground and among the rocks for signs of Light. As she proceeded a hyena flushed from its resting place near one of the many caves scattered along Fig Tree Ridge. Chui looked menacing for a moment, as if she would charge the hyena, but it quickly disappeared down through the rocks.

Dark rushed off ahead of Chui, as if he had seen something. Suddenly, out of nowhere, Light appeared, running towards Chui from the vicinity of Dwarf Rocks. His excitement was all too evident as he reached up to rub his forehead under his mother's chin. Dark joined the two of them, pushing his head against Light's face, sniffing and renewing contact with his brother. This was one of the rare occasions when I saw the cubs use any part of the ritual that they performed so regularly when greeting the arrival of their mother. But then it was unusual for the cubs to become separated from each other at this stage in their lives.

When I arrived back at Dwarf Rocks early next day Chui and the cubs had gone. I therefore decided to continue on my way east to visit the Mara Buffalo Female and her cubs. In fact I passed within twenty yards of the trees where Chui and her cubs sheltered, but failed to detect their presence.

On my way back later in the morning I saw a vehicle parked on the track ahead of me. Chui lay under an acacia bush close by, with Light and Dark huddled within the curl of her body. This was the last place I would have expected to find Chui and her cubs. It was two and a half miles from Dwarf Rocks and close to the eastern edge of Chui's home range, an area much frequented by hyenas. Her reason for leading her cubs on this dangerous journey hung in the top of a nearby tree: the half-eaten carcass of a male Thomson's gazelle.

Dark was the first to leave Chui's side, trotting over to the kill tree and clawing his way to the top. Light continued to suckle, kneading his mother's breast to stimulate the flow of milk, while Chui groomed his head. Having satisfied himself temporarily, Dark descended from the tree and rejoined Chui, who sat grooming.

When Chui decided to feed, the cubs left her and trotted to another tree seventy yards away, ignoring her calls for them to join her. Light and Dark seemed very nervous and within ten minutes they slithered down to the ground, head first, then sideways and finally backwards. With a few furtive glances in the direction of their mother they hurried away to the east, providing an indication of just how panicky and vulnerable young leopards are when they first follow their mother into unfamiliar areas.

Chui soon abandoned her kill and began searching for her cubs. Every so often she paused to look around, calling repeatedly before continuing forward with her nose close to the ground, tracking the cubs in the direction in which they had departed. Her plaintive calls were eventually answered.

The cubs had been hiding among the rocks and bushes 200 yards from the kill. As soon as they saw Chui and heard her familiar, reassuring voice they rushed towards her. The arrival of a bateleur eagle swooping from the sky to inspect the gazelle's stomach, left exposed on the grass, made Chui look up. As the bird plummeted to the ground Chui raced back, quickly forcing the eagle to abandon its meal. She climbed into the tree again and this time the cubs followed her lead.

The young leopards must have begun to feed on the gazelle during the night, for they both had well-rounded tummies, as did Chui. A full-grown male Thomson's gazelle weighs at least forty-five pounds and Chui had already feasted on her kill the previous day before departing to fetch her cubs.

Chui looked down on Light as he again deserted the food and moved away. He stopped thirty feet from the tree and turned to stare back at his mother, squawking and miaowing shrilly. He felt insecure in these strange surroundings, for this was a completely new and unfamiliar area, without caves for the cubs to hide in. Dark scrambled down as well, pausing to chew at the gazelle's stomach before trotting away in the opposite direction to Light. He chose the same patch of thornbush that he had retreated to earlier.

Chui turned around in the tree, peering this way and that in an attempt to follow the divergent paths that the cubs had chosen. The tree she sat in grew at the edge of a rocky outcrop that formed an island of cover among the plains. It is areas such as these that provide a leopard with access to the very edges of the grasslands. But there are large tracts of terrain in and around the Mara which are unsuitable habitat for a leopard; areas of open plain that provide none of the cover that a leopard needs if it is to compete successfully with the more powerful and numerous lions and hyenas which dominate the predator hierarchy.

It had been a stiflingly hot day with a thick wedge of cloud shrouding the sky and turning the area into a steam bath. Now the rain arrived like a hail of bullets, peppering the dry ground and throwing puffs of dust into the air. The smell of rain and dust-dampened earth, the musical pitter-patter on a tin roof, all helped provide a sense of relief from the oppressive heat.

When the rain finally eased, Chui climbed from the tree and called to her cubs. Dark appeared from the thicket to the west where he had been sheltering among the thorny branches of an acacia bush and trotted over to Chui. As he settled down to suckle, an old hyena hobbled into view. Dark felt his mother tense and heard the quiet growl which acted as a signal to the cub as well as to the hyena, who quickly veered away.

Dark did not immediately run at the sight of the predator, preferring to continue suckling. Chui followed the hyena with her eyes as it moved in a wide circle to join a second, younger hyena which was lying on the muddy path. Both moved north as it started spitting with rain again. The young hyena soon reappeared, wandering along the vehicle track to investigate the unmistakable smell of carrion. Chui bared her long canines in an open-mouthed threat and hissed as it moved closer.

Light now arrived on the scene and scrambled into the kill tree, while Dark fled in the opposite direction and climbed into the tree that his brother had rested in earlier. The hyena circled around the kill tree as Chui sat watching, her ears flattened and her mouth gaping in an expressive snarl. But the hyena took little notice of Chui's warning, sniffing around the base of the tree for any scraps that might have fallen from the kill.

Though perched safely in the top of the kill tree, Light looked nervously down at the hyena and then over to his mother. Chui ran forward in a swaggering trot, almost sideways on, which made her look bigger than she really was. She paused when she reached the base of the tree, peering towards the hyena, who ignored her disdainfully. Chui lunged forward, coughing explosively and hooking her outstretched claws into the hyena's rump. The hyena howled in pain, spinning round to face the leopard before grudgingly moving aside, growling and rumbling as it departed.

Chui backed away, keeping a wary eye on the hyena, and sat thirty feet from the tree. It was not long before the hyena returned, causing Chui to growl and snarl, blinking her eyes closed at the unwelcome attentions of the persistent scavenger. Again she slouched towards the tree, stopping to sit and watch before charging forward. This time the hyena barely moved aside, ignoring Chui even more pointedly and showing little sign of being intimidated.

As soon as the hyena departed, Dark left his tree and ran back towards where his mother sat. He did not stop when he reached her, but continued straight for the kill tree where Light crouched among the branches. Soon the rain returned, pelting down on the leopards and forcing Chui to creep away to the shelter of the thorn thickets.

Chui and the cubs were all in the kill tree when I arrived early next morning. Dark was busy picking over the remains of the carcass, while Light and Chui reclined along branches on the east side of the tree. Having scratched her claws on the branch, Chui climbed up to join Dark. Light soon followed. The three leopards fed together, each established in its own place at different corners of the kill, with Light and Dark crouched on either side of their mother. In this position Chui could control any disputes that might develop between her cubs. And develop they soon did.

Chui picked up the carcass and struggled to pull it higher into the tree, with both cubs vigorously resisting her efforts, hanging on to their portion of the kill as if their lives depended on it. Dark even hissed at his mother. Chui hissed back.

A succession of creatures passed the tree during the next hour. An African hare raced for cover as a jackal trotted into view, causing Chui to prick her ears up with interest. But the crafty canine was alert to the danger, leaving the scraps of meat at the base of the tree to bolder brethren the moment he smelt the presence of leopards. Hyenas skulked around, devouring whatever they could find, ignoring Chui's vocal threats, as birds of prey cast their shadows over the scene. Light miaowed and squawked at Chui, apparently distressed. But worse was to follow, for now he began to climb out of the tree, accompanied by Dark, who seemed anxious to follow his brother's lead. Surely though, they must have seen the hyena resting barely twenty yards away?

As Light backed down the tree the hyena sat up and stared at him. The young cub squatted to urinate before both he and Dark trotted straight towards the hyena, moving in a faltering, stop-start progression.

The hyena seemed surprised and confused by the sight of the leopard cubs running towards it. Light crept forward another twenty feet and crouched in front of the hyena, who yawned, exposing its powerful teeth. Perhaps it was intimidated by Chui's presence in the kill tree, though she gave no sound of warning to announce herself, nor did she attempt to rush down the tree to defend her cubs.

The hyena started to get to its feet, but the moment it did so Dark raced away to the nearest tree. Light stayed a moment longer, watching almost inquisitively as the hyena began to circle menacingly towards him. Then he streaked for the nearest acacia bush, climbing all the way to the top. Once the hyena had departed, Light climbed down again and trotted over to the tree where his brother had sought refuge. Before long the cubs were scrambling playfully among the branches.

By ten o'clock the kill had been picked clean. Chui called her cubs to her and led them away through the rocks and thornbushes scattered across the low hill to the north. She moved slowly and deliberately, and with good reason, for there were numerous hyenas resting in the vicinity.

The leopards moved deeper into the thickets with Chui keeping her eyes glued on a group of four hyenas lying barely a hundred yards away. Just as it seemed that the leopards would evade detection, a herd of impalas started to blast in alarm. One of the hyenas got to its feet, searching for an explanation of the antelopes' concern. The bush telegraph always made it doubly difficult for predators to move about undetected either by prey or by competitors.

Chui watched the hyenas, hissing and rumbling a throaty growl of warning while the cubs sat nervously on either side of her, ready to flee if necessary. Chui slipped away, the cubs following her every move, skirting well clear of the hyenas' resting place. But the hyenas were far too curious to abandon the leopards so easily. After all, the presence of leopards sometimes meant there was food to be scavenged and a hungry hyena might try to prey on the cubs.

The first hyena headed towards the leopards at a determined gallop. Chui sat and faced it, hissing and growling, giving her cubs valuable seconds in which to flee for the trees. But the hyena virtually ignored her threats, far more interested in the cubs. Chui circled, positioning herself between the hyenas and the cubs. A second hyena ran over to join its clan mate, moving even closer to Chui, sniffing along the ground to follow the scent trail left by the young leopards, each of whom had chosen a different euphorbia tree as his refuge.

Once the hyenas had returned to their original resting place, Chui moved away to the north, breaking into a trot as the tsetse flies swarmed around her. She too climbed into a euphorbia, which was the predominant species of tree growing on the hillside. Tiny green fingers grew from the dry, silvery tips of the cactus-like trees. The rain had started to work its magic.

The cubs lay in their respective trees, very exposed among the leafless branches. They stared across at each other, fifty yards apart, uttering high-pitched contact calls which carried clearly on the wind, interspersed with softer squawks which were barely audible. They paused occasionally to groom a paw or nibble at their own tails as they wandered around in their trees, searching for a shadow to lie in.

As midday approached Light left the euphorbia and slunk off into a nearby thicket. Though Dark watched his brother depart he chose to stay where he was, having finally found a fragment of shade cast by one of the euphorbia branches. Three hours later Chui hurried down from her tree and sought the cover of an acacia thicket sixty yards away. Here she dozed while Dark remained in his tree, unaware that his mother lay nearby.

Just before six o'clock one of the hyenas reappeared, earning Dark's undivided attention as it sniffed around the rocks a few yards from the base of the tree. A white-bellied bustard began to call from the edge of a croton thicket, not far from where Chui was resting. Her eyes opened at the sound, and she found herself looking straight into the dark eyes of yet another hyena that had tracked her scent to the thicket. The hyena sniffed around the bushes before moving off in search of something edible.

Before the light faded completely, Chui got up and walked quietly to the tree where Dark waited. The cub was still wary, looking carefully around before daring to respond to his mother's call. As Dark descended, Light reappeared from his own hiding place, calling as he ran to join Chui and Dark. Before she moved away, Chui paused to defecate, though on this occasion she did not attempt to cover her droppings.

In the distance a hyena uttered a series of mournful whoops as Chui lay down among the rocks. The cubs quickly established their positions and began to suckle, while Chui rested on her elbows to keep watch. The bustard called once more, sounding a final message at the end of another day.

Next morning the leopards were seen moving along Fig Tree Ridge, on their way back to Dik-Dik Lugga. For the cubs it was the end of a long and dangerous journey to a previously unfamiliar part of their mother's home range. The fact that they had travelled so far at such a young age cast considerable doubt in my mind as to whether I would be able to keep track of their movements for much longer.

6. Instinct and Experience

CHUI'S RETURN visit to Dik-Dik Lugga lasted only as long as it took her and the cubs to consume the topi calf which she had ambushed along Fig Tree Ridge. Now that Light and Dark had proved their mobility and were able to climb trees with ease, Chui seemed once more to be behaving like every other adult leopard, moving from place to place within her home range, killing where she could, feeding for a day or three and then continuing on her way again.

This new era in the cubs' life was fraught with danger for Light and Dark. Though they had gradually become familiar with some of the basic elements of their mother's world, they still had a lot to learn and experience along the road to independence. Growing up would not be easy, though as they gradually became stronger and more alert to danger they would learn to look after themselves.

On the third morning after Chui had killed the topi calf she led her cubs cautiously from the croton thickets and began the long trek east along Fig Tree Ridge. By nine o'clock they lay resting in the shadows among the rocks, high up on the ridge face, with Light as usual lying closer to Chui. Dark, however, decided to explore by himself, distracted by the multitude of sights and sounds surrounding him. Wherever he moved he caused a reaction: lizards scurried away from him, birds twittered and hopped from branch to branch above him in the acacia bushes, and dwarf mongooses spluttered and churred from the safety of the crevices.

As Chui and Light moved away, Dark's inquisitive behaviour was interrupted by the sudden appearance of a hyena from over the top of the ridge. The sight of the shaggy-coated predator was quite enough to send Dark scuttling down the rocky incline to the safety of a slender a cacia bush.

Fortunately the hyena took little notice of the startled leopard cub and continued on its way. Dark waited until he was sure the danger had passed, before quickly descending from the bush and hurrying off in pursuit of his mother. But no sooner had he done so than he found himself face to face with yet another hyena. For a moment they stared at each other, then, before the hyena could react aggressively, Dark walked, then trotted, then galloped back down the ridge as fast as he could go. He chose the same bush, though this time he climbed to the very top and perched there, twelve feet above the ground, looking anxiously around him.

Chui and Light plodded eastwards, quite unconcerned by Dark's disappearance, more interested in reaching their own destination. A young hyena dogged their footsteps, though it stayed some distance behind them, engrossed in their intriguing smell. On reaching the Cub Caves, Chui sniffed inquisitively around the base of the fig tree, searching for signs of previous visitors. Satisfied, she leapt into the tree and settled along the armchair. Light for once seemed content to lie quietly by himself on Top Rock, sprawled in the shade below his mother, while nearly a mile away Dark dozed fitfully among the prickly thorns of the acacia bush.

Vervets stuttered incessantly from the baboons' sleeping tree, busily plundering the ripening fruits in the absence of their larger relatives.

Eventually they ceased calling and for a moment everything seemed quiet and timeless. Clouds filled the sky and a pleasant coolness replaced the midday heat.

Chui rested throughout the afternoon hidden among the leaves and branches of the fig tree. But by 4.30 the first baboon had arrived. He sat at the base of the tree and looked up, his keen eyes quickly picking out the shadowy form of the recumbent predator. He climbed into the lower reaches of the tree and started to feed on the ripening figs. A smaller baboon leapt into the west side of the tree to join his companion in shaking the branches and threatening the leopard.

A few minutes later both baboons suddenly descended, slithering down the main stem like firemen. Chui relaxed visibly as the baboons strode away. But the peace was short-lived, for the younger baboon soon turned back. This time he climbed to within a few feet of Chui, who hissed and rumbled, until the baboon retreated to a safer perch on a branch below her. The rest of the troop made their way east, moving slowly through the acacia thickets to the south of the ridge, seemingly unconcerned by Chui's presence once they had been warned of her position. The young baboon soon departed as the troop headed for their night-time destination.

Chui descended to the lowest fork in the fig tree as the sun dropped from behind the grey clouds. She peered warily through the thick canopy of leaves to watch the baboons climbing into their sleeping quarters. A few loitered below, grooming and murmuring as the light faded from the sky.

Morning found Light and Dark playing among the open branches of a small tree half a mile to the west of the Cub Caves, only yards from the acacia bush where Dark had sought shelter. Chui must have retraced her steps during the night, smelling and calling to her stranded cub and reuniting him with his brother. Whatever the circumstances had been, Chui was now nowhere to be seen.

By eight o'clock the cubs were resting, eyes tightly closed, heads across forepaws, slumped together near to the base of a termite mound. Much to the cubs' alarm a banded mongoose suddenly erupted from within the mound. The cubs almost fell over each other in surprise at the sudden movements. For a motionless moment the mongoose and the leopard cubs stared at one another. But the spell was broken as the mongoose shot back down the tunnel again. Having recovered from their shock the cubs crept forward to investigate the mongoose's hiding place, only to be greeted by furious churrs and splutters of alarm from deep within the hidden chambers of the mound.

Thwarted, the cubs retreated to the base of the tree, whose roots had neatly split a slab of rock, producing an ideal hiding place, a narrow cleft just large enough for them to squeeze into. Here it was cool and they were protected.

Not long afterwards, and unknown to the sleeping cubs, a party of elephants appeared from the west. They had begun their journey near to Musiara Marsh and now moved methodically along the edge of the ridge, pausing wherever suitable vegetation allowed them to feed. Closer and closer the trundling giants plodded. The sounds of the elephants noisily dismembering the thornbushes, tearing up plants and growling throaty rumbles would have been enough to frighten anything. It was certainly not the time to be caught slumbering among the branches of a slender tree or fragile bush.

The largest of all the elephants, a giant cow, paused to feed at the edge of the croton thicket, only yards now from where the cubs lay. Light and Dark must have felt the ground tremble as a fallen branch snapped under the weight of an elephantine foot. Once they had ravaged the thicket of food the family herd filed up through a gap in the ridge and headed for fresher pastures, leaving the cubs safe and sound within their rocky hiding place.

The troop of mongooses who had remained hidden within the bowels of the termite mound were restless. Usually by this time they would be scouring the land below Fig Tree Ridge for insects and other food, resting beneath bushes or within burrows only during the hottest part of the day. But they were wary of the leopards, who even as cubs dwarfed the mongooses. So they waited, until certain of leaving safely.

Just before two o'clock a pointed muzzle peeped from the entrance to one of the air vent holes which provided both exit and entrance to the termite mound. Cautiously the mongoose looked around, searching for signs of danger. The cubs were both fast asleep and did not even stir as the mongoose crept quietly into the open. Soon a dozen troop members disgorged from the mound's interior and made a collective dash for the acacia thicket thirty yards away. At last they could feed.

The afternoon brought rain, though it was short-lived, driven onwards by a stiff breeze from the east, rolling the grey clouds back over the Siria Escarpment and replacing them with a beautiful blue sky. Dark was the first to emerge. He soon found a convenient pebble to play with, carrying it in his mouth to the crevice where he had rested. When he dropped the stone it clattered noisily over the edge of the rock, prompting him to pounce on it again. The rattle of the falling stone caused Light to emerge, sleepy-eyed, from beneath the rock. Dark crept forward and pounced on his yawning brother, wrestling Light to the ground.

The sounds of members of the Ridge Clan giggling made both cubs sit up, recognising a sound that they had learned to respect. Dark was the first to move, clawing his way into the tree again. Light followed and they climbed into the very topmost branches of the leafless, silver-barked tree. Here they were safe.

The sky had lost its earlier clarity and in the distance rain was already falling along the Siria Escarpment. Dark lay his head on a branch and closed his eyes, content to rest. Light, however, was now fully awake, and had climbed to a position directly above his brother. The larger cub was like a hyperactive child. First he dabbed his floppy paw on Dark's neck and when that failed to provoke a reaction he simply stood on his brother's head. Dark's attempts to ignore these abuses only served to frustrate Light even further, causing him to move to a new location providing better access to more of Dark. There were so many small confining branches between the two cubs that it was difficult for Light to launch a full-scale attack. He finally solved the problem by moving to a position below Dark from which he could completely smother his brother's head and neck. He bit down on Dark's soft, upturned throat before turning to tear more vigorously at the branches instead.

Chui returned to her cubs after dark and led them back towards Dik-Dik Lugga. I met them curled beneath a stand of tall acacia bushes at the base of the ridge not far from Kampi ya Chui. Chui rested up on her elbows, her head bowed forward, eyelids droopy. Light and Dark dozed contentedly on their mother's teats, while in the distance hyenas cackled and giggled. Though Chui did not look round, her ears twisted to locate the direction of the sounds. It was obviously time to move to a less exposed position.

Chui walked slowly towards the ridge while the cubs trotted over to a partially collapsed pappea tree. Dark clambered on to the thick fallen limb as Light climbed past him and continued up the main trunk. Chui came back and sniffed around the base of the tree. She seemed anxious to continue, but now Light found that he was stranded in a narrow fork near the top of the tree. He called in distress to Chui, who sat and stared up at her son, then chuffled twice to encourage him to come down. Eventually he did.

Dark had stayed on the broken branch, looking down at his mother a few feet below him. Chui sat rubbing her face, forehead and throat along the underside of the fallen limb where another leopard had recently sprayed. Then she turned, arched her long tail and added her own scent message to that left by the previous leopard.

Two or three times Chui moved purposefully away towards the ridge, chuffling at the cubs, doing everything possible to draw them with her. But each time she walked away the cubs found some new game to play. Eventually

Chui tried more persuasive methods, biting down on the cubs, rolling them over and nipping them, even picking Light half off the ground in her mouth. The cubs squealed in protest, though they acted almost as if it was just part of some new game. Then Chui leapt away and bounded up the vehicle track leading over the ridge. This time the cubs galloped to catch up with her.

A thin band of light peeped from beneath the grey cloud blanket as Chui paused briefly to sit on a huge termite mound to reconnoitre the way ahead. The cubs joined her and all three watched alertly in the direction of Dik-Dik Lugga, which was now within sight. But Chui turned away and headed east again along Fig Tree Ridge.

It was very hot, the blue sky streaked with hazy clouds. The cubs trotted behind Chui, their heads low, mouths open. When they reached the massive rock that marked the mid-point along Fig Tree Ridge, Light and Dark stopped to rest in the shade cast by a wizened tree stump. Finding she was alone, Chui turned back and rejoined the cubs where they lay panting. They were exhausted.

Meanwhile the Masai and their hungry cattle flooded along the west side of Dik-Dik Lugga, pausing to feed around the green edges of the pools. Perhaps Chui had sensed their arrival, heard the distant sound of cow bells and decided to move on.

When Chui plodded forward again the cubs tarried, sniffing and exploring the caves and rocky ledges. But when their mother was a hundred yards off the cubs quickly trotted after her. Dark caught up and flanked alongside Chui, forcing her to a halt. Light meanwhile moved up to the topmost rocks on the ridge, sending a wave of rusty-brown dwarf mongooses hurrying for cover. The tiny animals responded with a barrage of scolding alarm calls from the safety of the narrow crevices between the rocks.

Light was fascinated by the reaction he had caused. His whole bearing changed as he proceeded forward with his ears cocked and neck arched high, stepping daintily. The sounds emanating from the rocks proved irresistible to

Dark as well, and he soon joined his brother to investigate the area like two bloodhounds, pressed close together.

Chui continued, ignoring such juvenile curiosity, set on reaching her predetermined destination. Their journey leap-frogged from one patch of shade to the next, but always the tsetse flies were waiting to swarm around the leopards and force them onwards, though for some reason they seemed to bother Chui far more than her cubs.

Light and Dark moved out ahead of Chui, but she soon passed them as the biting flies forced her into a run. When she stopped to lie under the next bush the cubs kept moving, trotting side by side as if they already knew where they were going. Chui got up and followed, chuffling to the cubs. Impala blasted once more and topi and zebra snorted to the south, filling the air with an array of alarm calls. Chui stopped, carefully checking for signs of the dangers that might lie ahead.

Finally all three leopards arrived at the Cub Caves. Dark flopped down in front of his mother, who carefully stepped over the exhausted cub and slumped down on the smooth stone surface of Top Rock where it was cool, shaded and flyless.

The cubs lay side by side, panting, only a few feet from their mother, whose throat throbbed with the heat. Dark nestled in a shallow depression that almost perfectly mirrored his own shape. Chui got up and looked into the heart of the fig tree. Three or four times she stared upwards before leaping into the lowest fork. A party of four hyrax spotted Chui's ascent from their hiding place along a narrow ledge to the west. One of them started to screech in alarm. But as soon as all three leopards ceased moving the alarm cries stopped.

A male agamid lizard bobbed up and down only three feet from where Dark lay sleeping, issuing his distinctive challenge. But when a bateleur eagle soared overhead in the muggy heat, the lizard quickly scuttled for cover, acknowledging a threat that he could not afford to ignore. Dark sat up and watched the lizards, then looked up into the trees and called twice. Light heard him and emerged from the cave where he had been resting. Both cubs craned their necks to look at Chui, though she chose to ignore them and they soon moved off again and lay together in the shade behind Top Rock.

At last the rain arrived to relieve the heat. Light reappeared and wandered around restlessly. Then without further ado he started to climb into the fig tree. If Chui refused to come down he would have to go to her. The young leopard climbed higher and higher, making his way along the thinnest of branches until he was forced to a halt barely six feet from where Chui rested. A moment later Dark followed.

Finding that he was unable to reach Chui, Light retraced his steps and crossed from the central trunk to the thick western limb. Dark meanwhile had arrived at the same dead end of thin branches that had separated Light from their mother, for neither cub had yet mastered the route that Chui used.

Chui lay with her eyes closed, ignoring the cubs, while Light explored all the avenues along the branches to the west. It was like being in a maze: despite being so close to their mother the cubs were still unable to reach her. They were hungry and wanted to suckle, miaowing to attract Chui's attention. Finally Light reached Chui by an alternative route, but his reception was anything but friendly. Chui hissed and coughed, rebuffing the cub and making it quite obvious that she did not want Light to disturb her while she was resting. Eventually both cubs descended and left Chui alone.

The December rains now began to show their effect. Luggas filled once more with pools of muddy water. The clay soils turned soggy brown, crisscrossed by a maze of animal and bird tracks, while delicate lace-like wings, cast aside by ants and termites, patterned the ground like enormous snowflakes.

Chui poses in late evening light on the top of Fig Tree Ridge.

A huge male leopard marking his territory along the Talek River. A male's territory may overlap that of two or more females and is often double the size.

Dark and Light aged four months, at the Cub Caves on Fig Tree Ridge.

The Mara Buffalo Female, Chui's mother, emerging from the rocks where her cubs were hidden.

Half-Tail stretching as she sets off to hunt through the long grass.

Half-Tail and Zawadi, then ten months old, during the first series of *Big Cat Diary*, 1996.

Half-Tail stashing a young impala kill in one of the ancient fig trees along Fig Tree Ridge.

Zawadi on the hunt late one afternoon in 1998, when she was nearly three years old. She lived to the remarkable age of sixteen.

Zawadi with a hare she has just caught. Young leopards and mothers with cubs invest time hunting for hares in clumps of long grass and under fallen acacia trees.

Zawadi gazes out from the top of Fig Tree Ridge in 1983.

Bella and her male cub Chui, aged eighteen months, resting in the shade o
a giant fig tree along the Talek River in 2004. Large fig trees are favoure
resting places for leopards

Zawadi with her daughter Safi, aged three or four months, along Fig Tree Ridge in early 2000. Safi survived to independence and established herself in a territory slightly overlapping her mother's, where she raised cubs of her own.

Nkaiyoni at two and a half years old attempting to mate with his mother, Olive
He was already independent, but their paths still crossed at times

Malaika about to pounce on her mother's tail. Stalking, pouncing and biting are innate behaviour patterns for all cats, and leopard cubs spend much of their time with their mother and siblings refining their fighting and hunting skills through play.

A martial eagle, Africa's largest, is capable of killing and eating a three-month-old lion cub.

Hyenas are a major danger to leopard cubs – and steal food from adults.

Leopards have been known to kill giraffe calves, but their mothers defend them with chopping kicks from their plate-sized feet.

The arrival of the wildebeest migration provides all the Mara's predators with a glut of prey.

Olive grooming her three-to-four-month-old male cub, Nkaiyoni. Cubs are virtually weaned by this age but may continue to suckle for another couple of months. They begin eating meat at around eight weeks old.

Nkaiyoni and Paja at around one and a half years old.

Malaika greeting Zawadi and inviting her to play. She is thought to have been killed by hyenas shortly after this.

The Kicheche female known as Supuu with one of her two cubs, aged six to eight months. We filmed her for *Big Cat Diary* one year when it was tough finding Bella.

Nkaiyoni, now independent and soon to begin searching for a territory of his own.

The new young female in Leopard Gorge, born around October 2008. Could she be Zawadi's daughter?

Chui lay on the rocks in the lugga floor, elevated from the damp earth. A gentle breeze lifted the long white hair of her chest and belly, except around her teats where the fur was grubby brown, matted from the cubs' constant attention. She watched impassively as two dozen steppe eagles circled overhead. Their appearance did not indicate a recent kill, only the bloated bodies of the winged termites which would provide a variety of birds and animals with nutritious food.

A mile away along Fig Tree Ridge baboons clustered to feed in the honey tree, plucking fresh fruits from the larder. Others sat and devoured the floundering termites trapped among hundreds of discarded wings where some of their kind had descended back to earth. The solitary slender mongoose busied himself near Dwarf Rocks, where his smaller relatives gathered to capitalise on the windfall of insect food.

Chui climbed out of the lugga and reclined on an ancient termite mound. It was a giant structure long since abandoned by its architects and builders, after generations of use. The earthen spires had eroded to leave a comfortable, grass-covered platform. Such structures are a regular feature throughout the Mara, providing a perfect lookout point for lions and cheetahs, topi and kongoni – and sometimes even for leopards.

Twenty-five yards away a party of banded mongooses emerged from below ground and busied themselves around another termite mound. One adroitly heaved up a small boulder and diligently scraped among the exposed soil with rapid bursts of scratching, using its long, curved claws to ferret for insects and grubs.

When the rain arrived it fell as a fine drizzle, causing Dark to sit up and shake the tiny droplets of rain from his coat. Birds broke into song: flappet larks called – a soft two-note refrain, *tooee*, *tooee* – instead of just flapping, and slate-coloured boubous duetted. Chui bowed her head forward, eyes drooping shut, like a weary commuter on a long train journey. But there was to be no peace for her while she rested so close to her cubs. As Dark pressed against her, she lifted her tail and curled it sinuously around his neck. On seeing this Light came to join his brother and both played with their mother's tail. A grey wall of cloud blanketed the sky as it continued to drizzle. Chui sat and groomed herself while the cubs played around the termite mound.

Chui participated enthusiastically during some of these play sessions. Such occasions were a joy to observe, for the birth of cubs allowed me a glimpse of another, previously hidden, part of Chui's world. Behind that cold, withdrawn exterior lurked a warmth of mood that was totally captivating. Our image of the leopard tends towards that of the cold-eyed killer, but there is another leopard hidden deep within that spotted coat. It was a rare privilege indeed to be able to watch one of the animal world's most secretive creatures abandoning its cautious ways to romp and frolic in a manner I would never have believed possible.

As I watched, all three leopards rolled around on the wet ground, a mass of feet, fur and forepaws. The cubs hared after each other like young cheetahs, eventually returning to Chui, who in turn galloped away with Light and Dark in hot pursuit. When she stopped suddenly, the cubs bumped into each other and collapsed like a pack of cards in a heap at Chui's feet. As soon as they rushed off again Chui charged them, rolling Dark over and softly biting him, then walked away. Chui's movements ensured that she was not ignored, not simply a stooge in the cubs' games. It was a constant succession of chase, leap, tumble and bite while the neglected cub hurriedly stalked up from behind.

Next morning mother and cubs were in the same place, playing the same games. It had rained intermittently during the night and the ground was greasy-wet underfoot. The sky hung grey and soggy above the lugga, though it did not seem to be of any consequence to the leopards, except perhaps to make them even more active.

Chui paused to groom, veering away each time a cub approached, then stopping to watch as they played together. Light ran back and jumped onto

Chui's shoulders, straddling her and holding on to her neck with his forepaws, riding her like a jockey. Chui unseated Light and swaggered towards Dark, sinuously rolling on the ground and spinning up and away as he ran to meet her.

Briefly Chui climbed into a croton bush before walking into the open, where a solitary acacia bush grew. She sat, head lowered, inviting the inevitable charge from her cubs. As they closed in Chui held her position until the very last moment, then sprang sideways into the air with her back feet perfectly positioned together and her long tail looped in a graceful arc behind her. Dark found himself clutching at thin air as his mother easily cleared the top of the five-foot bush, and hung in the air before landing softly on the ground again.

Gradually the frantic pace of their activities slowed. Chui walked down to the lugga, drawing Light with her. But Dark preferred to stay where he was, nothing like as slavish in his relationship with his mother. Vervets called in alarm from the acacia thicket to the west, though they in turn were the cause of concern for the crowned shrikes that nested in the same bushes. Protective of their eggs and nestlings, the shrikes noisily mobbed the monkeys. A female vervet with a young baby clutched to her belly galloped across the open ground, scolded and pecked on the head by one of the furious shrikes pursuing her.

A gentle breeze stirred in the east, building into a gushing wind which rushed like a swarm of bees down the lugga, chased by the rain. Now it was pouring, lashing down on Chui who, for a moment, sat facing into it. But this was no mere shower, and Chui soon sought more substantial shelter deeper within the lugga. Eventually the rain eased to a trickle and Chui once more crept to the edge of the bushes.

Shortly after two o'clock Chui sat up alertly, as if she had heard something. Bee-eaters swept low on golden wings, but the leopard ignored them. From out of the emptiness of the rocks and thorn thickets covering the hill to the west, a mixed group of topi and zebra appeared. They moved in a disturbed trot and Chui watched them with a combination of curiosity and concern. Something had forced their departure.

It soon started to rain again, causing Chui to lie down under one of the bushes. But she remained wary, continually looking in the direction whence the zebra had come. For their part, Light and Dark were unconcerned, interested only in trying to suckle from their mother, though she tucked her legs up beneath her and refused to co-operate.

Suddenly a strange mixture of high-pitched yelps and squeals drifted down to where the leopards lay. Chui sat bolt upright again. Zebras scattered from the hillside, careering over the rocks less than a hundred yards away. Chui took one final look before turning to flee in the opposite direction, keeping low to the ground. She moved like lightning, causing her cubs to dive for cover among the rocks in the lugga floor. The reason for her alarm became apparent as three large warthogs and three piglets appeared over the rocky horizon, closely pursued by a pack of four Masai dogs.

The lead dog soon caught up with one of the piglets that had lagged behind, exhausted from the chase. But before the dog could secure a meal the mother warthog rushed in, grunting aggressively, and forced the dog away just long enough for her piglet to follow its relatives into the safety of a nearby burrow.

Instead of staying below ground, the frightened warthogs had no sooner disappeared than they dashed back out again. The dogs were waiting.

One dog in particular, a spotted brown and white one, kept the chase alive, driving the biggest pigs ahead of him before switching tack to close on the weary piglet again. For a moment the pack leader held the squealing youngster securely by the hind leg, until two of the adult warthogs raced back and bowled the dog over. But this particular mongrel was no newcomer to the art of pig chasing. In a flash the dog was back on his feet and racing after his attackers, despite a slashing wound which seeped red against his white shoulder.

Just then a young Masai boy rushed excitedly down the hillside carrying a bow and arrow, anxious to join in the fray. He was so intent on goading the dogs to further action that at first he failed to notice the vehicle partially concealed behind a large acacia bush. But the moment he realised that he had unwanted company he sped away, barefoot and nimbly negotiating a path through the rocks.

Accompanied by dogs and armed with a variety of weapons suitable for a life in the bush, Masai youths, understandably enough, did sometimes relieve the tedium of long hours guarding their father's herds by finding a suitable target for arrow, spear or throwing stick. It was not exceptional to see Masai boys indulging in sport with warthogs. Sometimes they would track the pigs to their burrows and then try to spear them – hence the warthogs' reluctance to stay below ground in these circumstances. If the boys had dogs with them, they were provided with an easy meal.

Some years earlier two of a litter of cheetah cubs were thought to have been killed by a pack of Masai dogs, just outside the northern boundary of the Reserve. Dogs might well endanger young leopard cubs too, if they ever came across them in the open or when they were too small to escape up bushes or trees.

Even though Chui and her cubs were extremely tolerant of vehicles, their response to them was a learned form of behaviour, conditioned from an early age. Usually leopards avoid contact with humans and Chui reacted just as warily as the Mara Buffalo Female, or any other leopard for that matter, when confronted by people on foot.

When Chui had fled, she was not trying to divert the attention of the dogs or the Masai youth from her cubs. She had moved away as quickly and stealthily as she could in the hope of avoiding detection. To have stayed with the cubs in the lugga would have been a futile gesture, for the drought had robbed her of cover: there was nowhere there for her to hide, no caves large enough to protect her from dogs, or a man on foot. But there were such places for Light and Dark, who had been able to shelter until the danger had passed.

Chui's own safety was ultimately more important than that of her cubs, who were still far too young to fend for themselves in the event of her death. At five months, the cubs had nothing to contribute reproductively to the leopard population. Chui, however, would be able to produce another litter of cubs within a relatively short time if her young were killed or died. Avoiding injury is essential to any solitary predator. Chui knew her own limitations. When and if she were forced to defend herself she would prove to be a formidable adversary. Until that time, running away was the most obvious means of ensuring her own survival. There is no such word as cowardice in the animal world.

It had poured during the night. The day following a really heavy downpour does not show the Mara at its best. Large areas become inaccessible and driving becomes a chore. Vehicles get stuck and windows steam up in the damp conditions. Fortunately it dries out quickly once the rain has stopped, leaving everything and everybody looking refreshed from the oppressive conditions that precede a storm.

Early in the morning of Christmas Eve, Chui was seen collecting Light and Dark from Dik-Dik Lugga and accompanying them east along Fig Tree Ridge. Later on the same day she was chased by a mother topi who defended her young calf vigorously, forcing Chui to flee with her cubs to the safety of the bushes.

Now Chui rested high in the east side of the fig tree. To the north, marabous and white storks searched for food among the acacia thickets, congregating to feast on a plague of army worms that reposed like dark seed heads on the grass stems.

It started to rain, fulfilling a threat that had loomed all day. The storks clustered in the tops of trees, swaying in the breeze like black and white flags as the light ebbed away. As another evening faded with the sun and the rain faltered, Chui suddenly got up and left her cubs playing together. Light and Dark sat and watched as Chui slipped away, then they carefully stalked forward together. But they stopped thirty yards from their mother as if they knew not to join her.

Chui sat, slightly hunched among the thunder, the rain spitting a fine, silvery gloss over her coat. She turned and looked back at her cubs. That single furtive glance was just enough to break the spell, prompting Light to stalk towards his mother again. Chui seemed undecided as to whether to lead the cubs back to the Cub Caves or try to continue on her way. There was little doubt that she wanted to leave by herself.

Chui trotted off, cautiously lowering her head from view as she came over a rise or around some natural obstacle. The cubs stared after her as her dark shape passed across the setting sun. But when she finally disappeared from view their confidence departed with her. Suddenly the cubs felt vulnerable without their mother there to protect them, alone and exposed in the open country above the ridge. So they turned back towards the Cub Caves. At one point Dark stopped, one forepaw cocked in mid-air, his ears pricked up again. All he could hear were the sounds of lions and hyenas – quite sufficient to intimidate any young leopard. But once the cubs were within thirty feet of the familiar surroundings of Fig Tree Ridge their confidence returned and they started stalking each other again.

I could think of no better way to spend Christmas Day than with Chui and her cubs. My friends seemed to find this behaviour extreme, intimating that I was becoming as anti-social as the leopard. Surely one day away from the leopards would not hurt, they said. It was not that I preferred leopards to people, more that I could rely on seeing people with far greater regularity than I could the leopards. I knew that at any time Chui might disappear with the cubs. In the past, one day with a leopard had been followed by months without. Consequently every day of observation was something I treasured.

It had rained heavily during the night and now everywhere was damp and grey. The cubs lay on Cub Rock, a slab of stone that roofed an open-ended cave, halfway down the ridge, below Chui's fig tree. They crouched together, their coats soaking wet.

A pair of red-rumped swallows fluttered back and forth to build their delicate mud nest halfway up the sandwich of rocks beneath Top Rock. The graceful birds glided in below their new home, hovering as they added to its structure. Their choice of site made it safe from most forms of predation and the cubs, despite their marvellous agility, were unable to reach it, though they often stopped to watch as the birds came and went.

As it began to rain again a cuckoo called in the distance, while a group of topi stood looking dreary among the acacia bushes below the ridge. Only the storks seemed busy as they paced along the vehicle track, feeding in the drizzle.

Finally, after nearly four hours, the rain subsided, leaving the rocks shiny black. Among them a tawny eagle diligently preened its wet feathers while temporarily grounded. Green leaves glistened in the fig tree, others, mainly brown, littered the ground beneath it. Buffalo appeared, huge bovine lumps that looked like movable parts of the rock face, feeding on the coarse grass growing between the boulders.

Dark wriggled from the dry interior of his cave, looking about him as if expecting to find his brother nearby, though Light had already climbed to the top of the ridge. Dark crept forward, peering carefully over each new level of rocks as he ascended to where his brother waited. What a lonely life it would be, I thought, for a single leopard cub, with a mother who spent many long hours away, and no litter-mate to play with.

On a day such as this, when the leopards looked drab and grey, the white undersides of their tails shone like beacons among the sombre rocks. But their activities were anything but dull. Light, for instance, soon found a rock with a distinctive tilt. The cause of the wobble was a smaller rock beneath, which turned the rock he was standing on into a perfect seesaw. Light rocked backwards, trying to lift the edge of the stone platform, which proved difficult since he was still standing on it. His original solution was to clasp it between his paws and bite it, sending himself somersaulting forwards.

One of the leopard cubs' favourite games was their own particular brand of plant bashing. There really was no other way to describe it. A cub would launch himself into the air, making exaggerated leaps towards the large-leafed clerodendron plants that grew around the edges of the Cub Caves. He would land in an undignified belly-flop on the surprisingly resilient bushes. Having once secured the plant between his paws he would tumble forwards, or at times backwards, bringing his feet up to clutch at the willowy stems. Then, releasing his hold, he would barely wait for the weary plant to refloat itself before subjecting it to another round of battering.

For a while Dark raced around alone, leaving Light preoccupied with something hidden behind a large rock. Suddenly all hell broke loose. The cubs growled and squawked, ears back, feet drawn up, clawing and biting at each other in real earnest. They tumbled almost to the bottom of the ridge, a bundle of absolute fury. The fight continued for nearly half a minute with Light apparently the instigator, though Dark fought back fiercely to defend himself against his brother's vicious assault. Finally the smaller cub broke away and trotted along the base of the ridge towards Cub Rock, looking thoroughly scolded and leaving Light to retreat behind the rock where the dispute had started.

Whatever had provoked the violence must have been worth fighting for. Previously I had only ever seen the cubs react like this in a dispute over food, never over an inedible object of play. Possibly Light had some morsel he was defending that I could not see: a lizard perhaps, a beetle, or a scrap of meat from an old kill.

The cubs settled down some forty yards apart, and after a few minutes Dark disappeared into his cave. Light moved towards him, but then circled behind Cub Rock and climbed up to the top of the ridge. He stayed there for a few minutes before returning to lie curled up behind his brother.

The fight seemed to have subdued the young leopards temporarily, for they remained hidden for nearly two hours afterwards. When they did reappear they separated and groomed themselves, easing the tension. As Light moved along the base of the ridge, Dark followed him and before long the cubs were playing as if the fight had never happened.

Suddenly, as they approached the rock again, the cubs started to fight. They batted each other with their paws, pushing and following up with bites and open-mouthed threats. But this time the outburst subsided quickly, though again it was Dark who gave way and hurried off to a quieter place. It had to be food.

Just before six o'clock Dark climbed up on to Top Rock, followed by his brother, successfully negotiating the steep west wall of the vertical cave. They could do this reasonably easily now, whereas only a few weeks earlier it had proved almost impossible. The cubs climbed into the fig tree, moving around confidently in the east side of the tree where Chui liked to rest during the afternoon. By now there was nowhere they could not reach, twisting and turning, following each other's movements in a dizzy display of climbing skills.

So absorbed in their adventure were the cubs that the first they knew of the baboons' arrival below them was a loud bark of alarm. But that was all they needed to hear. No time now to turn and clamber carefully backwards from the tree. Down they came, rushing headlong, never stopping to consider or negotiate the easiest path. It was pure reflex all the way to

Top Rock, where three baboons sat waiting. But the cubs' speed and agility swept them safely past the startled primates who were poised only yards from them.

Fortunately for the cubs the baboons were all youngsters. There were no large males to take the offensive. The cubs streaked away to their respective hiding places: Light to the vertical cave and Dark to Cub Rock. Within a few minutes they were out playing again, grooming and nit-picking, though both remained alert as the baboons moved south of the ridge and marched towards the honey tree.

Light and Dark had now established a familiarity and loyalty to their own personal hideaways when danger threatened. The cubs were less likely to respond simply to each other's fears. They often paused to assess a situation more carefully rather than rushing immediately for the nearest cover, though not where baboons were concerned.

It was some days since I had last seen Chui, though that was not unusual in itself. She often spent a day away from her cubs and so far they had managed to survive the many hours when she left them alone. There was no sign of her in the immediate area so, as it was still early morning, I decided to visit the Mara Buffalo Rocks. Even if I failed to find Chui I might still be able to see the other leopard family.

Imagine my surprise, then, when I saw a car parked close to the tree where Chui had stored her Thomson's gazelle kill three weeks earlier. Sure enough there she was, though this time she had a freshly killed impala calf in the tree with her. Sixty yards away stood a female impala, snorting in alarm as she faced the tree where Chui sat.

Chui began to feed on the carcass, every so often staring nervously to the northwest. Following her gaze I saw four lions of the Gorge Pride lying in the open plain, flanked by a motley array of vultures. The lions had killed a large bull buffalo during the night and now rested alongside it: one adult lioness and three subadult males of approximately three years of age.

A few hundred yards away, among the acacia thickets surrounding the entrance to Leopard Gorge, the two Gorge Pride males were slowly making their way towards the kill. They were in their prime – magnificent animals, considerably heavier and more powerful than the three young males. It was one of these same pride males – the dark-maned one – that had passed beneath Chui's fig tree seven weeks earlier.

The buffalo herd from which the lions had selected their victim stood watching them as they rested. At some subtle bovine signal they advanced on the predators, driving them away and in the process unwittingly presenting the patient vultures with the opportunity to move in and feed.

There were only twenty-five buffalo, a small herd by Mara standards, but quite large enough to cause problems for the lions. When the lioness tried to return to the kill three of the bulls charged forward and forced her away again. The lioness looked particularly nervous and with good reason, for out of the corner of her eye she could see the dark-maned pride male moving assertively towards her. The three young males got up and hurried away towards the rocky hill bordering the plain, not far from the tree where Chui lay watching.

Dark Mane moved slowly, with an air of considerable purpose. He held his great head outstretched, the dark hair of his mane flowing in the breeze, his muzzle thrust forward, shoulders hunched. The menace of his approach was clearly visible to the other lions, even if it failed to intimidate the buffalo bulls, who stormed straight towards him, sending the lion galloping in a wide detour around them. But it was the young males that Dark Mane was interested in, not the buffalo. He roared as he ran forward, thundering his challenge after the fleeing lions, and immediately echoed by his light-maned companion, who hurried to join him in the chase. The light-maned lion veered south, pursuing one of the young males through the rocky country only yards from Chui's tree. Dark Mane cornered sharply, and together the lions closed in on their hapless victim, showing a frightening turn of speed for such large animals.

Finding himself hopelessly cornered the young lion rolled sideways submissively, baring his teeth and grunting – escaping with little worse than a quick flurry of heavy paws and a bite in the backside. Even though he was from the same pride as the older males, their increasing hostility towards him signalled that the time had arrived when he and his companions must begin to lead the life of nomads: compulsory outcasts from the pride system until they were mature enough to contest ownership of a pride of their own.

During all this excitement Chui remained quietly in her tree, watchful among the leaves as the lions pursued their adversaries. Meanwhile, the female impala whose fawn lay next to Chui had been forced to abandon her lonely vigil in the confusion. An hour later, she stood by the same acacia bush where she had been earlier, staring towards Chui's tree and calling incessantly. The noise she made wavered between a bleat and a grunt, softly repeated. It was as if she expected her calf to reappear at the sound of her call.

Impala mothers usually leave their newborn calves to lie out in a place providing cover, returning to the herd to feed and ruminate between visits to suckle their young. I had often seen such calves lying among the rocks of Leopard Gorge and along Fig Tree Ridge, vulnerable to an experienced predator, one that might see through the young animal's powers of concealment. Perhaps this female had not even seen Chui kill her youngster and, as must often happen, returned to the place where she had left her calf only to find it gone.

A small group of impala appeared among the acacia bushes, drawing the lone female to them. But her maternal instincts were still too strong for her to seek the comfort of the herd. After only a few minutes she turned about and moved even closer to Chui's tree.

The sun finally broke through the cloud cover again as Chui climbed back up to her kill. She crouched over it, plucking out bunches of hair where necessary and pulling the skin back to feed on the tender flesh.

By the time Chui finished feeding there was little left of the impala carcass, which had probably weighed ten or twelve pounds. After carefully grooming her face and paws she squatted, sway-backed, and raked her claws along one of the branches.

Chui was near the edge of her home range and before leaving she carefully marked the area. On descending from the tree, the first thing she did was defecate. Next she walked to the base of the tree and, turning about, jetted four or five squirts of urine at leopard-nose height. A little later she sprayed again, this time onto a low bush. But it was her tail that caught my attention, for as she walked away she curved it higher into the air than I had ever seen her do.

The positioning and movements of a cat's tail convey various levels of excitement. The leopard's tail is relatively longer than that of either the tiger or lion, and is certainly a more striking visual signal. An angry leopard, when charging, curls its tail high into the air, revealing the underside like a startling white flag as it bounds forward. Female leopards also sometimes carry their tails held high when accompanied by young cubs, providing them with a visual signal to follow. In this circumstance the white underside is usually only clearly visible from behind. But now, whether viewed from front, side or back, the white undersurface and sides of Chui's tail-tip stood out like a spotlight in the twilight hours, a time when other leopards might also be beginning to become active.

The impalas bounded away, plotting Chui's path for me with the sound of their alarm calls. She continued in a wide arc that would take her south of Leopard Gorge and back towards Fig Tree Ridge where her cubs waited, hungry for food. In the end Chui did not return to the cubs straight away. She doubled back to the tree and ate her fill. By the morning all that was left of the kill was a small scrap of skin dangling from the branches. There was nothing for Chui's cubs when she arrived back at the Cub Caves. Nothing except her milk.

7. Struggling for Food

IT WAS just after 5.30 in the morning when I left Kichwa Tembo Camp. My vehicle headlights picked out the congregations of animals that flittered across the track ahead of me. A herd of impala faltered, dazzled by the lights. I switched them off and the antelope quickly re-orientated themselves and melted back into the darkness. Giraffes, gazelles, zebras, wildebeest and lions all followed my progress from the shadows.

Chui had dictated my daily route by her consistent use of Fig Tree Ridge and Dik-Dik Lugga. As I left for camp each evening I felt fairly confident that I would find her or the cubs again the following morning. If I was lucky I was able to steal an hour or more at either end of the day alone with Chui and her cubs. On these occasions there would be no angry hissing or snarling from Chui and I found myself virtually ignored. It was not that Chui recognised me, just that one or even a few quiet vehicles had little visible effect on her behaviour.

Each new morning arrived with the delicious sense of anticipation as to what might be in store during the day ahead. Something new, perhaps: an insight into an unfamiliar aspect of animal behaviour or possibly the chance of capturing a previously unrecorded incident on film. I just never knew what lay around the next corner. But it was much more than that when leopards were involved. They were something very special.

Such were my thoughts as the vehicle scraped against the familiar snagging branches of the thornbushes lining the narrow track leading to the base of Fig Tree Ridge. Baboons and warthogs had already ventured from their sleeping places and were now preparing for another day of feeding, feeding, feeding.

I paused to scan the rocks beneath the fig tree, searching for signs of life. Nothing. Perhaps the cubs were still curled up, snug and warm in one of the caves, not yet ready to greet a new day. The stars faded from the welcoming blue sky and the warming African sun peeped encouragingly from over the far horizon as I continued in my search for Chui. I longed for a cup of coffee, but there was no time to waste now. I would check on the cubs later.

It was just after seven o'clock when I drove back over the ridge. On occasions such as this I would usually scan up and down the trees with my binoculars, follow along each lugga and scrutinise beneath every bush. Then onwards, crisscrossing the area in the hope of finding some clue to Chui's whereabouts. Eight times out of ten I would find nothing and with any leopard but Chui the success ratio would be even more meagre.

But this was one of those special days, a day when I did not just stop and pause to re-check a suspicious-looking shadow or a tail-like branch. Today she was there. There is no other sight in Africa that I would rather have seen: a leopard reposed on a leafless branch, unobscured by shadows and bathed in the soft orange glow of early morning light.

Chui lay in one of the Three Trees, framed among the open branches like a delicate stained-glass window. Not the eleaodendron tree that she had climbed to avoid the buffalo herd, but the pappea that a month earlier had been bare of leaf. Now its crown was shrouded in a soft green canopy of foliage.

She sat up, looking not at me but at the two hyenas that paced around, twelve feet below her. They in turn looked upwards, trying to locate the position of what their noses were clearly telling them was meat. Lying across the same thick branch as Chui was a half-eaten impala fawn.

The enticing smell of fresh meat was almost more than one of the hyenas could endure. Momentarily the shaggy-coated hunter reared up on its hind legs, its blunt, dog-like claws pressed impotently against the rough surface of the tree trunk. Chui hissed and rumbled at the foul-smelling creature which stared into her eyes. Yet she had no real cause for concern. She and her kill were safe for as long as she chose to remain with it in the tree. Satisfied that there was nothing to be scavenged, the hyenas departed to their retreat among the rocks some distance away.

In some parts of Africa, where leopards exist without fear of competition from hyenas or lions, they often consume their kills on the ground, having little need to store their food in trees. But not in the Mara.

Chui relaxed, spread-eagled along the comfortable limb, her chin stretched forward, all four paws dangling. She stared towards the impala herd that loitered at the edge of the acacia thicket cloaking the ridge top a hundred yards away. Among them stood the female whose fawn now hung next to Chui.

When the next vehicle arrived Chui simply closed her eyes and ignored it. The occupants remained silent, mesmerised by the beauty of the golden, spotted predator. In the distance a white-bellied bustard competed for air space with the raucous cry of a coqui francolin, and flappet larks flapped incessantly in the sky, serenaded by the soothing sound of ring-necked doves.

Gradually the impala settled back into the most time-consuming activity of their lives. Like all herbivores the impala must spend most of the day feeding, for their vegetarian diet contains less than a tenth of the protein that meat can provide. Consequently carnivores such as Chui can afford the luxury of resting for most of the sixteen to eighteen hours that the herbivores spend feeding. Chui had already eaten the protein-rich rump and thighs of the impala calf which would help sustain her during the hours that might pass before she managed to make her next kill. Storing her kills in trees not only protected them from competitors, it also increased the time available for Chui to hunt.

Though prey might appear to be abundant in Chui's range it was subject to seasonal fluctuations, rarely over-plentiful and at times scarce. Carnivores tend therefore to range over far greater areas than that needed by herbivores of comparable body weight.

Yawning cavernously, Chui sat up and groomed the inner side of her forelimb. With supple ease she turned about on the branch and stooped to sniff at her kill. Fastidiously she began to pluck the soft hair from the carcass where she had already been eating, just as she did when she killed hyrax and hares. Drawing her lips back in a distasteful grimace, she used her incisor teeth to tear out small bunches of hair stuck together with saliva. These dropped to the ground, falling like feathery seed heads to form neat piles beneath the tree, leaving a telltale message for leopard watchers after her departure.

Chui repositioned the kill before turning and calling twice, uttering the same imploring moan sound – *aaaououuu* – that I had heard her use so often in the past when calling her cubs. Within seconds Dark emerged from his retreat among the uppermost branches of the tree. He must have been there all this while, silently watching the proceedings below him. The cub rubbed alongside his mother in a friendly greeting before pushing past her to get to the kill.

Chui lay down again, content to rest while her cub gorged himself. But where was Light? He was certainly not in the same tree as Chui, who was now busy raking her sharp claws on the branch that grew vertically above her.

Soon Chui's eyes closed once more. The sun edged around, replacing its golden glow and casting thick black shadows across the leopard's spotted coat. Dark paused for a moment from his feasting and turned his bloody face into the sun, red droplets glistening like tiny rubies on his whiskered muzzle.

Clumsily the young leopard picked the impala up by its neck and tried to move it. Chui watched, somewhat concerned, as the carcass slewed precariously to one side, throwing Dark momentarily off balance and nearly sending cub and kill hurtling to the ground. Fortunately Dark already possessed prodigious strength in his legs, neck and jaw muscles. He hung on, frantically straining to right the carcass. Eventually the exhausted cub reached a compromise with the kill: it was not quite where he had intended it to be, but at least it was secure.

Dark was obviously greatly excited by the carcass and continually attempted to drag and lift it by the neck and throat. I had previously witnessed this kind of activity while watching the Mara Buffalo cubs. When presented with freshly killed impala and wildebeest calves, the female cub had dissolved into a spasm of the most frenzied activity before settling down to feed. It is possible that this is one way for a young leopard to expend some of its frustrated eagerness to hunt while refining its instinctive skills. Substitute hunting and killing behaviour might even make the budding predator more eager to eat.

Having feasted, Dark lay sprawled five feet from Chui. The leopards rested like two book-ends, head to head. But the peace was soon interrupted. Chui's eyes flew open at the sound of the tawny eagle's long wings slicing through the air towards her. Twice the hungry bird passed overhead, manoeuvring skilfully on the wind so as to inspect the inviting carcass carefully. Chui immediately sprang into the centre of the tree, lunging towards the eagle.

The sight and sound of his mother protecting her kill proved too much for Dark. By now far too big to be considered suitable prey for the tawny eagle, Dark was nevertheless frightened by all the hostile activity. So the young cub bolted down the tree and headed for what he seemed to consider was a safer place.

Once the eagle had departed, Chui climbed back down to the lower fork and stared across to the east where Dark crouched among the rocks. He looked very small and vulnerable out there on the ground, alone and exposed in the open. But instead of running back to rejoin his mother, Dark turned and trotted further away. Chui watched anxiously as he disappeared from view among the maze of rocks, not far from where the two Ridge Clan hyenas had gone to rest.

Chui called, but if Dark heard he chose to ignore her. Quickly now, Chui grasped the impala by the neck and squeezed around the awkward fork, searching for the easiest route to descend by. She hugged her belly against the vertical incline and flowed down the trunk, jaws clamped firmly over the neck of the carcass which drooped awkwardly from her mouth. It would have been far simpler for her to drop her kill to the ground and then hurry down after it, but Chui was not prepared to risk losing her meal to a hyena.

Chui dropped the carcass at her feet, looking nervously about her. Again she called and this time a cub raced towards her, but he did not come from the direction of the rocks where Dark had fled. Instead he galloped from the thornbush thicket where the impala herd had paused earlier in the morning, responding instantly to the sight and sound of his mother as she stood by the tree. It was Light.

Chui looked around and called again. But there was no sign of Dark and she could no longer afford to wait for him. She was vulnerable: on the ground and in the open, a kill at her feet, a cub by her side. She must move quickly to a safer place before hyenas, lions or baboons found them.

Light's intentions were quite different from his mother's. He had probably become separated from Chui due to the intimidating and dangerous presence of the hyenas, either before or after his mother had carried her kill safely into the tree. While Dark had gorged himself, Light had been forced to wait patiently in the top of one of the acacia bushes. All Light was interested in now was the kill. He grasped the impala by the neck and started to pull the carcass away, just as his mother would do. But this was neither the time nor the place for practice sessions. There was only one refuge that Chui was interested in and that was the Cub Caves. The urge to be hidden and to store her kill outweighed all other considerations.

So, with undisguised urgency, Chui wrenched the impala from under Light's nose. She moved away quickly, her powerful neck muscles helping to keep the carcass clear of the ground. Chui carried her tail looped high, white underside marking her progress as she moved east, with Light trotting alongside her.

Ten minutes after she descended from the tree, Chui disappeared from view over the lip of the ridge. It was just after nine o'clock and leopard, kill and cub were safe. Chui dropped the impala in the grassy depression behind Top Rock and lay on the smooth rock surface nearby. Light immediately began to feed.

Chui sat and groomed a forepaw, moaning and *aauu'ing* as she walked over to the base of the fig tree. For a moment she stared into the welcoming branches above her. But she could not rest yet. Something was obviously amiss. She gazed into the distance – out across the rocks and scattered acacia bushes – searching for signs of her missing cub.

Light moved away by himself to lie in the shade of the cub-sized depression on Top Rock where Dark so often liked to rest. But Chui found it impossible to relax and before long she set off on a complete tour of the Cub Caves. She called, ignoring the alarm snorts of the impala whose peaceful feeding she had disturbed.

First Chui searched the horizontal cave, but there was nothing there except agamid lizards and fresh hyrax droppings. A brief inspection of the deep interior of the vertical cave revealed nothing of any greater interest than a cool emptiness. Chui bounded back up the ridge, passing through the shrubby passages among the rocky fortress that she knew so well. Light got up and trailed along behind his mother, meaowing plaintively.

It looked as if Chui was not absolutely certain where Dark had disappeared to. Yet she had seen for herself the smaller cub trotting off among the rocks near to the Three Trees. Had Chui really expected that Dark might make his own way back to the Cub Caves? She certainly knew that he was missing, that was only too plain to see.

Light did not even see his mother leave. One minute she was in front of him and the next she had vanished. I had read that a female leopard may use a particular sound which signals to her cubs that she does not wish them to follow. I have found no evidence to support this. Chui certainly hissed and snarled at her cubs when she wished to stop them from trying to suckle or bite her tail, or when they prevented her from resting in peace. But she used none of these signals or any other form of vocalisation prior to trying to leave them. If she moved away rapidly and silently, the cubs were usually deterred from following, at least while they were still quite small.

Light wandered around looking lost. Eventually he flopped down, resigning himself to being left alone. He lay straddled on a low branch at the base of the climbing tree, patiently facing north in the direction that Chui had departed.

It soon proved too hot to remain exposed in the open and before long the fat little leopard got up and plodded wearily back to the fig tree. His stomach was full and it was far too exhausting even to consider playing with the impala carcass that lay twisted and exposed in front of him. Light continued all the way down to the base of the vertical cave, pausing to sniff carefully at the grass before sitting in the shade of a slender bush. White, wispy clouds dragged across the hot blue sky and soon the cub settled down, curled up on himself with eyes tightly closed to await his mother's return.

Chui followed her nose, calling intermittently to Dark. She searched carefully among the rocks in the area where she had left him, doubling back every so often to investigate a narrow cave or patch of scrub. It was nearly eleven o'clock when she found him, perched high in the thorny branches of one of the acacia bushes. Dark looked down as his mother approached and squawked gruffly at her. He waited until she was almost beneath him before scrambling down and excitedly rubbing up against her face and throat. But when he tried to suckle, Chui hurriedly led him back towards the safety of the Cub Caves, driving an overly curious hyena away as she did so.

Chui sat on Top Rock and licked the two cubs. At last she could relax. A cool breeze wafted along the ridge, gradually slowing the frantic rhythm of her panting as she sprawled in the shade of the fig tree. She made no attempt to feed from her kill or to take it into the tree, and if she had done so one of the cubs would almost certainly have dropped it out again, for the impala was small and there were no horns to help wedge it securely between the stout branches.

Chui climbed into the fig tree. She lay almost completely shaded on the armchair, sprawled along the thick branch, all four legs lolled out to one side, the white underside of her chin and throat turned skywards, reflecting back the sun. Except for the occasional look up or around, the odd lick of a patch of tangled fur, Chui rested. Below her a large tortoise stumbled awkwardly through the rocks. But it passed unnoticed.

Life ebbed back and forth. The apparent emptiness of one area was inevitably filled with animals and birds. Vacuums seemed to develop only to draw life to them. Nothing was constant. In such circumstances it is tempting to drive and drive and drive; nothing to see here, nothing there. But if one stops for a moment one finds that there is something of interest everywhere, all the time.

Half an hour after the tortoise had disappeared from view a small herd of impalas drifted towards the Cub Caves, their large hair-filled ears pricked alertly. They paused collectively, as if part of a single creature, only forty feet from the fig tree, their sensitive noses filling with the familiar predatory odour of leopard. Anxiously they strained every sense and muscle as they attempted to locate the source of their alarm while at the same time preparing to explode into dramatic flight if the predator revealed itself.

Cautiously, oh so cautiously, they peered over the lip of the ridge, oblivious of Chui's watchful green eyes, unblinking from behind her concealing cloak of leaves. For a moment the impalas' dainty, pointed hooves clattered nervously on the rocks as they bumped and jostled against each other. Then they were away, cascading into the air like a stream of toffee-brown lava, turning and twisting in graceful leaps and bounds as they fled blindly from the danger that they could not even see. Chui watched them go, then closed her eyes again, and retreated into her own darkness.

Rain spat from the grey clouds that had all but obliterated the blue from the sky. On the plains to the south, white specks littered the green grass where the cycnium flowers had blossomed to greet the arrival of the rain. Baboons clustered to pluck the delicate flowers and stuff them greedily into their mouths.

Light lay on his side on Top Rock and watched his mother above him. He did not call to her, apparently content to rest, his head and one forepaw flopped over the edge of the rocks. There was so much of interest for a young leopard to focus on that it was hard for Light to concentrate his attention in one place for more than a few seconds at a time. Above him a bateleur once more scanned the area for possible food, while a pied wheatear hopped and fluttered along the base of the ridge in its search for insects. And, as always, agamid lizards scurried across the rocks.

Chui was still hungry, her stomach noticeably lean in comparison with the bloated bellies of her cubs. But as soon as she came too close to where Dark was chewing on a leg bone the cub circled away from her, shielding the food with his flank. Chui lay down beside him, watchful. As she bent forward to sniff at the bones, the young leopard lashed out with a pawful of sharp, ivory-coloured claws, catching Chui on the nose and forcing her to jump aside.

Even though she was hungry, Chui respected the cubs' possessiveness, patiently waiting for the moment when she might steal a morsel for herself. At times she lay almost submissively, her head turned aside on her forepaw, in the wake of some threatening rumbling from the young leopards.

In the distance the faint sound of cow bells and the lowing of cattle signalled the drawing to a close of another day as the Masai herdsmen began the slow trek back to their thornbush enclosures. Just as slowly and methodically, dark menacing shapes appeared from among the thornbushes. As six o'clock passed, the first baboon came into view, moving alertly along the base of the ridge.

One of the baboons, a male, climbed into a low acacia bush and began to bite and tear off pieces of bark, exposing his awesome array of teeth. Another stooped to pluck green grass deftly between thumb and forefinger. Yard by yard the troop moved closer with three of the larger males strutting purposefully towards the place where Chui and Light now lay.

Briefly Chui raised her head. As she repositioned herself she flicked her long tail, revealing its white underside among the dark rocks. The sight of that tail was all the nearest baboon needed to see. He barked in alarm, instantly bringing Chui's head up again. Light moved even closer to his mother as Chui's tail lashed and thumped on the rocks.

The troop were now fully alerted to Chui's presence and one of the younger males raced up the ridge towards her. The baboon stopped just long enough to snatch a bird's nest from the bushes that Chui's cubs regularly tried to flatten during their boisterous play sessions. He pressed the nest to his mouth and ate the contents as he ran forward. Close by, the red-rumped swallows' nest remained protected under its rocky ledge, seemingly inaccessible to even the most opportunistic baboon.

As more baboons arrived Light turned and fled for the safety of the caves while Dark, who had been gnawing on the remaining bones behind Top Rock, paused before running off as well. A large male soon joined the younger baboon, pausing to rear up on his hind legs for a better view as he approached.

One of the largest males strutted around Top Rock as other troop members scaled the ridge face and advanced towards Chui. It was like an army of ants swarming remorselessly forward. But Chui was hungry. She had watched patiently while her cubs ate their fill and now that they had fled to the safety of the Cub Caves she could at last chew on the meagre remains of her kill. Chui had no intention of moving.

By this time the leopard was almost surrounded by baboons as yet more climbed into the fig tree above her. The baboons strutted, bared their canines, flashed their white eyelids and jumped this way and that. In fact they paraded their whole repertoire of intimidation in front of Chui. But it was still not enough to force her to flee.

The pungent odour of baboon faeces wafted down from the ridge as the majority of the troop continued on their way. Some paused to groom; others squabbled and screamed at some unseen transgression. The more persistent of the baboons – and it was often the younger animals – moved to within thirty feet of the leopard, but eventually even they chose to leave.

A grey and misty blanket shrouded the Siria Escarpment, and the only sounds were the crunch and snap of tiny bones and the distant murmuring of baboons. Gradually the sun transformed into a huge pink orb, dying in the grey sky and warming the haze above it with a saffron glow.

As the sky grew darker the baboons began to climb into the fig trees where they would sleep for the night. The distant whoop of a hyena drifted on the wind, mingling with the fainter sounds of cattle. Thunder growled in the south, adding a voice to the lightning which fractured the dark sky.

Not far away, in the west, two hyenas stood alongside each other. They stretched, then greeted by cocking their hind legs and carefully smelling each other's genital region, renewing and reinforcing the social bonds between clan members. The hyenas had rested during the heat of the day in the shade of a large slab of rock, surrounded by the cool shadows of a croton bush. Other members of the Ridge Clan – including the two that had stood beneath the kill tree early in the morning – were also beginning to stir from their favourite resting places in the vicinity of Fig Tree Ridge. This was their time of the day.

The two hyenas began to wander east on their nightly forays in search of food. They moved in a shuffling sort of manner that masked their ability to run like the wind when the occasion warranted it. Their well-developed forequarters made their back legs appear weak, but they were not.

Earlier the hyenas had listened to the noisy baboons and heard their barks of warning. Though they recognised the sounds they had seemed to ignore them. Now as the hyenas moved almost casually towards where Chui lay hidden from their view they could hear the inviting sounds of cracking bones.

Dark sat and watched as the first hyena came into view along the ridge top. The young leopard easily recognised the slouching silhouette of a hyena and his curiosity was tempered with wariness. When the hyena walked directly towards him the cub wisely slipped away to the safety of one of the caves.

Chui growled, prepared to hold her ground and confront a single hyena in this situation. The moment the hyena attempted to barge forward aggressively and steal the impala leg bones from in front of her, Chui lunged towards him, snarling. Grudgingly the hyena gave way, rumbling its own warning to the leopard. But it only retreated a few feet, for now the second hyena emerged from below the ridge. The two of them whooped and growled as they prepared to advance on Chui together. The noise alone was an intimidating and persuasive threat.

There is nothing more expressive than the face of an angry and frightened leopard: ears laid back and pale green eyes blazing; teeth exposed like jagged glass between snarling black lips. Chui seethed with hostility, keeping her vulnerable bottom tucked close to the ground. But the hyenas were just as determined as she was and, with the arrival of a third member of their clan, they drove forward. The animal closest to Chui darted in to snatch for the food. Chui sprang towards it, but as she did so one of the other hyenas moved in behind her and bit savagely into her rump. As she felt the hyena's powerful teeth tear at her flesh, Chui spun high into the air to face her attacker. Before she could retaliate with her claws the giggling creature moved out of reach.

Chui half-heartedly charged after one of the scavengers. She protested vociferously from a few feet away, but it made no difference. The hyenas were completely confident in their ability as a group to dominate the smaller predator. Having disposed of the last of the food, the largest of the hyenas, a female, wandered down on to Suckling Rock West and sniffed along the narrow cleft leading into the vertical cave. Chui rumbled a warning from out of the darkness, concerned now only for the safety of her cubs.

It would have been impossible for any hyena to reach the inner recesses of the cave which Light and Dark had chosen to hide in, though Chui was taking no chances. She charged explosively over Top Rock and sank her claws into the rump of the hyena, raking her off balance. The hyena spun away with a howl and fled for a few feet, growling deeply. Other members of the clan whooped and giggled supportively from higher up on the rock face as they listened to the sounds of the confrontation below them. But eventually they all moved away. For both animals the night had only just begun.

Later, under the cover of darkness, Chui moved with the cubs back to Dik-Dik Lugga, leading them carefully through the maze of thornbushes along the ridge top. By the next morning, when the baboons clambered from their roosts and sauntered warily towards the caves, Chui's cubs were sleeping safely among the rocks of the lugga floor, more than a mile away.

It was nearly four o'clock in the afternoon when the stuttering alarm calls of vervet monkeys led me to where Chui rested. She sat, panting heavily, in a euclea tree. Dark had already joined his mother and was busily struggling with the young impala that Chui had just killed.

The impala was wedged precariously by its slender neck among the highest branches of the tree. Dark tugged, lifted and wrestled so vigorously with the carcass that it soon fell from his grasp and crashed to the ground, landing only a few feet from where Light lay patiently waiting to feed. The larger cub wasted no time in taking possession of the kill.

In an instant Dark scrambled down the tree. But he was too late. Now it was his turn to watch and wait as Light fiercely drove him from the vicinity of the kill. Dark retreated into the tree and sniffed around, licking at the patch of drying blood where the impala had rested against the branch. He seemed almost surprised that the kill was no longer there. But the evidence lay on the ground below him and eventually he gave up and joined Chui in the lugga, shaded by the overhanging bushes.

It was that magical hour at the end of the day. A beautiful soft light crept from beneath the clouds and transformed the scene, intensifying the colours of the green foliage of the trees and turning the grey sky a heavy purple. The Fig Tree Troop strolled south over the eastern plain, wending their way towards Kampi ya Chui where they would roost for the night. Fortunately they failed to detect Chui or her cubs hidden in Dik-Dik Lugga.

A nightjar fluttered into the air, revealing itself from among the camouflage of dead leaves and dull-coloured rocks. It perched fleetingly on a slender branch, only a few feet above the place where Light lay. Then the eerie silence was broken by a sound not unlike a tiny diesel generator springing into life. The cub looked up, curious as to where the familiar sound was coming from. But as he did so the noise stopped and the nightjar fluttered onwards.

All the vehicles had departed and the noises that enveloped Chui and her cubs were the undiluted sounds of the African night. Diurnal birds finally quieted, their songs replaced by the melancholy refrains of nightjars and eagle owls. The trees and luggas reverberated to the piping of tree frogs, the zizz of insects and the soft repetitive grunt of a lion.

Chui's breathing slowed and her head lolled wearily forward as she dozed. The sharp sound of a twig snapping underfoot brought her head upright in an instant. As her eyes flew open she hissed and snarled at the bulky shape emerging from further down the lugga. Chui turned, bristling, and circled back to her kill, where Dark was already straddling the impala and trying to drag it up the steep bank. The loss of those few precious seconds prevented Chui from escaping with her kill up the nearest tree. Now she must defend it as best she could.

The male hyena ambled forward, determined, ignoring Chui's defensive hiss of warning. Once he actually saw the impala carcass he rushed headlong towards it. Dark turned tail and scrambled up the nearest tree where Light already crouched, wisely leaving their mother to confront the intruder alone. But Chui was not going to surrender her kill easily.

The situation quickly turned into a roughhouse: the animal equivalent of a bar-room brawl. I had seen hyenas acting boldly and with a considerable degree of violence before, but I had never seen Chui quite so determined. The gathering darkness seemed to increase her aggressiveness. She charged, switching from defence to attack, clawing at the hyena and sinking her dagger-like canines into his neck as he attempted to snatch the impala away. Fortunately for the hyena, his muscular neck was well protected with a ruff of coarse fur, though for a moment he seethed and writhed on the ground with Chui. The combination of sounds was awesome.

The two animals continued to struggle ferociously for possession of the impala, fighting in the manner of hungry lions contesting ownership of a small kill. Neither dared to release their grip on the food so as to bite the other, for fear of losing it altogether. The hyena outweighed Chui by at least thirty pounds and the crushing power of his jaws was second to none. But it was Chui's food and she possessed muscular strength which, pound for pound, rivalled that of any hyena. The leopard wrenched the kill and the hyena towards the euclea tree where the impala had originally hung. Inch by inch Chui forced him to follow.

Eventually it was the hyena who dropped the kill, biting savagely at Chui's back leg. She did not even pause, ignoring the pain, for nothing at that moment seemed more important than her food. Sensing that the battle was nearly lost, the hyena lunged forward again, locking his powerful teeth around the trailing back leg of the impala. Still Chui pulled and tugged, hauling herself closer and closer to the base of the tree. Suddenly she felt the weight release behind her as the hyena toppled backwards in an untidy heap, the back leg of the impala still clutched between his teeth. Chui scrambled into the tree – she was too tired to leap – leaving the hyena to race away with a portion of his own.

For a moment Chui paused, twelve feet above ground, desperately sucking air into her lungs through her large nostrils. Her back legs trembled with the exhaustion of the battle as she balanced unsteadily in the fork of the tree. Most importantly Chui still had the bulk of her kill clenched between her teeth.

Within a minute the hyena was back, scouring the lugga floor for more food. But it was too late. Chui moved even higher into the tree. If she felt the injury to her back leg it did nothing to affect her ability to feed. Soon the sounds of the shearing of flesh and the crunching of bones testified to that. On this particular occasion she had managed to turn the tables on a member of the Fig Tree Clan. The only food he or any other clan member would get from Chui this night would be the scraps that fell from the tree as she and her cubs satisfied their hunger.

One of the most interesting aspects of watching Chui was learning more about the complicated relationship that exists between hyenas and leopards. Usually a single hyena wins its disputes over food with the solitary leopard and the presence of more than one hyena leaves the issue beyond doubt – unless the leopard can reach the safety of a tree first. Chui was particularly vulnerable while she had cubs, as they frequently managed to drop her kills out of the trees where she had stored them, particularly if they were small carcasses. The cubs seemed to find it easier to feed if a kill was on the ground, though by the time they were four months old they both showed signs of the urge to store small portions of food safely above ground, even if they had little success.

The habit of food thieving has undoubtedly had its effect on the relationship existing between the different species of large carnivores. In general, weight and body size correlate closely with the ability of the various predators to win their encounters over food. Certainly the hyenas – which in most cases are heavier – showed little sign of being intimidated by leopards and recognised them immediately as a potential source of food. In consequence they always investigated the presence of a leopard in the possibility of scavenging a meal.

There is little doubt that the Ridge Clan hyenas were familiar with Chui as an individual and probably responded to her partly on the basis of previous encounters, as was the case when she encountered the baboons of the Fig Tree Troop. Degree of hunger, original ownership of the kill and the number of hyenas present also influenced the outcome of any encounter between the two species. Leopards have been known to chase a hyena from its kill and carry the stolen food into the nearest tree. But on most occasions it is the leopard that loses its meal, not the hyena, which is the most abundant of all the larger predators in the Mara.

I think the fact that Chui and the Mara Buffalo Female were managing to raise their cubs successfully outside the protection of the Mara Reserve was not without significance. Lions and hyenas seem to be less able to avoid conflict with the Masai herdsmen and less capable of hiding from them than the more secretive and solitary leopards and cheetahs. Consequently, the leopards outside the Reserve were faced with less competition from these more powerful rivals, who were even more numerous within the Reserve.

Next morning Light and Dark were back among the pile of multi-shaped rocks that lay buried in the floor of the lugga. It was hot, with little breeze to ease the mugginess, and the cubs lay fat-bellied and sleepy, huddled together in the shadows of their temporary home. As Light rolled onto his back, stretching his paws skyward, a topi snorted from west of the lugga. Chui had returned.

The cubs began playing, energised by their mother's presence as she lay with them on the bank of the lugga. Light curled around Chui's neck while Dark rolled on his back and gripped her face between his paws, kicking boisterously as she licked his white belly.

It was just after three o'clock when Chui decided it was time to move. The cubs chased after her as she headed north in the direction from which she had arrived. She broke into a trot as they passed Hyrax Rocks, with the cubs gambolling along beside her. When Light and Dark stopped to do some investigating of their own, Chui turned back, chuffling.

The cubs' playfulness soon evaporated with the sheer effort required to keep pace with their mother. A hare flushed from its resting place in a patch of grass and for a moment the cubs forgot their tiredness as they turned to watch it bouncing away in exaggerated leaps and bounds. But the further they travelled the more subdued Light and Dark became. Sometimes Chui was up and moving ahead, even before the cubs could reach the shaded spot where she had been resting. Perhaps that was Chui's way of keeping them on the move; it certainly prevented them from trying to suckle.

After a few hundred yards the cover provided by Dik-Dik Lugga petered out, exposing the leopards to view. Chui slunk quickly away, leaving the open country behind her and seeking the protection of the thorn thickets that ran alongside the rocky hill to the west. Light and Dark hurried after their mother, looking thoroughly put out by the whole experience. Eventually Chui moved back to the lugga at the place where the croton bushes grew thickly again.

There, wedged beneath a fallen tree and surrounded by the shade of the bushes, was a freshly killed impala male, its feet spread stiffly in the air like an upturned table. For a while Chui rested a few feet from the fly-ridden carcass before starting to tear at its groin. As soon as she had sheared through the skin with her specialised carnassial teeth, Light burrowed his way in beneath Chui's belly to feed. Dark was there too, straddled over the impala's bloated stomach.

At first, the cubs did not squabble over the kill. But when Chui departed to groom her face and paws, they started to rumble and cough at each other. Chui got up and walked to the edge of the lugga for a drink. On seeing this Light left the kill to join his mother and together they lapped at the cool water, replenishing the liquid that they had lost on their long trek to the kill.

The cubs reverted to their normal feeding regime. As one left to drink or socialise with their mother, so the other cub would take the opportunity to feed. Chui stopped to glance around at the acacia and croton thickets that surrounded her, though it was the trees that interested her most. She bent and lifted the impala by the chest, struggling with all her might to free it from the snagging branches. But her original efforts to conceal the heavy kill had been too successful and now it was firmly stuck. Chui was left with only one alternative and that was to feed as quickly as possible. She tore at the impala's rump until her face was transformed into a bloody mask. Then once more she tried to dislodge the carcass, but to no avail.

In the distance a jackal barked. Chui looked nervously around her and slunk closer to the kill, fearful of discovery. Hyenas soon added their voices from lower down the lugga as they rushed from their resting places to join another clan member who had stolen the impala fawn that a pair of jackals had just killed.

Dark meanwhile had climbed into a dilapidated tree, thirty feet south of Chui's position. He lay slumped over the point where a thick branch had broken down. When Light heard the all too familiar whoops and cackles he ran to Dark's tree and scrambled up, just as another Ridge Clan hyena galloped into view. Chui remained motionless, her outline invisible among the lengthening shadows of the croton bush.

As darkness closed around the leopards, striped kingfishers trilled their final songs for the day. Chui lay just a few feet from her kill while the cubs drifted with the wind in half sleep: meat-filled and contented, safely ensconced on their aerial perches.

During the night, the Ridge Clan found the leftovers of Chui's kill. The wind answered their questioning noses and led them unerringly to the place where the impala's stomach and intestines lay stinking in the lugga floor. But Light and Dark paid little attention to the hyenas, for they were already stored in the treetop with Chui and the remains of the carcass. There was so little left that I wondered if Chui had again fought a tug-of-war with the hyenas, or if she and her cubs had managed to consume so much meat between them. Perhaps part of the carcass had fallen from the tree and the hyenas had been there to gobble it up.

As morning dawned Dark lay in the same spot where he had rested the evening before. The bloody kill hung red raw, wedged securely in place by the impala's horned skull. Above it lay Light, straddled along one of the impala's curved horns like a tiny circus performer. I felt dizzy just watching as he wobbled precariously among the branches. His belly was already fit to burst, but like any predator in similar circumstances he continued to gorge himself.

It might be days before he ate meat again and the food would quickly pass through his swollen stomach.

Chui lay curled beneath the concealing curtain of orange and green leaves near to the base of the tree. A rumbling growl brought both cubs' attention back to earth as two large hyenas shambled towards where Chui lay hidden. Ignoring Chui's warning, they proceeded to sniff carefully around the kill site. When they had gone Chui left the croton bush and fed briefly on a scrap of meat that had fallen from the tree. But suddenly she abandoned her meal and crept back to her shady retreat as the Fig Tree Troop made their first appearance of the day, preceded by shrieks and screams from the rocky hill to the west.

Slowly the baboons advanced towards the place where Chui and the cubs were resting. The sight and sound of the primates made the cubs visibly nervous. Insecure in this unfamiliar place, they were desperate for somewhere to hide and there were no rocks or caves in this part of the lugga. Trees might protect them from hyenas, but they were no place for small leopards to be when the Fig Tree Troop were in the area. Light and Dark were frantic, not knowing which way to run for the best. They had yet to learn the secret of Chui's success, for she remained calmly where she was, doing nothing to draw attention to herself.

Dark put his ears back and nervously trotted south along the edge of the lugga, followed at a gallop by his brother. Fortunately the baboons did not see the cubs and as vehicles milled around in an effort to obtain a better view they forced the baboons to hurry on their way.

Once the baboons had moved out of sight Chui slunk cautiously towards her cubs. Light and Dark were not consoled by their mother's presence, so they quickly trotted off through the bushes. But the further they went the more their confidence ebbed from them. Before they had travelled far Dark turned and preceded his brother back to where Chui lay watching.

Gradually the cubs settled down again as the sights and sounds of hyenas and baboons retreated from their minds. Chui groomed Light as he rolled on his back in front of her, while he reared up, clutching and licking at his mother's bloody face.

It was a journey of nearly half a mile back to the rocky island which the cubs had adopted as their most favoured resting place on Dik-Dik Lugga. Light and Dark seemed to sense that they were going in a direction that suited them, that they recognised. That did not imply that it was easy, for they were hot and heavy-bellied. But this time when Chui paused it was the cubs that trotted ahead, anxious to keep going, to be on their way again.

The moment they arrived at the familiar island of rocks, Light and Dark flopped down in the soothing womb of the lugga floor, exhausted. Gone now was the anxious pacing from bush to bush, the nagging urge to be somewhere else. The cubs could rest. It might only be for a few hours, it could be for days. That depended on Chui.

Once the cubs had settled down, Chui left them and returned to her kill. There was little more than skin and bones remaining, so she did not feed for long. On descending Chui took a final look up into the treetop where the bare mask of the impala stared back at her. Then she turned away, making no attempt to conceal herself even though the alarm calls of impala soon attracted the attention of a hyena who briefly trailed along behind her. Chui ignored it, unconcerned by its presence now that neither cubs nor food were threatened. But the hyena had been in the vicinity of the kill earlier in the day and, on smelling the scent of blood and meat that still clung to Chui's fur, turned back and followed its nose to where she had been feeding.

During the last four days Chui had killed an adult male impala and two impala calves. Little had gone to waste, even though the hyenas had tried their best to steal from the leopards. The impala calves were usually consumed in their entirety, for Chui would crunch up the paper-thin skulls, and only the occasional leg bone or scrap of skin would be left behind. The larger kills, however, could not be consumed so completely, though Chui was capable of eating the equivalent of between a fifth and a quarter of her body weight in meat. Approximately 30 per cent would be inedible – skulls, bones and digestive tract contents. Chui would usually feed on a Thomson's gazelle buck for three days if she were eating alone, and an impala male lasted even longer. Smaller kills were usually devoured within twenty-four hours. During one week the Mara Buffalo Female and her daughter killed a dik-dik, a male Thomson's gazelle, two wildebeest calves and an impala calf. Apart from the dik-dik, which was stolen by hyenas, the edible portions of all these kills were devoured by the end of the eighth day. Feeding fast-growing leopard cubs is no easy task.

Now, an hour before dark, Chui continued on her way, blending grey and spotless in the dull light. As she entered the lugga near to the cubs' resting place she stopped and called them to her. Chui knew they were just ahead of her and on cue they ran from the rocks to join her. She climbed back out of the lugga and lay on the termite mound where the cubs could suckle. Before long they slept contentedly against her well-rounded belly.

8. Growing Independence

THE ISLAND of stones was still the cubs' favourite hideout. Such places were essential to the cubs' survival and, once firmly established in their minds, these special localities of shade and security were never forgotten by the leopards.

At rest during the heat of the day the cubs often appeared to be sleeping quite deeply, though in effect they were only cat-napping. The important sounds, sounds that announced the possibility of danger or the arrival of their mother, still filtered through to their consciousness.

Light now slept less and was more active than Dark during the daytime. He was a fidgety, restless cub who would often suddenly get up to grasp at overhanging branches or play with stones, stalk after birds and mongooses or simply molest his brother. Dark usually tried to ignore these friendly and playful interruptions, preferring to sleep, though at times the smaller cub would help turn some brief form of contact into an all-out wrestling match. In fact, Dark acted much more like the male cub at Mara Buffalo Rocks, showing greater signs of independence in his relationship with his mother.

I was told that for the first months of their lives the two Mara Buffalo cubs stayed close to each other, playing and resting in the way that I had seen Light and Dark do so often. But as they grew older there came a time when the larger male cub started to go off by himself or to stay away after accompanying his mother and sister on a journey from the caves. From the time he was eight months old he was spending more and more time by himself. At eleven months, even when the cubs were in the same area they spent little of their time socialising together, and usually rested alone unless occupying the large cave. They hardly ever wrestled with each other, in marked contrast to the behaviour of younger cubs. Sometimes, though, they raced into a tree together in pursuit of birds, chased up and down in the croton bushes after each other, or tore over the rocks after lizards. While there was an undisguised playfulness in some of their activities the young leopards now seemed far more interested in investigating and stalking around their environment than in playing with each other. There was a new air of detachment to their relationship. Life, particularly for the male cub, seemed to have taken a more serious and impersonal turn, a sign of his steady development towards a basically solitary existence.

By four o'clock it was still very hot, without the slightest trace of a breeze to relieve the oppression. But as the sky turned ever greyer it began to cool and Light and Dark started to stir again. For a while they moved quietly around the rocks, dabbing at a stone, pausing to sit and groom a muddy paw, or trip a brother. The storm that had threatened, full of promise, blew past, leaving a gentle breeze in its wake, rustling through the croton bushes and stirring the hyenas that waited in their shadows, waited for the beckoning signs of some other hunter's predation. Trees swayed with a melancholy sigh, illuminated by a soft light that painted pastel colours, and for the moment the Mara seemed a peaceful place.

Shortly after six o'clock Light and Dark appeared along the east side of the lugga, with Dark strutting provocatively in front of his brother. As they approached my vehicle a little bee-eater swooped low over the smaller cub's head, causing Dark to flip round and half-heartedly chase the tiny bird.

I remained motionless as the young leopards edged nearer and nearer to my car. The sight of the cubs so close was breathtaking. I was used to the detachment of seeing them through binoculars or a telephoto lens, but now as I watched I could almost feel their long stiff whiskers, the blacker than black spots and rosettes, still slightly overlapped by white guard hairs. I could look directly into the hazel brown eyes which were filled with youthful curiosity at the large green box that came to watch them each day.

Every so often Light stopped and dropped into a half-crouch, fascinated, though wary of the vehicle. But Dark moved closer still, rocking back and forth, stretching his neck forward until he finally plucked up enough courage to press his nose to the front tyre.

The cubs' boldness towards vehicles worried me. If Chui were present to witness such behaviour she might attack a vehicle in trying to keep the cubs away from what she could perceive as being a dangerous situation for her young. Worse still, the cubs might inadvertently be injured by a vehicle as they crept around it.

At five and a half months, the cubs were beginning to look like real leopards. They suddenly appeared lean and leggy, like slightly gangling adolescents. Their full bellies of yesterday now looked slim and taut, for they soon digested the largest meal. But it would be another two years before they were fully grown adults.

There was one particular rocky platform that the young leopards liked to lie on, situated halfway between the termite mound and the bottom of the lugga. There was really only sufficient room for a single cub to lie on the platform at any one time, and occupation of the site virtually ensured the initiation of a game of 'king of the castle'. One cub would try to stalk up from the lugga floor, using a variety of approach routes and at times deliberately rolling back down through the rocks, something they seemed to enjoy as much as the chase itself. This action would precipitate a mad dash around the base of the rock, ending up in a race to see who could get back to the castle first. The winner would lie, head dangled over the rock, looking imperiously down upon his brother. The cubs repeated this whole process endlessly.

During the night the cubs played intermittently, stopping every so often to groom or to curl up and sleep. Sometimes they simply sat or lay listening attentively to the sounds of the night, interpreting their messages and acting accordingly. If hyenas or lions approached, the cubs would quickly take cover in some secure place in the lugga floor or among the branches of a tree. They paused sometimes to look into the darkness, straining their eyes for signs of their mother's approach. But usually Chui was some distance away, searching for food to satisfy the young leopards' hunger.

As the sun rose jackals began to yelp, scolding to the north of Dik-Dik Lugga, where Dark and Light now rested. The Marsh Lions added a distant voice to the dawn, though the cubs ignored the sounds, intent on playing their game around the castle.

Chui's arrival, shortly after eight o'clock, was heralded by the same jackals that had sounded earlier in the morning. Jackals and leopards take a particular interest in each other, though for very different reasons. While sometimes killing one another as competitors, carnivores are generally disdainful of each other's flesh as a source of food. Leopards, however, are well known for their habit of killing and eating small carnivores such as genets, mongooses, civets, servals, wild cats, bat-eared foxes and jackals. Lion cubs, cheetahs, wild dogs and domestic dogs have also at times supplemented their diet.

Whenever a jackal came trotting into view Chui would react with the greatest of interest, trying her best to ambush it. Usually she failed to kill her quarry and was then forced to endure the scolding barks that I now listened to. The jackals did not need to be chased to elicit this mobbing response: the mere sight or smell of a leopard would set them off, and usually the leopard would hurry away to a quieter place. Jackals do sometimes manage to scavenge scraps from a leopard's kill or even to kill unguarded or straying leopard cubs when they are very small. So the leopards do not always have things their own way.

Later during the morning, Chui led the cubs east along Fig Tree Ridge, a journey that they had made together on a number of occasions. With the compulsory stops for rest beneath shade, and the caution necessary to circumvent possible danger, it took an hour and a quarter for Chui and the cubs to reach Dwarf Rocks.

Chui carefully sniffed around, then leapt up into the emerald crown of the pappea tree. At its base was a shallow depression recently covered with a flush of green grass and fringed by rocks. It was in this arena of shade that the cubs now whiled away the heat of the day. They lay flat out, their cheeks pressed against the cool grass, as the clouds swept up into the afternoon sky. If danger threatened, they could always retreat quickly into the tree where Chui lay.

At intervals, the cubs tried to gain their mother's attention, either by calling or by climbing into the tree to join her, but Chui hissed and rasped, making it quite obvious that she wished to be left alone.

It was a relief when the storm finally broke. The ice-cold hailstones fell like a shower of white marbles. They bounced and clattered on the rocks, matching the distant sounds of thunder and leaving the rocks sparkling shiny grey. The cubs crouched side by side, their backs pressed against the wall of stone. A small dry patch encircled their bottoms, mirroring the image of the rock that sheltered them from the rain.

Once the rain eased to a drizzle the cubs started to play, freed by the cool conditions. They circled each other from below the rocky ledge, walking round and round, each with a tail in his mouth. Dark changed the rules after a while, releasing Light's tail and grasping him by the back leg instead. Light hopped around like a spinning top, still clutching his brother's tail in his mouth while desperately struggling to keep his balance.

The place where the cubs played was similar to a huge rocky slide, leading to a lower level a few slippery feet below them. The rain had transformed the rocks into a slick black surface, on which Dark sat trying to retrieve his abused tail from between Light's sharp teeth. As Dark pulled and struggled to free himself from his brother's grip Light suddenly let go, inadvertently sending the smaller cub tobogganning right over the rocky step to the ledge below. Before Dark could recover, Light leapt after him and once more grabbed for his tail. Just then Chui appeared, causing both cubs to abandon their game and join her along the top of the ridge.

During the night Chui led the cubs back to Dik-Dik Lugga. She had seen and heard the baboons approaching the fig trees from the east and probably wished to avoid a confrontation early the next morning. Later still she left her cubs and went off to hunt.

Light was the first to stir, creeping onto the top of one of the boulders and peering wide-eyed down the lugga, where birds fluttered around a termite mound, busily feeding on the insects. But he soon returned to where Dark lay sleeping, pawing and biting at his brother's tail. Once he switched his attention to an overhanging branch and bit that instead. But tails were better, especially those of other leopards, for they moved by themselves and this one twitched and curled between his forepaws. Initially Dark failed to respond, acting as if he did not even own a tail, but eventually he obliged and provided Light with the playmate he wanted.

A little grooming, some nit-picking and branch biting helped pass the time until a hamerkop came into view, fifty feet south of where Dark now crouched. Named for their hammer-shaped heads and classed in a family all their own, these drab brown birds are best known for their enormous stick nests which they construct in the fork of a suitable tree near to water. These huge structures are often commandeered by other birds: tawny eagles, various species of kestrel and Egyptian geese have all been known to parasitise these elaborate nesting sites. However, it was the giant Verreaux's eagle owls that were most often to be seen occupying the old nests along nearby Leopard Lugga.

The hamerkop flopped into the air on slow wing beats, calling weakly with a piping whistle – peep, peep, peep – before landing on a small rock a few feet closer to where Dark crouched. The bird began feeding, busily searching for frogs at the edge of one of the grass-fringed pools which had collected in the floor of the lugga. As soon as the bird turned its back on Dark the young leopard eased forward a few inches, the tiniest portion of his tail twitching with excitement.

Dark crouched, quivering, stretching his neck and half raising a paw, stirring as if about to edge further forward, yet remaining riveted by the presence of the bird. The wind suddenly picked up, rippling the surface of the water and rustling through the croton bushes along the lugga, though Dark never took his eyes from the strange object standing hunched in front of him.

Light, who had been quietly watching his brother and the hamerkop, now walked casually to the water's edge. He lay on his belly, lapping noisily at the water, sending the hamerkop scuttling away and ending Dark's hunting effort.

It was nearly six o'clock when Chui returned to her cubs. Her arrival caused instant havoc among a party of guinea fowl busily scratching for food. The birds scattered in all directions at the sight of the leopard, noisily grating in alarm as they raced away like colourful, motorised tea-cosies. They soon regrouped and followed Chui, scolding her like a column of broody old hens.

The cubs rushed to greet their mother. But before they could settle down to suckle, Chui noticed an impala male feeding alone among the acacia bushes some sixty yards away. The leopard ran low and fast, her head pushed forward, shoulders hunched and belly almost touching the ground. But it made no difference – the impala looked up, halting the leopard dead in its tracks. For a moment neither animal moved; they simply stared at each other. Then the antelope blasted nasally in alarm. As was often the case, the prey animal's acute senses had saved its life, neutralising the predator's superlative stalking ability. Evolution has made it a close-run race between predator and prey, ensuring the survival of both species and helping to maintain the balance of nature.

Though the cubs followed their mother when she wanted to move with them from one place to another, they still did not attempt to accompany her while she actually hunted. They had sat attentively at the edge of the lugga and watched every move as Chui flowed, snake-like, towards the impala. But once the antelope had snorted in alarm and Chui had sat upright, abandoning her stalking position, the cubs ran forward to join her.

Later Chui investigated the area carefully, circling and sniffing around the rocks and bushes, searching perhaps for a hare, impala fawn or gazelle baby, any of which might lie concealed in such a place. It was not unusual to see the leopards employing their sense of smell to hunt the smaller prey animals that sought to survive by hiding themselves.

Next morning Chui looked well fed, though there was no sign of a kill stored in any of the trees. There were probably many times when she killed some small animal or bird and was able to consume it on the spot, concealed by darkness and without the need to seek the shelter of a tree. Though the large Mara Buffalo cubs supplemented their diet by killing small prey animals for themselves, I think that generally Chui and other adult Mara leopards were able to satisfy the bulk of their food requirement by killing medium-sized antelopes – particularly impalas and Thomson's gazelles – rather than investing much time hunting the smaller fare such as hares, dik-diks and hyrax. However, diet varies from area to area.

Once more Chui led the cubs away from Dik-Dik Lugga and journeyed east along the ridge, with Light rock-hopping to try to keep pace with his mother. But the leopards were headed on a collision course this particular morning, for out of the east strode a large male baboon. Chui was the first to notice him, though she did not move until she was certain that she herself had been seen. The cubs watched intently, their eyes riveted on the baboon as it passed to the south of where they crouched.

The baboon paused to sit and look carefully at the cats before announcing their presence by barking loudly in alarm. Then he murmured a low sound and barked once more, as he moved closer and postured in front of Chui. That was all the cubs needed to see or hear; they turned and fled to the west, hurrying back to the safety of Dik-Dik Lugga, but none of the other troop members appeared on the scene and shortly the male moved back in the direction from which he had arrived.

Chui did not try to attack the baboon, and not once did I see her or the Mara Buffalo Female respond towards baboons as if they were prey. All the leopards I have watched did everything possible to avoid contact and confrontation with these formidable primates. When Chui's cubs were smaller there were a few occasions when a baboon male came upon the leopards unexpectedly. She responded to these encounters with a charge of terrifying speed, robbing the baboon of his advantage while the cubs fled for the safety of the caves. But it did not take long for the baboon to recover from the shock and challenge Chui, usually rallying other troop members in the process. Even when the adult leopards were unaccompanied by cubs and could have attempted to prey on the baboons they did not do so – at least not during the hours of daylight.

Baboons invariably move around as a group and provide little opportunity for a lone leopard to attack them. I do not doubt that leopards sometimes kill baboons – it is a fact – but there is no reason for them to do so in a habitat such as the Mara, where far easier prey is available.

Chui slowly made her way back towards Dik-Dik Lugga, calling and smelling for signs of her cubs. But Light and Dark ignored their mother's calls, preferring to remain at their familiar patch of rocks in the lugga floor. As soon as Chui located the cubs she reappeared from the croton thickets and lay in the shade of an acacia bush at the lugga's edge. Though temporarily thwarted by the sudden appearance of the baboon, Chui now seemed ready to resume her journey.

But before she could do so a large male warthog trotted jauntily into view from the east, journeying purposefully towards Dik-Dik Lugga. He held his tail ramrod stiff in the air, unaware of the leopard and her cubs observing him from beneath their bush.

Chui did not move, watching the warthog carefully, though it was quite apparent that she did not view him as a possible source of food. Adult warthogs are rarely killed by leopards in the Mara, though I did once see a large male leopard attack and successfully strangle a boar which he then carried into a tree.

Chui groomed her throat, ignoring the warthog until he suddenly stopped and wheeled round in her direction. He stood stock-still as if he had just been slapped in the face.

It is said that warthogs have rather poor vision, but what is certain is that they have a highly developed sense of smell, and this particular warthog now smelt leopard. As he turned towards Chui the warthog thrust his flat, rooting nose even higher into the air. His tail lowered to half-mast and then subsided completely. Now he could see the smell and, what is more, he was not in the least bit intimidated.

Chui hissed defensively, baring her long canines as the warthog moved towards her. But he had weapons with which to defend himself that were just as formidable as the leopard's. His huge upper tusks that looked so impressive were not the real danger. It was the lower tusks, slender and dagger-like, which caused those slashing cuts on face and shoulders that an incautious or inexperienced lion sometimes suffered when attacking a fully grown boar.

The cubs raced for the nearest tree. Light reached it first, though Dark was right behind him; they were virtually sitting on top of one another in their efforts to scramble higher into the spindly branches. Chui hissed again, though she did not attempt to charge the belligerent pig who now circled downwind of her. As often seemed to be the case, the cubs felt insecure exposed in the tree, even though they were quite safe where they were. While the warthog confronted Chui, Dark tried to slip unobtrusively back down the tree trunk. He would rather be in the lugga, concealed from view. But as he scuttled down he missed his footing and tumbled the last few feet to the ground.

The warthog spun round, emitting a blood-curdling roar. In the ensuing confusion Light fled from behind his brother and disappeared into the lugga. But the sight of the fierce 150-pound pig at ground level was quite sufficient to persuade Dark to race straight back up the tree.

The warthog swung back to face Chui again. If anything was going to cause him trouble it was not the young leopards. He strutted towards Chui, the long stiff hairs on his neck rising in a bristly mane that made him look even larger and fiercer. Chui lay on her belly facing him, reluctant to concede ground, hissing and growling at the pig. If she had turned to move away he might well have charged after her. But as long as she refused to be intimidated the pig continued to act with more bluster than real intent. In the event the issue was a stand-off. The warthog did not know that this particular leopard had not been intent on ambushing him.

The problem was finally resolved by a vehicle which arrived upon the scene and unwittingly sent the jittery warthog on his way. As soon as he had disappeared, Light emerged from the edge of the lugga, where he had remained hidden. Chui coughed aggressively and stood up as he tried to reach her teats. Dark descended from the tree and slunk towards his mother, still showing signs of caution.

Wisely Chui abandoned any further attempts at leaving the relative safety of the lugga. Eventually she went off to rest by herself, away from the unwanted attentions of her hungry cubs, leaving them to their own devices at the island of stones.

As yet another day drew to a close I prepared for my journey back to camp. One last cup of coffee and I would be on my way. I was always loath to leave the leopards. Yet it seemed only appropriate that I should. In some ways, night time was their day. True, Chui was often active during daylight hours, but she was undoubtedly more comfortable and at ease as the light faded from the sky. To have been able to see everything would have seemed almost indecent. Most important of all, the night was the leopards' only chance to rest from the mob of vehicles that, understandably, so desperately wanted to see them. Like it or not I was one of them too. Trying to strip away the mystery of the leopards' ways eventually filled me with depression. I, with others, had helped to condition Chui to vehicles during the six years I had known her. But now the situation had grown out of all proportion. I felt at times almost as if I had betrayed the trust that Chui had developed towards my vehicle, yet I found it impossible to ignore her presence while I could find her so easily.

Leopards remain elusive because it is the best way for them to survive. They conceal themselves because they have to. The choice is not theirs. Evolution has moulded them to fill a position in wild habitats that allows them to hunt and compete successfully with lions, hyenas and others that would rob them of their food or even their lives, coating them in spots and bestowing on them the ability to conduct nearly every aspect of their lives out of sight of human or animal eyes. It has therefore always struck me as cruelly ironic that the leopard's spotted coat, designed to help conceal them from their enemies and their prey, should be cherished as a garment to be flaunted in public as a means of drawing attention to the wearer. Yet no human wears it with more grace and beauty than its rightful owner.

I have heard it said that leopards can sustain themselves against the effects of poaching and hunting, that leopards killed are soon replaced in an area by transient animals waiting to occupy the vacancies. But where are these leopards originating from? Is it not from the same small litters of cubs that female leopards such as Chui produce and struggle against all odds to raise to maturity? Strictly controlled hunting of leopards may be the only way they will be allowed to compete with the interests of ranchers outside the Parks and Reserves. But the utmost caution is needed in resolving these issues, just as the Kenya government has shown.

Next morning there was no sign of Chui or the cubs, so I drove east through the Gorge to see how the Mara Buffalo leopards were faring. My journey proved worthwhile as both the adult and her large female cub were in residence, though there was no sign of the male cub.

On the last occasion that I had seen the two cubs together at the rocks they looked thin and hungry. At that stage they were nearly eleven months old and their mother was finding it increasingly difficult to provide all three of them with sufficient food, even though she sometimes killed animals the size of zebra foals and young wildebeest. Longer separations between mother and cubs therefore became inevitable as she searched for food.

By the time the cubs were a year old the young male had abandoned Mara Buffalo Rocks as a resting place. He acted in a much more independent manner than his sister, who seemed to require a closer relationship with their mother. The male, being larger, stronger and faster, was probably better equipped to supplement the food that he still sometimes obtained from his mother's kills and he was already killing smaller game. Perhaps in situations when only one cub is being reared, a male cub can maintain a closer association with his mother for a longer period. But in these particular circumstances there was just not enough food to go round.

I watched the year-old female during the afternoon as she wandered through a patch of forest at the edge of the massive rock where her mother lay hidden. At one point the youngster crept up on a huge warthog that resided in the area. The two animals were by now old acquaintances and at times seemed to treat their encounters almost as if they were a game. Though the young leopard was incapable of proving little more than a mild irritation to the elderly pig, she was still able to give him a fright once in a while when she sneaked up on him unawares. However, she usually ended up in a tree when he decided to call her bluff.

Shortly after six o'clock the Mara Buffalo Female emerged from the cave where she had rested throughout the day. Cautiously she moved away in the direction that I had left her daughter, pausing once to spray her scent on to a low bush.

Later as I sat listening to the darkness, the night erupted with the sound of three sharp, rasping coughs which preceded the methodical and familiar wood-sawing call of an adult leopard. The call elicited no vocal reply, though, when I turned my vehicle headlights on, two leopards stared back at me from the shadows, their night eyes glowing brightly. Mother and daughter had found each other and now stood at the base of the tree in which the adult female had stored her impala kill.

On the way home my car headlights cut out. I suddenly felt hopelessly ill-equipped for night-time activity. Leopards have a special layer of cells called the tapetum, situated at the back of the eye, which reflects light back through the retina, helping them to see at a sixth of the light level required by human eyes, and creating the 'cat's eye' effect I had just seen. Lucky leopards.

The clouds had ballooned into the sky leaving a patchwork of blue. Next morning I found Light and Dark lying beneath the pappea tree at Dwarf Rocks, though there was no sign of their mother. The cubs dozed a few feet apart in the grass, crawling to a new patch of shade whenever the sun became too hot.

Quite when the giant tortoise arrived, or when the cubs first saw it, I do not know. At first the leopards seemed not to have noticed it. Perhaps that was part of the game. It was poised precariously on a flat rock next to Dark, though it was Light who looked up as the tortoise slowly extended its head from beneath its shell. The cub crept forward, dabbing a floppy paw on to the tortoise's shell and sending it skidding towards his brother. Dark jumped up with a start as the tortoise almost landed in his lap, though he quickly recovered his composure and enthusiastically joined in the fun. Light grabbed at the tortoise, rolling onto his back and bracing his feet against its shell. He chewed and bit, his sharp white teeth grating over the bone-hard surface.

The leopard cubs and this particular tortoise had met on a number of previous occasions, though that did nothing to detract from the fun of the encounters for Light and Dark. The same could hardly be said for the tortoise. The young leopards pawed and prodded the unfortunate reptile, sniffing it inquisitively at both ends, though it quickly became apparent which was less attractive. But their interest soon flagged. After all, a tortoise is not the most animated of objects for animals as boisterous as young leopards to play with. So as soon as the tortoise retreated inside its shell again, the cubs turned their attentions on each other, rolling around in the grass, batting and biting, sinking their teeth into something a little softer.

Sometimes a cub would sit beside the tortoise, waiting for it to move. But nothing is more patient than a tortoise. Dark slowly walked away, stopping every so often to look over his shoulder for signs of life from the house-bound creature. The moment it started to move away again Dark turned back and carefully stalked after it, extending a large paw and patting down onto the tortoise, forcing it to withdraw its head. Light galloped over to join his brother, up-ending the tortoise with an expert flip of his paw.

Adult lions and hyenas similarly paw and gnaw on tortoises. In fact nearly all the larger specimens in the Mara bear the imprint of vice-like teeth on their shells. But they are the survivors, the more fortunate individuals, for some of the smaller tortoises are crushed and eaten by hyenas and lions, and even pecked to death and prised from within their shells by ground hornbills. Often the ancient reptiles manage to escape harm by remaining camouflaged from view. But those that do not must rely on the strength of their shells to protect their vulnerable interiors and compensate for the painfully slow pace of their lives.

Eventually the tortoise made a determined bid for freedom. While Light and Dark tore up and down in the trees, the tortoise capitalised on the cubs' fickle nature and trundled off as fast as its legs would carry it. By the time the cubs returned to where they had left it, the tortoise looked just like one of the dull-coloured rocks further along the ridge.

It was Sunday 8 January. During the last two weeks Chui had started to move with her cubs almost daily, leading them backwards and forwards between Dik-Dik Lugga and the Cub Caves. Dwarf Rocks had become established as a suitable stop-over if for some reason Chui decided not to continue all the way to the fig tree. That decision was often dependent on whether or not the baboons were in residence.

From where Light and Dark rested on Dwarf Rocks they could hear the baboons. Light stopped to stare as the Fig Tree Troop emerged to feed among the acacia scrub a hundred yards to the south. As they did so the larger cub retreated behind the shroud of tangled vegetation surrounding the rocks, leaving Dark crouched in the open. To the north a pair of jackals began to bark. Light opened his eyes and stared in their direction and I wondered if we both associated the distinctive sound with the possible appearance of his mother.

It was just after eight o'clock when Chui appeared from north of the ridge. She often seemed to arrive back from her nocturnal wanderings at this hour of the morning. She paused to smell the trunk of the pappea tree, then sat and watched as the last of the Fig Tree Troop disappeared from view. She chuffled to her youngsters and led them away to the east, the cubs racing along in front of her, as sure-footed as their mother over the rocky terrain. Dark crouched on a boulder as Chui approached, then leapt over his mother's back as she passed by. At times the cubs bounded and twisted into the air or performed other acrobatic feats which distinguished them from any other large cat I had ever watched before.

Chui stopped a hundred yards west of the fig tree, though there was no doubting that it was her real destination. A tawny eagle flew low overhead, scrutinising the leopards, causing Chui to stop and lash her tail irritably. The eagle landed on a dead tree, forty yards away, prompting Light to stalk quickly back to where the tawny perched.

The eagle cocked its head inquisitively, peering down at the cat. Light quickly proceeded up the tree, forcing the eagle to flap clumsily a few feet into the air. As soon as the bird flopped back on to its perch, Light climbed right to the top of the tree, not in the least bit intimidated by the eagle, which hissed aggressively before departing to a more peaceful roost.

While Dark hurried to join his brother, Chui continued to the fig tree where she could rest away from the heat. Before long the cubs raced towards the Cub Caves, rediscovering the pleasures of the climbing tree on their way. Later still they climbed into the fig tree with their mother, who for once encouraged them, chuffling as they clambered up to join her. Perhaps she now felt more confidence in their ability to look after themselves in the open.

During the afternoon vervets began to stutter, drawing attention to the leopard cubs who were busily chasing around Top Rock in pursuit of the hordes of agamid lizards. The cubs paused to look in the direction of the agitated monkeys, then continued with their own activities. But the Fig Tree Troop were already on their way back to their sleeping trees.

This time Chui did not wait for the baboons to congregate around her. As soon as the first few young males climbed into the fig tree to join her, she turned and streaked down the main trunk, leaving a trail of startled baboons in her wake. Her sudden departure provoked an outburst of grunts and barks from the baboons, who hurriedly dropped from the branches to follow Chui's movements as she fled to the safety of the vertical cave.

Thunder crashed in the distance as Chui led her cubs back along the ridge. When she reached the place where the cubs had played with the tortoise she stopped and called to them before lying down. Both cubs quickly started to suckle, though after barely a minute they moved away again.

Light and Dark raced up and down the euphorbia tree as Chui lay staring after them. She called softly and each time they returned to her she rolled towards them with outstretched paws, inviting contact with the cubs, who tumbled on top of each other in their efforts to reach her.

The cubs broke away from their mother and wrestled briefly, tumbling from the rocks. They play-fought head to head, faces bent back as they pushed and swatted each other with clubbing blows. They feinted this way and that, sparring like boxers seeking an advantage. When a suitable opening appeared they lunged in to nip at throat or neck. At times Light seemed to be getting particularly rough, causing Dark to try to escape from his brother's determined assaults. Light showed an extra yard of pace too, when chasing after Dark, catching up with him and tripping and swatting at his brother's flying heels.

Sometimes Light tried the same tactics on his mother, forcing her to close her eyes as he batted at her face. When he did this Chui would suddenly lunge in hard with open mouth to get a bite in on the boisterous cub, restraining him.

So it continued, Chui relaxed and playful, the cubs storming back and forth, confident in their movements. Chui looked lean and so did her cubs; she would have to kill again for them all soon, for the six-month-old cubs were virtually weaned now. Chui trotted away with a swaggering, playful stride, the cubs bounding ahead of her. As she caught up with them Chui accelerated, drawing the cubs with her in a mad caper over the rocks and through the thorn thickets.

The young leopards – and they now looked like young leopards, not just cubs – climbed into yet another tree, elevating themselves above the dim shape of the Siria Escarpment. Framed by the dark clouds, they formed brief silhouettes against the last glow of sunset. A burst of lightning flashed across the sky, illuminating the leopards' golden coats. Chui sat at the base of the tree and called – *aaouuu* – and again – *aaaouououuou* – even more drawn out. Then she turned and walked into the darkness.

As Chui disappeared I could hear the familiar thud, thud, of the cubs' feet as they chased after their mother. I listened carefully as she called once more, a mournful, fading sound as the leopards vanished into the night.

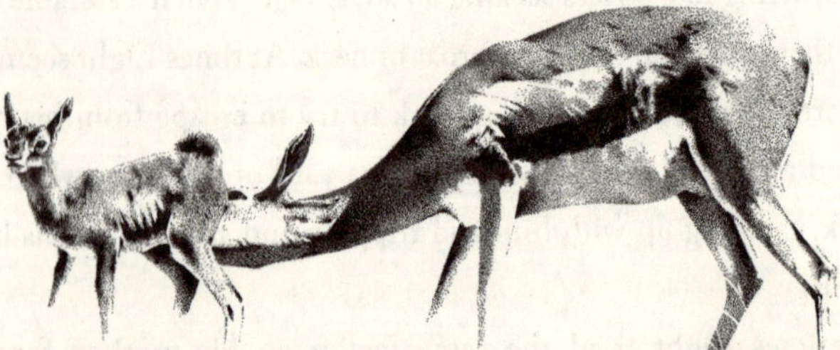

9. The Leopard's Future

UP UNTIL now Chui had confined her cubs to a relatively narrow corridor of land which provided security for Light and Dark and sufficient food for them all. But there had been many times when she ventured further afield alone, leaving the cubs a number of miles away. Food was certainly not the only motive for these safaris, as Chui sometimes left an area harbouring abundant prey within easy reach of where the cubs were hidden. She may simply have been investigating and re-affirming her presence in those parts of her home range which she had been forced to neglect while shackled with young. It was probably essential that she should do this, as an area left unused for any length of time might be appropriated by another female leopard.

Finally, during the second week of January 1984, the leopards vanished. At first I was confident that somewhere among the croton bushes of Dik-Dik Lugga or the caves of Fig Tree Ridge and Leopard Gorge, Chui and her cubs would be found. Yet the more carefully I searched the more daunting the task of finding them seemed to become. I knew only too well from my previous experiences with leopards how difficult it could be once they were permanently on the move.

Wherever I looked I found signs of Chui's absence. Hyenas wallowed in the flooded recesses of the lugga floor where Light and Dark used to rest during the heat of the day. Warthogs rooted and clipped the green shoots beneath Chui's fig tree while vervet monkeys fed on the ripening fruits above them. Hyrax clustered in groups along the ledges surrounding the Cub Caves and the slender mongoose had free rein inside. The leopards had gone.

Even though Chui was very approachable by leopard standards, she had sometimes disappeared for months without anybody being able to find her. It was only when she had cubs and remained with them in a fixed location that she was visible for any length of time. In my heart, much as I wanted to see them again, I felt a tremendous sense of relief. At last, however briefly, Chui and her cubs were free.

Light and Dark were by now highly mobile young leopards who could climb the tallest trees in order to feed on their mother's kills or if danger threatened. They no longer needed the massive security of the Cub Caves and had abandoned the rocky shelter provided by Dik-Dik Lugga. The cubs could now follow Chui wherever she chose to take them and, no longer confined to a small part of her range, she could disappear back into the shadows of her former existence.

I would often pause in my search to try to imagine where Chui and the cubs were located at that precise moment, in the knowledge that I had certainly driven close by the three of them on a number of occasions, yet failed to detect them. Days soon turned into weeks without sight or sign of the leopards.

Then one day in February, six weeks after I had last seen Chui and her cubs, a driver from Kichwa Tembo Camp told me that he had found one of the cubs resting in the fig tree, Chui's old haunt. He also mentioned in passing that the cub had grown considerably since he had last seen Light and Dark.

I could hardly wait to find out which of Chui's cubs it would be; how big it had grown and whether the colour of its eyes had finally dimmed from dark brown to the pale green – or is it yellow? – of adult leopards.

I made my way as quickly as possible to Fig Tree Ridge, stopping briefly to talk with Jock Anderson, an old friend from Mara River Camp. Jock confirmed having seen an adult leopard with a single cub in the same area two days earlier. I began to wonder if either Light or Dark had been killed. Apparently the cub had been eating the remains of an impala fawn in a euphorbia tree along Leopard Lugga, not far from where it cut across the ridge. Earlier the cub had been lying in the lugga within a few feet of a hyena, once again affirming the ambivalent relationship these two species maintain. Both animals seemed quite willing to rest close together as long as there was nothing to compete over.

When I finally arrived at Chui's fig tree it was horribly bare. I could find nothing to suggest that only an hour earlier a leopard had draped itself elegantly over one of the thick branches. Disappointed, I re-checked that part of Leopard Lugga where Jock had seen the leopards two days earlier. A single back leg, wedged high in the euphorbia tree, was all that remained of the impala kill.

Having searched the area carefully I drove back to Dwarf Rocks and followed the track leading towards the Three Trees, as Chui often wandered off in that direction when leaving the fig tree. Here at least there was still some vegetation remaining, providing cover for a leopard to stalk up on the impala herds which frequented the edges of the acacia thickets. Suddenly I heard the warning snort of an impala, immediately echoed by that of a topi standing alertly nearby. Surely it must be the leopard. But where?

The moment I saw the impala female she turned and bounded away, followed on high springy steps by a young calf. As I strained my eyes to locate the cause of the disturbance a leopard streaked from the tangle of thornbush and boulders. It sprinted like a cheetah, a blur of spots on an olive-brown background, its rudder-like tail flying behind it. The speed of the chase was electrifying. In a matter of seconds the leopard closed with the calf, which stumbled as it tried to negotiate a path through the rocks. The cat was on it in a flash, pouncing forward and biting into its neck.

The mother impala rushed back, snorting as the leopard picked up the struggling fawn and began to carry it to the safety of the nearest tree. But the leopard was not alone. A hyena had heard the warning snorts of the antelopes and had left its resting place beneath a wizened gardenia tree. Before the leopard could cover the last few yards to safety, the hyena rushed forward with its tail cocked aggressively and bit at the leopard's vulnerable bottom. The smaller predator had no alternative but to drop its kill or risk being injured; without turning to defend itself the leopard ran off, leaving the hyena free to grab the dead impala and hurry away among the thorn thickets.

When I looked again the leopard had disappeared, and I could find no trace of it in the failing light. Then, just as I was driving away, I saw her. She lay curled among the rocks, making no particular effort to conceal herself. She did not need to. Her coat blended so perfectly with the rocks that if she had not turned her head towards me I would have missed her completely. Now she held her position, perhaps assuming that I had not seen her, that she still remained hidden from view and I would continue on my way.

I looked carefully at the leopard through my binoculars. I already knew it was not Chui, for this leopard was bigger and darker, almost the size of some male leopards. She had an older, fiercer bearing, a muscular thickness around her neck and chest, and the first signs of a loose jowl of soft white fur beneath her chin. The heavy muzzle and deeply notched right ear now confirmed my suspicions. It was the Mara Buffalo Female.

How could I feel disappointment when I had just watched a leopard hunting, revealing all its speed and power as it gracefully twisted and bounded after its prey? When I was able to sit, no more than fifty feet away, and enjoy the beauty of such a magnificent animal? Yet I now knew for certain that the long search for Chui and her cubs had not ended. The fast-growing cub that had been seen lying contentedly among the branches of the fig tree would certainly not be either Light or Dark, as I had hoped. Instead it would be this leopard's large female cub, who was six or seven months older than Chui's cubs.

Later the leopard moved off in the same direction that the hyena had fled, sniffing at the ground as she went. Her belly was taut, curving tightly upwards to her groin: she was obviously hungry. All that remained from her kill was a piece of wet skin. She picked it up and shook it, then lay with it behind a termite mound. But after gnawing and licking a few tiny scraps of meat from its inner surface she abandoned it. She continued along the ridge, pausing every so often to sniff the ground. On reaching a dense clump of bush she sprayed her scent over the leaves before turning towards Leopard Gorge and disappearing into the darkness.

What, I wondered, had prompted the Mara Buffalo leopard to move so far? I had never seen her in this area before and it was more than four miles from where she now stood to the Mara Buffalo Rocks. Unfortunately I had no previous information on the range of this particular leopard, as I had only become aware of her presence at the time of the birth of her two cubs. During this period she, like Chui, had concentrated her main activity in a relatively small area, even though her home range was undoubtedly considerably larger.

Possibly the two females' home ranges partially overlapped, even though they had carefully avoided each other's presence by interpreting the various clues that every leopard leaves as to its whereabouts. In this way Chui and the Mara Buffalo Female could have been conducting their activities in that part of the shared area not being used by the other.

It soon became apparent that this was not simply a fleeting visit into alien territory by the Mara Buffalo leopard and her cub. It seemed somehow strange to see these other leopards disappearing into the Cub Caves, clambering over the rocks and resting in the same trees that Chui and her cubs had occupied during the last few months. The young female, now nearly fourteen months old, soon acted as if she had lived in the area all her life, quickly becoming familiar with every facet of Fig Tree Ridge and the surrounding luggas. During the day she often lolled in the fig tree while her mother, when in attendance, sought the greater privacy of the deep vertical cave.

It was as if a locked door had suddenly been flung open for the Mara Buffalo Female. By absenting herself from the area and consequently not leaving fresh marks of residence, Chui had provided the other female and her cub with the front-door key. It proved just how effective the spacing mechanism employed by leopards really is.

Sometimes I would find the young female exploring along the northern reaches of Leopard Lugga or even as far west as Dik-Dik Lugga. At other times she might be found chasing hyrax or creeping around the caves of Leopard Gorge which had been vacated by the lions, now that their cubs were also old enough to venture further afield. Her mother was usually somewhere in the area, though she avoided detection where possible and sometimes roamed far from her daughter. But sooner or later the two leopards would find each other.

The Mara Buffalo Female would hunt in the proximity of her daughter as well as further afield, often returning to the cub from these sorties and staying in her vicinity during the daytime if she had failed to make a kill. When she did kill and it was too far away or too big to bring back to the cub, she would store it and then come and fetch the cub so that she could feed with her.

The young female was also making her own attempts to hunt, though at this stage she only managed to kill occasional smaller game animals such as lizards, hyrax, dik-dik and African hares. Though she accompanied her mother on some of her nocturnal wanderings I felt that the cub's hunting experience was gained as much through trial and error as by learning directly from her mother. I witnessed none of the behaviour adopted by cheetah females, who sometimes release small or injured prey for their cubs to kill, though perhaps the leopards did so at night.

There was little doubt that the Mara Buffalo Female favoured certain areas in her range, particularly while she still had a semi-dependent daughter. Chui and the Mara Buffalo Female were adopting the same basic pattern of behaviour. Dik-Dik Lugga, the Cub Caves and Leopard Gorge seemed ideally suited as focal points of activity for any leopard with cubs. Such places seemed to strike a chord in the minds of the leopards and they returned to them time and again when in the area. In fact they seemed almost essential to their survival, somewhere to raise their cubs and a place to shelter for themselves.

There still remained one aspect of this story that had intrigued me from the very first day I had become acquainted with the Mara Buffalo Female. What, I wondered, might her relationship with Chui be: did they ever see each other, did they already know each other, had they ever confronted one another? What was their history?

At first I was not even sure that they were neighbours. It was quite possible that another unknown female might occupy a range separating these two leopards. But when the Mara Buffalo Female moved into the area temporarily vacated by Chui it seemed proof enough that they were in fact neighbours.

Yet there was a still more exciting possibility, an intriguing twist to this leopards' tale.

Once female cubs become independent they often continue to occupy an area partially overlapping their mother's home range. The possibility of home-range inheritance by female offspring suggests that two or even three females sharing all or part of the same home range may be related.

Chui still frequented the areas that I had seen her in as a cub: Dik-Dik Lugga, Leopard Lugga and Leopard Gorge were all places to which she had been gradually introduced by her mother prior to independence. But what I did not know was the full extent of Chui's mother's home range. As in the case of the Mara Buffalo Female, I had only become aware of her presence through the appearance of her cubs.

Now I pondered on the possibility that the Mara Buffalo Female and Chui might be related. More exciting still, they might even be mother and daughter. If only I had been able to photograph Chui's mother the mystery would have been solved long ago. The spots on a leopard's face and the markings on its tail provide a positive means of distinguishing one animal from another. The problem, of course, is trying to photograph them.

Certainly the Mara Buffalo Female was large, dark and shy, just as Chui's mother had been, and she was definitely older than Chui. In those respects at least she fitted the description. It is known that a female leopard can live for at least twelve years in the wild, possibly even a few years longer. Chui was now in her seventh year, so there was no reason why her mother might not still be alive. But would she still be breeding?

There was only one occasion when I had been able to snatch even the briefest glimpse of Chui's mother, and that was on the day I first saw Chui and her brother as young cubs feeding on the wildebeest carcass at the base of the eleaodendron tree above Leopard Gorge. For a moment, as Chui's mother reached the safety of the Gorge, she had turned and looked back at me. Then she was gone.

Now, six years later, I was once more driving through Leopard Gorge thinking, as I always did, what a perfect retreat this was for leopards. Just as I neared the west end of the Gorge, at the place where it opens out onto a beautiful view of the country surrounding Fig Tree Ridge, a hyrax began to screech. It was a sound I had heard many times before, yet it never failed to send a tingle of excitement through me in the knowledge that, except when they spotted a bird of prey, the hyrax invariably reserved this alarm chorus for leopards.

I stopped the vehicle. Four or five hyrax crouched along a narrow ledge bordering the huge cave where the old wall-eyed leopard sometimes used to lie. The giant fig tree that once grew proudly from the cave floor, guarding its darkened entrance and casting a cooling shadow over the rocky roof, had finally fallen. All that remained was a massive charred log. Now the cave and its stony surrounds looked somehow naked.

The sounds of my arrival had undoubtedly prompted the leopard to slink away, movements that had inadvertently brought it to the attention of the ever-watchful hyrax. Now their gaze directed me to the place where the leopard had disappeared from view. I scanned the rocks opposite the cave, pausing at favoured resting places where a leopard might hide.

I looked carefully along the lichen-covered ledge that lay partially obscured by a canopy of creepers and leafy undergrowth. It was a place where generations of leopards had sought shelter, for behind it lay the concealed entrance to a network of caves and tunnels. The wall-eyed male had once lain on the ledge and in the past I had seen Chui, the one surviving cub of her first litter, the area's resident male leopard and the young female from Mara Buffalo – all resting at this same spot.

It also happened to be the place where Chui's mother had disappeared that day when I came upon Chui and her brother for the first time. Now as I watched, a dark spotted head with ears flattened slowly raised itself above the level of the rocks until the pale green eyes, gun-barrel nostrils and white-whiskered muzzle came into view. It was the Mara Buffalo Female.

Perhaps this was indeed Chui's mother, a survivor from a bygone era that I hoped would never be seen again. More importantly I rejoiced in the fact that, despite all the problems that have faced leopards in the past, Leopard Gorge could once again provide them with a safe refuge.

And what of Chui and her cubs? Not a trace could be found of the leopards for months after they first disappeared during those early days in January. Then, in September, Chui was seen with both Light and Dark at the west end of Fig Tree Ridge, not far from Kampi ya Chui. By that time the Mara Buffalo Female had long since disappeared again, and her daughter and independently minded son were occasionally to be seen separately in an area closer to Mara Buffalo Rocks.

I paid a fleeting visit to Chui's old haunts in December 1984. The Mara looked sparkling fresh and green, invigorated by the heavy rains which had at last arrived to ease the drought. One of the Kichwa Tembo drivers led me to a place along Fig Tree Ridge where the grizzled remains of a Thomson's gazelle hung from a pappea tree which Chui often sprayed and clawed when in the area. The kill was less than a week old and there, indented on the smooth bark, were the telltale signs of its owner. Alongside the deep claw marks of the adult leopard were a tramline of somewhat shallower scratches, made by smaller leopards. Imprinted in the mud beneath the tree were a maze of pug-marks, some large, others smaller. Chui, Light and Dark had returned.

Perhaps one day, many miles from Fig Tree Ridge, a car will stop to watch a male leopard resting on some rocky ledge or in a leafy tree. The people will watch in wonder at his apparent lack of fear, providing them with more than just a fleeting glimpse of a creature that is still thought by many to be the most beautiful of all Africa's animals. Then in his own good time the leopard will slip quietly away to some more concealed resting place, and Light or Dark will have been seen once more.

Epilogue 1

The Paradise Female

FOLLOWING CHUI and her cubs remains one of the highlights of my life. There was an almost mystical quality to spending hours at a time in the company of these elusive predators. The years of hoping and waiting made the experience all the more satisfying. The first edition of *The Leopard's Tale* took me six years to complete – that is how hard it was in the 1970s to *find* a leopard, let alone *photograph* one. I felt that I had put the time in and earned the privilege.

Though I gradually resigned myself to Chui's disappearance, I took comfort in the knowledge that Light and Dark were now old enough to follow their mother. I never gave up hope that one day I would see them again – or that someone would bring me news of them. How realistic was I in believing this? Fairly, I think. At six months a leopard is a very different cat to a lion or cheetah of the same age. It has almost certainly made its first kill: an agama lizard, perhaps, or a baby hyrax plucked from a cave with those razor-sharp claws. A leopard's ability to hide thanks to the camouflage of its spotted coat, to scramble into the densest bushes or to claw its way up into the treetops gives it an advantage over other big cats. But it is primarily the leopard's secretive way of life that sets it apart. It must conceal itself from its enemies *and* its prey, the stealthy shadow passing unseen and unheard on the most silent of paws. Leopards are more adaptable and less 'needy' than lions and cheetahs. A lion cub unexpectedly separated from its mother is liable to become alarmed, perhaps moving into the open and calling, while a young cheetah in the same position will utter high-pitched bird-like calls of distress, anxious to be reunited. A leopard meanwhile embraces solitude and, while a leopard cub can be playful and attention-seeking when accompanied by its mother, from the age of six months onwards its instinct is to explore and seek out prey, quite content to wander off on its own and to rest alone at times. Little surprise, then, that leopards are capable of becoming independent at an earlier age than lions or cheetahs and this gave me hope that Light and Dark had survived. My biggest concern was lions; they are always a danger to a leopard.

As I set out from camp each morning I often found myself imagining what the two cubs might be doing. I wondered how their characters were developing; whether Dark would grow larger and more dominant than his brother; how far they would have to disperse to claim a territory. As adolescents they would have continued to enjoy each other's company, particularly whenever their mother was away hunting and patrolling her territory, reminding other adults in the area that she was still in residence. They would have spent their time playing and sparring with one another, fast and athletic youngsters wrestling and tumbling, rearing up on their hind legs and cuffing each other with their large forepaws, mouths ajar as each tried to pin the other to the ground with a throat bite, back legs bicycling wildly – refining the fighting techniques that they would need to employ in earnest as they grew older and challenged for a territory of their own.

This is a difficult time for a young leopard. Unoccupied territories are in short supply and competition fierce, with the younger generation often having to fight for the chance to take possession. Those who fail are squeezed into less desirable areas, where natural prey is in short supply; this can lead to conflict with pastoralists or to the leopards being forced to pick off dogs or stray cats from villages – or even from city dwellers. Many are poisoned or trapped.

Occasionally during this period I found the Mara Buffalo Female's cubs, who were six months older than Light and Dark and fully independent by now. One afternoon I watched as the young male feasted on an adult topi he had killed and then dragged to cover among a clump of croton bushes at the edge of the plains. He had grown into a magnificent animal, but still had some tough lessons to learn if he was to survive among so many dangerous competitors. As he gorged himself, two young lions ambushed him, intent at the very least on stealing his kill. I could tell by the look of utter hostility on their faces that they would not hesitate to kill the young leopard if the opportunity presented itself. Slowed by his bloated stomach and with nowhere to hide, he could only crouch and rumble a warning to his larger rivals. As I sat imagining what might happen next, another vehicle arrived and drove straight at the lions, enabling the leopard to run for the nearest trees. While I have always believed that nature should take its course and been unwilling to intervene at a time like this, I felt relieved that the young male had escaped unharmed.

True to their reputation for stealth and concealment, I saw very little sign of leopards over the next two years. Then in October 1985 I was told by the American film-makers Warren and Genny Garst that a shy female had been spotted in Leopard Gorge. They felt sure she had cubs, as her belly skin was loose and pendulous, with dark rings around her nipples indicating that she was suckling young.

My heart leapt with excitement at the news. I hurried to the mouth of the Gorge via Fig Tree Ridge, passing all the old familiar landmarks, the giant fig trees and euphorbias, clumps of strongly scented leleshwa bush and massive caves that added to the allure of this patch of country. As I drew closer I slowed the vehicle to quiet the sound of the engine. Knowing that this leopard was shy and almost certainly had cubs, I decided to approach from the top of the Gorge. This would offer the best view without unduly disturbing the mother. I scanned all the favourite hiding places that I knew so well. Nothing. Not even a hint of a spotted coat or a flicker of an ear, no gun-barrel nostrils peering over the rocks. I had been in this situation so many times before, felt the first flush of elation on hearing that a leopard had been sighted, only to find that it had disappeared by the time I reached the appointed location. I fought back the sense of deep disappointment, knowing that often the best thing to do was simply to stop, wait, look and listen, hoping for some clue that might pinpoint the leopard's position.

Suddenly, there they were. Halfway along the northern lip of the Gorge, three tiny leopard cubs no more than three months old, the long guard hairs of their sooty greyish coats partially concealing the distinctive pattern of spots and rosettes. I was overjoyed. The cubs knew I was there, had heard my vehicle approaching, seen me drive up. But they were unperturbed, feeling secure in their rocky hideaway, scrambling around in the bushes and creeping in and out of the labyrinth of nooks and crannies that make Leopard Gorge such a perfect spot for a mother leopard to hide her cubs. I could see a large cave beneath the place where the cubs gambolled about, the same cave where Joseph Rotich – Bwana Chui – had told me that Chui and her brother had been born in early 1978.

I stayed at the Gorge for the rest of the day, hoping that at some point the mother of the three cubs might make an appearance. Perhaps she had gone off hunting in the middle of the day to avoid the attentions of the hyenas and lions and would return before it got dark. There was always the chance that she was tucked away close by, avoiding the cubs to give herself a few hours' respite to take a nap. I scanned all the likely trees. Nothing. Imagine then my delight when the mother leopard suddenly melted into view, moving cautiously along the lip of the Gorge. She paused as she spotted my car and hissed, revealing her dagger-like canines – an impressive defensive gesture that I had seen leopards use on many occasions when warning a hyena to keep its distance. I was 100 yards away but still hardly dared breathe with the tension. On she came. She hissed again, so I edged back further, noting that her canines were more toffee-brown in colour than ivory-white, marking her out as an adult in her prime.

She paused as she drew close to where the cubs had been playing earlier, and as she did so I could hear her chuffling, uttering that lovely puffing sound that I had so often heard Chui use when calling Light and Dark from their hiding place along Fig Tree Ridge. Chuffling or prusten is the quietest, most intimate and subtle way for a leopard to communicate to her cubs or her mate that 'it is me', 'I am friendly', 'I mean no harm'. In this instance she was telling them, 'It is safe to come out.' The cubs needed no further encouragement, bundling into view, falling over themselves in a frenzy of excitement, reaching up to push their heads against their mother's chin, winding their long white-tipped tails around her neck, demanding to suckle.

Though I did not recognise this female, I did manage to take a single photograph of her with my 800mm lens. Thank goodness I did, for when I returned at first light next morning she and the cubs had gone. The Garsts told me that they reappeared briefly a few days later at the Cub Caves along Fig Tree Ridge. The cubs were obviously mobile enough to follow their mother without needing to be carried individually from one hiding place to the next. But the threat of a deadly encounter with lions is never far away in the Mara. Two lionesses from the Gorge Pride were camped further along the Ridge and it seems likely that this was sufficient to prompt the leopard to move on. The following day I departed for England for the publication of the first edition of this book and an exhibition of the photographs at the Natural History Museum in London. I never saw the mother or her cubs again.

There was a pleasing twist to this tale. A year later, while sifting through a mountain of slides at my mother's house in England, I happened upon the solitary close-up I had taken of the mother leopard at Leopard Gorge. Each leopard has a pattern of spots and rosettes as individual as a human fingerprint, so if this was one I had photographed before I should be able to identify her. I picked up a copy of *The Leopard's Tale* and as I flicked through the photographs I paused at one particular image of Chui. There was something about her eyes (they looked squinty at times) and the broadness of her face that told me that it was Chui I had seen at the Gorge. And my photograph proved it.

How on earth could I have failed to recognise Chui? I felt almost guilty, embarrassed, disrespectful even for not knowing a creature who had been such a pivotal and emotional part of my life. It was like meeting someone in the street you know well, only to find yourself struggling to put a name to their face. I wanted to go back in time, to have one more look at Chui, to absorb her essence. Not as the stranger she had become, but as that other Chui – the one I had watched since she was a small cub – to celebrate her achievements as a mother. At least I had the satisfaction of knowing that Light and Dark had almost certainly survived. If a mother leopard is successful in raising her cubs, the birth interval between litters is usually around two years. This would fit with having found Chui with small cubs. I was later to discover a leopard may give birth much sooner than this – sometimes when the previous generation is barely one year old and still partially dependent on its mother – but even so my instincts told me that Chui had reared Light and Dark to independence.

Much as the leopard will always be my favourite big cat, I had also dreamed of following the migration of wildebeest and zebras on their southern journey back to the fabled Serengeti National Park – the Masai Mara's 'big brother'. I had been living almost permanently in the Mara for the past eight years and wanted a new challenge. The wildlife film-makers Alan and Joan Root, who owned Mara River Camp where I had been based for my first five years in the Mara, had produced an epic documentary called *The Year of the Wildebeest,* employing the resonant tones of James Mason as narrator. I felt inspired by their work and wanted to see the migration for myself in all its many permutations. In early June each year the advance parties of the wildebeest nation spill across an intermittent watercourse known as the Sand River that separates the Serengeti from the Mara, spreading like dark treacle across the rolling grassy plains and scattered acacia thickets. I now wanted to visit the ancestral calving grounds in the south of the park; marvel at the sight of a million animals scattered like ants across the short grass plains; see half a million newborn calves wobble to their feet during the height of the calving season between January and March; witness the great predators feasting to exhaustion on the profligacy of the herds.

For the best part of the next three years I spent more of my time in the Serengeti than in the Mara. I always maintained a keen interest in the big cats that I had come to know so well and continued to document their lives – in particular the lions of the Marsh Pride and a female cheetah with the habit of jumping on to the bonnet of safari vehicles, earning herself the name of Queen from the drivers of Governors' Camp (*Big Cat Diary* viewers later came to know her as Amber). But from 1985 to 1987 I lived out of my Toyota Landcruiser for months at a time, soaking up the essence of the Serengeti and following not only the wildebeest but another predator that had always fascinated me, a pack-hunting animal that was as different from a leopard in its behaviour as it was to look at. The African wild dog's scientific name *Lycaon pictus* means 'painted wolf', aptly describing its mottled coat pattern of brown, black and white. Smaller and lighter than a leopard, it is the epitome of a social predator. It was thrilling to watch the dogs racing across the short grass plains in pursuit of a Thomson's gazelle or haring through the woodlands after impala. These are the same prey species favoured by leopards but hunted in a totally different way. I was able to get to know a pack of dogs intimately, so that three years after my next book, *The Great Migration,* was published in 1988, I produced *Painted Wolves.*

Between my safaris to the Serengeti I headed north again to the Mara, crossing the Bologonja border post and on into Kenya via the Sand River entrance gate, a two-hour drive from my base at Kichwa Tembo tented camp in the Mara Triangle. It was around this time that I met Angie Bellamy, the lady with long blonde hair and startling good looks. Angie was the buyer for a chain of curio shops and was struggling to find copies of my wildlife books. She left a note with my friends at the Nation Book Shop in Nairobi asking me to contact her. My greatest love up to this point had been my work. Now I found a soul-mate who was not only from Africa – Angie was born in Alexandria and raised in Dar es Salaam in Tanzania – but was passionate about art and photography and relished time spent on safari. It was – and 25 years later still is – the perfect match.

My books completed, it was time for me to immerse myself once more in the world of the Marsh Pride and the other animal characters I had been following in the Mara since 1977. It was also the beginning of a new chapter in my lifelong obsession with leopards, due to the arrival of a young female the likes of whom none of us had ever seen before. Every visitor wants to see a leopard, but with only a few precious days on safari they don't have the time to invest in searching day after day for these enigmatic predators. So the sudden emergence of the Paradise Female around Fig Tree Ridge and Leopard Gorge was like a gift from the heavens.

Female leopards often carve out a territory adjacent to the area where they were born, sometimes overlapping part of their mother's home range while doing their best to avoid her by scent-marking and calling. So it would have been easy to assume that the Paradise Female was one of Chui's offspring or a relative at least – a younger sister, perhaps. But the drivers insisted that she must be the same leopard that they had occasionally seen as a cub in the Paradise Plains area, hiding up in the daytime with her mother in the croton thickets and rocky outcrops around the Two Hills overlooking the wildebeest river crossings. That is why we named her the Paradise Female.

The drivers told me that the young female had furtively made her way across the rocky landmark known as Rhino Ridge that separates Paradise Plain from the Musiara area and then continued along the Miti Mbili Lugga (now known as the Bila Shaka Lugga), clinging to the cover that the intermittent watercourse provided in a journey that took her months rather than weeks. On her way she had to tiptoe past the resident leopards, and the lion prides that cover the whole of the Mara with their tawny and dangerous presence, avoiding first the Paradise Pride, then the Marsh Pride and on into the realm of the Gorge Pride, who at times also favoured the rocky sanctuaries of Fig Tree Ridge and Leopard Gorge as a place to hide their young cubs and seek respite in the heat of the day.

The first time I saw the Paradise Female, in early 1990, I remember thinking what a handsome creature she was. Her nose was bright pink and her ears beautifully rounded without a hint of damage: none of the telltale nicks or notches that you so often see with older females who have earned their battle scars defending their territory. I estimated that she was at least two years old and in search of a permanent place to settle.

The Paradise Female wasn't the only leopard staking a claim to this area. A shy female with a large male cub also frequented Chui's old haunts, so their home ranges must have overlapped to a degree. But though we never saw them fight it wasn't long before this other female disappeared. We did see the young male trying to mate with the Paradise Female, but their union was unsuccessful. A few months prior to this he had been surprised by a Masai honey hunter along Fig Tree Ridge while resting up in the largest of the Cub Caves where Light and Dark had loved to spend time. The man had been probing around the mouth of the cave for honeycomb with his long stick – honey hunters often cut into the thick limbs of the fig trees along the Ridge and the Gorge to encourage bees to swarm. Jolted from his slumber on the cool of the cave floor, the leopard sprang forward, sinking his claws into the man's face. As the honey hunter stumbled backwards, blood pouring from his face, the leopard made good his escape. Fortunately a tourist vehicle on the lookout for the spotted cats happened past at that moment and took the wounded man to the nearby dispensary at Mara Rianta, where he was stitched up.

A few days later, disaster struck. The young male was ambushed by members of the Gorge Pride along the Ngorbop Lugga. As he moved away from two safari vehicles he failed to notice the lions stalking towards him, cornering him as they would a rival from another pride. The vehicles tried to intervene, but to no avail. Alerted to the incident, Angie and I went to see what had happened. We stood there in silence, reflecting on the life of the young male as we examined his body. Spending as much time as we do watching wild animals, getting to know them as individuals, sharing the highs and lows in their lives, marvelling at their tenacity and will to live, we cannot help becoming emotionally involved.

Looking at the young leopard, it was all too apparent how he had died. Brutally efficient in their execution, the lions had simply done what they are evolved to do: defending their territory against competitors for food and space, employing their size and social advantage to gang up on their smaller rival, assaulting him without mercy, biting into his hindquarters and ripping at his stomach before finishing him off with a bite to the neck. This distressing event meant that, now more than ever, the drivers and guides in the northern Mara focused their efforts on finding and following the Paradise Female.

So began our association with one of the most remarkable big cats that Angie and I have ever known. There would be others down the years – how could we ever forget the cheetahs Amber, Kike and Honey, or Khali and White Eye from the Marsh Pride, or the magnificent males Scar and Notch, Clawed and Romeo? But these cats were always more strongly connected in our minds to their wild habitat than to us; yes, they fascinated us and we felt a sense of closeness in our spirit, but none of them caught our imagination quite the way the Paradise Female did. She somehow transcended (in our minds, at least) the distance that so often seems to separate man and beasts – a discontinuity on our part in clinging to the idea that we humans are not animals at all. There was something about the Paradise Female that drew you closer to her very essence, allowing you a glimpse into her world and hinting at a deep connection and reverence for all life.

Throughout the 1990s Angie and I followed the Paradise Female's story as closely as possible. Whenever we were absent from the Mara we made a point of networking with drivers and guides, photographers and film-makers, to ensure that we could record the details of her life. One particular incident was to mark the Paradise Female out from every other leopard: the loss of half of her beautiful spotted tail.

At first we thought this would be debilitating for her. A leopard's tail always seems to be a vital part of its anatomy, integral to the surefootedness and lightness of touch that make it such a consummate climber: a counterbalance when walking along the narrowest of branches, a rudder when running swiftly after prey, as well as an important means of conveying its intentions. As well as a mother arching her tail so that her cubs can track her movements, a leopard in the open will sometimes make itself even more visible by holding its tail aloft, demonstrating to prey that it is passing by rather than hunting. Most demonstrative of all, an aggressive leopard will twitch the tip of its tail when about to charge, lashing it from side to side before lifting it high above its body, revealing the startling white underside as it launches a head-on attack of frightening speed and intensity. But despite this multitude of uses, after losing half her tail the Paradise Female still caught as much prey as she needed to feed herself and her cubs, climbed effortlessly into the tallest of trees and conducted her affairs as ably as she had always done – at least as far as her human observers could tell.

Nobody to our knowledge saw the incident, but it gave the Paradise Female a wound so severe that it all but severed her tail in two, leaving more than half of it hanging limply by a scrap of fur which soon afterwards tore free. We speculated as to what might have happened. Had she been ambushed by a lion? If so she was lucky to survive with her life. Alternatively, a spotted hyena certainly has the jaws to crunch through a leopard's tail. More likely she had been involved in a catfight with another female leopard; it isn't only males who fight over territory.

But what about baboons? It might have been them. A large troop of olive baboons overlapped the core of the Paradise Female's territory, often roosting in the giant fig trees. Baboons are quick to chase a leopard in daytime and, if the cat is caught unawares or in the open, a frenzied mob-attack may ensue that occasionally ends with a dead leopard. I had seen Chui running for her life on more than one occasion, the Paradise Female too, saved only by their intimate knowledge of the caves along Fig Tree Ridge and Leopard Gorge.

Whatever caused the Paradise Female's injury, it only added to her unique status and character in the eyes of her human admirers. From that day on she became Half-Tail.

Wonderful as it was to have a leopard like Half-Tail to work with, she struggled to raise cubs just as Chui had done. Chui had had her first litter in November 1980 when she was almost three years old, the age at which leopards usually start breeding, but had failed to raise either of the cubs; it wasn't until she was five years old that I was able to watch her with Light and Dark. Nobody knew if Chui raised the three cubs that I had seen briefly at Leopard Gorge in late 1985, and who knows how long she lived after that – she was in her ninth year at that time and a wild leopard is old at ten to twelve years of age.

It is not uncommon for a mother leopard – or lion or cheetah, for that matter – to lose her first litter of cubs. It generally takes experience as well as innate cautiousness to become a successful mother, and the first few months of the cubs' life are the most crucial. There are so many things that can go wrong, so many dangers to consider, so many unexpected contingencies to face. Not surprisingly Half-Tail lost her first litter in May 1990, when she was about three years old. The cubs' father was killed not long after this by Masai herdsmen along the Ngorbop Lugga in reprisal for his mauling a herdboy who surprised the old male as he hunkered down in the belly of the lugga. The boy survived, but the leopard had broken the unwritten pact: 'Keep your head down, mind your business, don't take livestock and stay safely in the shadows.' The Masai came looking for him later that same day, armed with spears and simis, surrounding the place where the leopard was hiding. Eventually he was subdued, but not before he had inflicted damage on his adversaries. Mortally wounded, he was left to die; when rangers were dispatched the following morning to look for the wounded cat they could find no sign of him. The spotted hyenas would have been quick to tear him apart, dead or alive.

In November 1992 Half-Tail gave birth to three cubs, one of whom survived. A friend of ours, the German photographer Fritz Polking – a warm and generous man – named the little female Beauty. She was a delightful cub, bold and playful, amusing herself for hours at a time when Half-Tail went hunting, leaping into bushes, chasing lizards and butterflies, dabbling with pebbles and elephant droppings, gnawing on sticks and anything else she could find to incorporate into her games. Once Half-Tail felt confident enough to move Beauty from Fig Tree Ridge she took up residence for the next few months around a rocky hill bordering the Ngorbop Lugga in the eastern sector of her territory.

This is ideal leopard country. Leopards favour places that provide access to prey but within reach of cover – the edges or ecotones, as they are known.

Thomson's gazelles and impalas were in abundance on the surrounding grasslands and when they ventured within range of the thickets the ever-watchful Half-Tail was ready to pounce. The lugga itself, apart from being stunningly beautiful, provided shade for our leopards among the croton thickets and acacia bushes, as well as olive and euclea trees in which Half-Tail could stash her kills. It also proved to be a refuge from lions when they moved into the area: on more than one occasion we found Half-Tail and Beauty perched in the top of a tree with a pride of lions prowling around below, making life uncomfortable for them.

Angie and I spent many happy weeks photographing the leopards during the long rainy season in 1993 and, with Half-Tail showing a total lack of concern about all the safari vehicles that came to watch her, Beauty quickly learned that she too had nothing to fear from these noisy metal boxes that at times belched acrid clouds of grey exhaust fumes in her direction. When a visitor accidentally dropped a safari hat or a film box, Beauty delighted in destroying them, much to the horror or amusement of the human onlookers. For her part Half-Tail would sometimes use a vehicle as a blind to shield her approach from prey. Sadly, though, when Beauty became independent and started to carve out a territory of her own, she quickly lost her tolerance of vehicles, hissing and charging those that got too close. Before long she simply retreated from all the attention, merging back among the cover of the acacia thickets and rocky hillsides, moving only when she was sure she was alone and seeking the anonymity of darkness.

In November 1993, with Beauty barely a year old, Half-Tail gave birth again. One of the three cubs soon disappeared, leaving a male the drivers named Mang'aa and a female called Taratibu, which is Swahili for 'careful' or 'self-possessed'. Mang'aa was bold and powerful – his name means 'the one who does not care' – and he soon began to dominate his smaller sister when they played. The cubs prospered during much of their first year and we all thought that they would survive to adulthood. But it was not to be.

One day a lioness trapped Taratibu on the ground and mauled her to death. Half-Tail and her brother could only watch from the safety of some nearby bushes. When the lioness eventually moved away Half-Tail came and sniffed at Taratibu's broken, twisted body, her sodden fur pale against the flush of green that had erupted with the rains. Taratibu was one year old.

Mang'aa meanwhile grew into a strapping young male, a giant of a leopard with a wonderfully tolerant temperament that made him a favourite with the drivers. He roamed around the area of his birth until he was well into his third year, making the occasional forays into alien territory that are so characteristic of newly independent youngsters. Sometimes he met up with Half-Tail, but never for long. Friends at Kichwa Tembo told us that Mang'aa eventually established himself as the territory holder in the Mara Triangle, on the other side of the river, and that he 'performed' beautifully for visitors, walking nonchalantly along the edges of the acacia thickets or reclining on a convenient branch in one of his favourite trees and living up to his name for not having a care in the world.

Two years after Taratibu died, in early 1996, Half-Tail gave birth to two cubs, one of whom was lost almost immediately after they were first seen. The surviving cub was a female whom we named Zawadi, meaning 'gift' in Swahili. And what a gift she would prove to be. When *Big Cat Diary* was first commissioned later that year we knew we had a winning formula. Half-Tail and Zawadi were key to its success. Without a leopard like Half-Tail, whom we knew we could find almost every day, the series would never have been made. Not only are leopards the most difficult of big cats to find, they often do very little during the daytime. The exception to this is when a female has cubs that are old enough to have begun to emerge from their hidden birthplace and move around. By three to four months leopard cubs are irresistible to watch and as cute as they come. Add to this that their mother socialises with them on an almost daily basis and you have the most charismatic of all the big cats at their most active and visible.

One of the keys to the audience's engagement with our leopards was that they were so easy to identify as individuals. Contrast that with the Marsh Pride, where each lion – unless of course it bore some distinguishing impairment such as White Eye's blind eye – looked virtually identical to the untrained observer. Not only did Half-Tail distinguish herself in the way she looked, but with just one cub she and Zawadi made the perfect combo. And as individuals they oozed character. Who could forget the moment when Zawadi – not yet one year old – gave us a hint of her resolve when Half-Tail tried to take a freshly killed hare from her hyped-up daughter to prevent a hyena from stealing it from under her nose? Zawadi launched herself at her mother with the white-hot ferocity so characteristic of a leopard under threat. Mouth open and claws extended, she forced Half-Tail to rear up on her hind legs to defend herself and deflect the challenge. I think we realised then that Zawadi was going to leave her mark on all of us.

By the end of the first series of *Big Cat Diary* everyone was talking about Half-Tail and Zawadi, whom the production team decided to name Shadow to cater to an English-speaking audience – much to our irritation. At home in Nairobi, Angie and I had a Labrador called Shadow, a lovely creature who was part of the family and as domestic as they come. Zawadi, by contrast, was a wild leopard with an African name, free to live the life she had been so perfectly designed for. So to the drivers and guides – and to Angie and me – she would always be Zawadi.

Epilogue 2
Half-Tail's Legacy

WE ALL realised how lucky we had been to launch *Big Cat Diary* with Half-Tail and Zawadi in starring roles. Not a day dawned during that first series without our finding at least one of our leopards, often both. But finding a leopard isn't enough when you're making a TV programme: you need things to happen. The key to success in this instance was Zawadi. Her presence ensured that Half-Tail was more active than ever, making her easier to find.

But if we have learned anything about leopards it is that once you have found one you must never take your eyes off it – it can slip away in an instant. Angie will always remember the day I left her watching over Half-Tail, who was taking a catnap in one of her favourite trees along Fig Tree Ridge. I had to head back to camp for a few hours and wanted to be sure I could still find the leopard on my return. Later in the afternoon I arrived back to find Angie sitting at exactly the same spot, but with no sign of Half-Tail. As I gesticulated with more than a hint of irritation to ask what had happened, Angie smiled, put her finger up to her lips and pointed beneath the open film door of her vehicle. There, sound asleep and as good as gold, was our leopard, curled up in the shade cast by the door. At one point Half-Tail looked up at Angie with those liquid golden eyes tinged with green; there was no sign of fear or alarm – just an acknowledgement, perhaps, that all was well in her world.

When the BBC crew departed for England we continued to do what we had always done – record in words and pictures the lives of the big cats we had come to know so well. During the first few days of October 1997 Half-Tail gave birth to two cubs, her fifth litter. Angie and I were thrilled at the prospect of watching our old friend with young cubs again, particularly as she had chosen Leopard Gorge as their birthplace. We had recently begun filming with Paramount TV for a series called *Wild Things* at locations around the world and knew that a leopard with cubs would make the perfect story – especially a leopard named Half-Tail. Little did we realise just how dramatic and disturbing our time at Leopard Gorge would be.

When we arrived at the Gorge early on our first day of filming there was no sign of Half-Tail. Instead we found a freshly killed hyrax abandoned on the ground – and a young male leopard acting very suspiciously. He slunk around the rocky outcrop where we had been told Half-Tail had hidden her cubs, who by now were four weeks old. We watched with mounting concern as the male disappeared into a cave, quickly re-emerging with the body of a cub dangling limply from his mouth, fresh blood on its throat. He entered the cave a second time and again emerged with a dead cub in his mouth. Not a sound had been uttered.

We could not see if the male ate the cubs, but there was no question that he had killed them, an act of infanticide similar to what we had witnessed when new male lions take over a pride. Losing her cubs prompts a lioness to come back into season and mate with the newcomers, rather than spending up to two years raising young sired by the previous pride males. Infanticide is now known to be part of the normal cycle of change when younger, fitter males replace ageing ones. These incidents are not without danger for the lionesses, who will threaten or attack a male intent on killing their cubs; with males being so much larger and more powerful, the females are sometimes injured as well. This is part of a leopard's life too.

Later we spotted Half-Tail resting up in a tree a few hundred yards away and wondered if it was she who had killed the hyrax; she might then have hurriedly moved away when she saw this new young male, to avoid inadvertently revealing where she had hidden her cubs. When she returned to the hiding place some hours later the male chased her into the top of one of the giant fig trees. Half-Tail defended herself fiercely, causing the male to tumble backwards onto the rocks. She then pursued him, walking parallel to him and ushering him away, threatening to attack each time he turned towards her. But the damage had already been done.

By now Zawadi was hunting and killing adult gazelles for herself. By the time we began filming the second series of *Big Cat Diary* in 1998 she was two and a half years old and had grown into a beautiful young female, easily identifiable by the row of five identical spots under her right eye. The resolve she had displayed from a very young age meant that as she became fully independent and prepared to breed she gradually forced Half-Tail out of her core area. We were now far more likely to find Zawadi prowling around Fig Tree Ridge and Leopard Gorge, while her mother spent more of her time further north, closer to the Mara River. Zawadi was very active and always up to some kind of mischief, so we decided to make her the focus of our story for the new series – until we discovered that Half-Tail had given birth again in March, just a few months before we began filming.

We knew that Zawadi would soon have cubs of her own, but in the meantime we could enjoy spending time with Half-Tail, who was as calm and tolerant of vehicles as ever. We watched one afternoon as, alerted by the strident yelping of a pair of jackals, two lionesses tried to sneak up on her as she hunkered down over a freshly killed hare, carefully plucking mouthfuls of fur to reveal the tender meat. At times like this you are overcome with the tension, the heart-stopping rush of adrenalin as predators pit their wits against each other – not as potential prey but as competitors. One part of your brain is screaming, 'Don't just sit there and watch, do something,' while the other part says, 'Don't interfere, don't play God, take the shot.'

As these thoughts flashed through my mind Half-Tail suddenly sensed danger and caught the lionesses' stealthy movement out of the corner of her eye. With all her years of experience she had no doubt assessed the risks of feeding on the ground. She bolted up the nearest tree, her meal clasped safely in her mouth, ears back, pupils wildly dilated and as black as night.

A lucky escape perhaps? A dramatic moment for us to observe most certainly. But for Half-Tail nothing out of the ordinary. She would soon face a far more testing adversary.

Living beyond the boundary of the reserve meant that Half-Tail shared her domain with the Masai livestock owners who traditionally show little tolerance for predators. Half-Tail had survived her fair share of run-ins with humans. Once, in 1997, when she was being courted by a male, she or her mate had taken a sheep or a goat, incurring the wrath of the herdsman guarding them and prompting him to fire his bow at Half-Tail. This caused an arrowhead to lodge deep in the roof of her mouth, its sharp tip lacerating her tongue each time she closed her mouth. A vet was called in to treat her and she survived; but even after that incident she was not averse to taking the occasional stray sheep or goat that wandered within range. 'Incidental' killings like this are grudgingly accepted: the pastoralists know that, if one of their animals wanders off or gets lost, predators will soon find it. But woe betide the predator that breaks into a boma and steals.

Half-Tail was now nearly twelve years old and the signs of ageing were visible to us all. She rested for longer, was a step slower and bore that grizzled look you see with old lionesses, the grandmothers of the pride. Over the years Half-Tail had endeared herself to millions of viewers, becoming an almost mystical figure for drivers and guides alike. We all felt good whenever we managed to spend time with her. But to the Masai a leopard – any leopard – is 'the goat killer', a crafty pest so cunning that it can steal food from in front of your eyes and be gone without your even knowing it; not only a thief, but a hardened enemy. When Half-Tail, hungry and with two demanding cubs to feed, came across a temporary boma hurriedly constructed by herdsmen moving through her territory, she could not resist the chance of an easy kill. Emboldened by the smell of sheep and goats, she burrowed through the tangle of thorny branches, grabbed her quarry and was gone. But when she returned a day or so later the herdsmen were ready for her. They had concealed a wire snare where she had forced an entrance, attaching it to a weighty log to anchor the predator they sought to destroy.

I have seen enough snared animals in my time to know what a brutal, ugly death awaits them, their desperate attempts to struggle free only pulling the wire noose tighter and tighter around their neck, or body, or leg, biting deep into their flesh as they thrash about. There is no quick release when a predator is trapped like this. Freedom comes at a terrible cost, the result of gnawing through its own paw or leg bone, as leopards and hyenas have been known to do.

When word got around of Half-Tail's death, people were stunned. There was a sense of despondency. How could such a well-known and well-loved character end her days in such an ignominious and tragic fashion? Surely we could have prevented it?

We had to keep reminding ourselves that observing Half-Tail from the sanctity of a vehicle was very different from having Half-Tail come calling at night, determined to steal your property. As far as the herdsmen were concerned this leopard had broken the rules and paid the price. However, once the Masai community realised exactly *which* leopard had been killed, people were reticent about discussing the matter. Better to move on, they said. But Angie and I were desperate to know exactly what had happened. Masai friends confided to us what they knew, that it was outsiders, an unfortunate incident they would rather lay to rest.

Some people simply refused to believe that Half-Tail was dead. Rumours as to her whereabouts abounded for months afterwards: that she had crossed the river and was now living in the Mara Triangle; that one day she would reappear just as she always had done. But a leopard does not change its spots. We had seen no recent indications of Half-Tail's being forced to cede territory to another female, so why should she have moved? In the end we decided to film a *Big Cat Diary Update* that I presented, giving me the chance to reconstruct what we thought had happened – and why.

Some years later a friend added a twist to this tale. He had heard that Half-Tail had managed to chew through the wire snare only to accidentally hang herself later, when the wire dangling from her neck got caught up in the branches of a tree; her body had then been dumped in the river – presumably by someone wanting to cover up her fate. Even if this were true, it still left the question of what had happened to her two cubs, who would have been almost a year old at the time of her death. They had been seen around that time, with one of them coming into a campsite on the lookout for scraps of food. Without an occasional meal from their mother to sustain them as they learned their way around and gained experience, they would have found life very tough. But there are records of leopards surviving on their own from that age – and if ever there was a cat that might, it would be a leopard.

All our hopes now rested on Zawadi. She gave birth for the first time in Leopard Gorge in 1999, but her two cubs were killed by hyenas when they were barely two weeks old. Then sometime in September/October that same year Zawadi produced a second litter, a male and a female, this time choosing Fig Tree Ridge as their birthplace. As soon as the cubs were old enough to emerge from their hiding place Angie and I drove down to the Mara. It was the dawning of the new millennium and what better way to celebrate it than to see the sun emerge soft and pink as Zawadi and her cubs frolicked along the Ridge? Even at three months old the cubs were easy to tell apart, and not just because the male cub was larger than his sister. He was bolder, too, reminding us of Half-Tail's son Mang'aa, his uncle. Perhaps it was this boldness that cost him his life, for he was killed by lions when he was six months old. Though rather small and timid, his sister Safi (which means 'clean' or 'neat' in Swahili) was a delightful cub to spend time with.

By the time we started filming the third series of *Big Cat Diary* in 2000, Safi's father had been expelled from his territory by an aggressive newcomer with a distinctive drooping lower jaw. Even though Safi was almost a year old and nearly two-thirds the size of her mother, Zawadi was taking no chances when Droopy Jaw tracked them down. An aggressive leopard is a terrifying adversary and Zawadi put on a display of such unbridled determination and ferocity that she forced the male to back off, repeatedly attacking him and giving Safi time to hide. Despite this success, Zawadi was so unsettled by the arrival of this new male that she moved out of the area and it proved impossible to find her over the next two weeks, reminding our audience that this was a real-life soap opera and that anything could happen.

One thing that Angie and I can be certain of is the date when Zawadi produced her third litter. On the afternoon of 28 September 2001, Shieni Ropiara, head driver at Kichwa Tembo Camp and an old friend of ours, was heading for Leopard Gorge in the hope of finding Zawadi, who was known to be in the area and heavily pregnant. Neither he nor his visitors could believe their good fortune when they not only quickly located her among the rocks at the east end of the Gorge, but witnessed her giving birth at the entrance to one of the caves. The two cubs were born within the space of twenty minutes as Shieni and his guests looked on in amazement. Zawadi carefully freed each cub from its birth sac and licked it clean before disappearing from view. Though she remained in the area for the next few weeks, neither cub survived. A few months later she was seen mating in the Gorge but failed to conceive.

Imagine then our delight when, the following August, Zawadi gave birth to her fourth litter just a few weeks before filming commenced. Angie and I were almost beside ourselves with joy. Over the years we had watched nearly every major transition in a leopard's development, so to be blessed with the opportunity of watching a mother leopard with three one-month-old cubs in as scenic a location as Leopard Gorge was more than we could have hoped for.

However, our delight was tempered by the realisation that the Gorge was proving to be something of a graveyard for Zawadi's cubs. Like Chui before her, Zawadi had been born and raised in the Fig Tree Ridge and Leopard Gorge area and it evidently had a reassuring familiarity: she knew every secret inch of it. Lions and leopards both often favour the place they were born as their den site and nursery – even, it seems, when times have changed. Though Leopard Gorge has everything a mother leopard could wish for in terms of trees and caves and cover – and prey – in recent years a clan of hyenas had taken up permanent residence among the labyrinth of deep caves and cool earthy dens. With their acute senses of smell and hearing, nothing of significance happened in the area that the hyenas did not soon come to know about. And for the leopards there was the constant threat posed by lions, too. In the old days the presence of the Masai, with the spears and poison they used to protect their livestock, had kept lion and hyena numbers in check, making the Gorge a safer place for a mother leopard. But with the

Masai now encouraged to share their land with tourism partners there was greater emphasis on conservation-friendly practices.

I would lie awake at night in camp chatting with Angie about our good fortune. Would we finally have the chance to photograph a mother leopard carrying small cubs in her mouth, for instance? And watching Zawadi with three cubs at play would be something really special. But though we were indeed blessed with the perfect filming scenario, it wasn't long before the hyenas found Zawadi's hiding place: they killed two of the cubs when they were barely four weeks old. Zawadi did herself no favours when she hung a freshly killed Thomson's gazelle in a tree almost directly opposite the place where she had hidden her cubs. The incident attracted virtually every hyena for miles around. We were heartbroken to witness just how difficult it was proving for Zawadi to raise cubs in this area, forcing her to carry her sole surviving cub four miles to the northernmost limit of her territory, a low hilltop known as Moses Rock, overlooking Serian Camp. When a bush fire swept through we feared for the cub's safety and, though it survived that incident, it disappeared shortly afterwards when barely six weeks old. Towards the end of 2003 Zawadi is thought to have given birth again and we were told that a male cub survived from this fifth litter.

With so many spotters on the lookout for our cats there were some intriguing discoveries during filming, such as in October 2002 when we were able to photograph and then identify the male leopard who had killed Half-Tail's cubs in Leopard Gorge in 1997. He had gone on to establish himself as the territory holder around the Olare Orok Lugga and mated with Zawadi's daughter Safi when she was three years old. Now in his eighth year he was a huge ginger tom with the massive dog-like muzzle and jowly dewlap beneath his throat that is the hallmark of the older and largest leopards.

When filming *Big Cat Diary* we had always known that at some point our luck in consistently finding leopards would run out. What would we do if that happened? The luxury of having three different big cats to focus on had always meant we could cut away to another story if one of our stars was lying low during filming. Fortunately for us, and the leopards, times had changed since I first arrived in the Mara. The trade in fur coats as fashion items had eased, thanks in no small part to some innovative and hard-hitting advertisements that underlined what a brutal, bloody and obscene business this was – and still is in parts of the world. Trophy hunting had been banned in Kenya in 1977 and has never re-opened; by now leopards were not being poached in the Mara. So apart from the occasional incidents when a leopard was killed after taking livestock, its biggest concern was competing with the large lion and hyena populations, and, for females, avoiding infanticide. That meant finding sufficient cover to raise cubs and stay hidden. However, the Mara's spotted plains have become more open, the acacia woodlands and croton thickets pared back by the burgeoning elephant population, dry-season fires and the attrition of hundreds of thousands of wildebeest and zebras that keep the regrowth of bush and forest at bay.

Such cyclical changes in the balance between grass and woodlands are to be expected. But for the moment competition with larger predators *and* the reduction in cover means fewer leopards. On the positive side more leopards are tolerant of vehicles than in the old days, due to the massive rise in visitor numbers. Given time and blessed with the right temperament leopards can become almost as habituated to vehicles as lions, as Half-Tail and Zawadi so elegantly bore witness. Outside the reserve and protected areas – and throughout Africa – it is a different story. The leopard faces growing pressure from man's hunger for land. Not just the leopard – all big cats.

With Half-Tail gone and fewer people following Zawadi (Mara River Camp had closed), we had to think about other options. Over the course of the previous two years the drivers and guides had often been heard talking about a female leopard that frequented the area around Mara Intrepids Camp. Intrepids is situated along the Talek River, the main tributary running into the Mara from the east. The Talek has always been considered prime leopard territory, a beautiful ribbon of country snaking its way west across the plains with the Olare Orok joining it from the north. The river is steep-sided in places, fringed with sandbanks and massive fig trees arching upwards to the sky. The architecture of the Talek allows a leopard to feel unthreatened and relaxed, sometimes providing visitors with an encounter they will never forget. To meet a leopard picking a path through the shallows, leaping from rock to rock with athletic ease rather than get its feet wet, is the photographic opportunity everyone is hoping for. Better still a mother leopard with young cubs scampering along beside her.

In the summer of 2000 when we were struggling to find Zawadi and Safi we briefly filmed a mother leopard with a female cub in a fig tree along the Talek River. This was Bella and her daughter Olive, the same leopards the drivers had told us about. Although we did not film them in 2002 thanks to Zawadi having young cubs at Leopard Gorge, from that time onwards Angie and I made a point of keeping track of what was happening in Bella and Olive's lives, thanks in no small part to our friend Paul Kirui,who was based at Intrepids Camp for many years. Paul is an outstanding naturalist and one of only a handful of guides rated 'gold' by the Kenya Professional Guides Association. He is also as obsessed by leopards as we are.

2003 was a year to remember. *Big Cat Diary* had developed such a worldwide following that the controllers and commissioners at the BBC decided that the show was ready for prime time on their flagship 'entertainment' channel, BBC1. Before this, apart from our opening season, we had always occupied a 'family' slot on a Sunday afternoon on BBC2, the channel for more serious and niche content. Now instead of going out once a week the programme would be shown on five consecutive evenings and re-branded as *Big Cat Week*.

A couple of years earlier, Angie and I had been commissioned to write and illustrate a series of three books, one on each of the big cats. We had completed *Lion* and *Leopard* and now needed to focus on cheetahs. Angie was one of our cheetah spotters as well as the stills photographer for *Big Cat Week*, so she was ideally placed to gather material for the new book. In the early series of *Big Cat Diary* I had always presented the lions' and leopards' stories, but now I asked to be 'transferred' to cheetahs. We concentrated on a female called Kike, who became the quintessential 'cat on a hot tin roof' thanks to her love of climbing onto safari vehicles. The fact that she also took the opportunity to poo and pee through my open roof hatch from her aerial perch – mimicking a cheetah's normal scent-marking behaviour when perched on a termite mound – meant that my claim to fame would forever centre around my being 'the bloke the cheetah crapped on'.

Meanwhile, Angie and I attempted to keep track of Zawadi through our network of friends among the drivers and guides, but for much of the rainy season we were thwarted by the shroud of long red oat grass blanketing the rocky hillsides and waterlogged plains and luggas in the northern Mara. News of Zawadi was always a bonus, but the golden era symbolised by our success filming her and her mother was drawing to a close.

As the time approached to begin filming *Big Cat Week* we were buoyed by the knowledge that all three of our big cats had cubs. But would they survive long enough for us to film them? The Marsh Pride was enjoying a boom period with more than a dozen cubs – twenty-nine lions in total. Pride male Simba's companion had been killed earlier in the year in a deadly encounter with a buffalo. This made the Marsh Lions vulnerable to a takeover by new males, with plenty of potential for the kind of 'jeopardy' that our producers and audience loved. Kike the cheetah and her three nine-month-old cubs were set to grab the limelight from their more dangerous cousins, but it looked as if they would be pushed for top billing by Bella, whose two three-month-old-cubs were old enough to follow their mother and up to all kinds of mischief. Both leopard cubs survived this period, but a few months after we finished filming the female known as Ntito disappeared, leaving her brother, Chui, to star with Bella in *Big Cat Week* 2004 and 2005.

Although filming *Big Cat Diary* dominated our lives between 1996 and 2008, Angie and I continued to track our favourite cats year in year out. Even when we were not able to be in the Mara ourselves we made sure to keep our journals up to date and it was always a big day when we heard word of Zawadi. Her territory extended to the west of Fig Tree Ridge and she could sometimes be found along the tree-lined lugga draining towards the windmill that pipes water from a perennial spring to Musiara Entrance Gate. Where the Windmill Lugga peters out, patches of croton bush erupt from a rocky rise, the perfect lookout point and hiding place for a leopard seeking to avoid lions – if the lions were not already resting up there.

Around December 2005 Zawadi gave birth to a sixth litter, and the following March the photographer Federico Veronesi found the partially eaten remains of one of the two cubs hanging in a tree. There was no doubt that whoever had fed on the cub was a leopard. Had the cub been killed in an act of infanticide by a male leopard – or had it been lions? Hyenas would have devoured the cub on the spot, but lions would have abandoned it after killing it, so perhaps Zawadi had then found it and carried it into the tree to eat. Macabre as this may seem to us, there is no room for sentimentality or waste in nature.

Two months later, Zawadi was seen again on the rocky escarpment to the north of the windmill; she had a Grant's gazelle kill and was accompanied by a six-month-old cub. That cub – a female – survived to maturity and in June 2007 Zawadi gave birth to her seventh litter, which Federico photographed along the Windmill Lugga. The female cub from this litter is also thought to have survived to maturity.

In February 2009 Federico photographed the two cubs of Zawadi's eighth litter – they had been born about the previous October – along Fig Tree Ridge, noting that one was much shyer than the other. People tell us that a female survived from this litter too.

During this period Angie and I spent very little time beyond the Reserve boundary, focusing instead on the Marsh Pride. But that didn't prevent us and other concerned parties from fighting tooth and nail to stop a lodge being built on top of Fig Tree Ridge – prime leopard breeding habitat – right next to the two magnificent fig trees that are such a feature of the area. Piles of stones, concrete plinths and half-finished outhouses are still in evidence, but for the moment at least the development has been abandoned.

In January 2009 Fig Tree Ridge and Leopard Gorge became part of the Mara North Conservancy (MNC), a beautiful wilderness area of more than 120 square miles. The conservancy was established as a not-for-profit company initiated by the Masai community and their tourism partners, with eleven tented camps leasing land from over 800 stakeholders, helping to ensure that the landowners receive substantial and direct income from the wildlife on their land. Mara North is just one of a growing number of wildlife conservancies bordering the Reserve with the aim of encouraging low-volume, high-revenue-yielding tourism while protecting wildlife, local communities and their shared environment. Vehicles from camps and lodges situated outside MNC are no longer allowed to game-drive here. Fortunately, due to our long association and promotion of the area, Angie and I have been granted access to the MNC so that we can continue our work.

In October 2009 Zawadi produced her ninth litter. One of the two cubs, a male, survived and I saw mother and son together near Moses Rock a year later. It was wonderful to see our old friend again. At one point during the morning she left her cub to explore on his own, moving towards my vehicle through a clump of long grass bordering a salt lick favoured by the Masai. She paused to sniff and scent-mark, and then later killed a dik-dik. We could tell by her son's self-possessed behaviour that he would soon be old enough to start wandering further afield and in mid-July 2011 Zawadi was seen mating. She did not conceive, but she mated again a month later and by the time she was seen in September around Leopard Gorge she was visibly pregnant.

Angie and I had always longed to spend some quality time with Zawadi again. She seemed almost ageless down the years, clinging on to Fig Tree Ridge and Leopard Gorge at the heart of her territory. When we heard she had given birth to two cubs in October 2011 we were overjoyed.

Like her mother Half-Tail, Zawadi had struggled to raise cubs and it is interesting to contrast the breeding success of these two females with that of Bella and Olive, who lived within the protection of the Reserve with little chance of falling foul of pastoralists. Also, although there is no shortage of lions in the Talek area and there were plenty of times when Bella and Olive had to seek refuge in trees to escape their attentions, there are fewer hyenas than in Leopard Gorge. Bella was at least twelve years old when she died in late 2008 or early 2009, having raised one male and two female cubs to maturity: Chui, Olive and a daughter known as Pili who has raised three cubs of her own. This is similar in terms of lifespan and breeding success to Half-Tail, with both females probably raising around 20 per cent of their cubs. Interestingly, though cubs are born at any time of the year, Half-Tail and Zawadi gave birth most frequently around the time of the short rains, which normally begin in October. At this time impalas and many other prey species also have their young.

Olive, on the other hand, has raised the remarkable number of seven cubs to maturity from five litters, according to records kept by Paul Kirui since

Olive was six years old (she must have given birth to cubs prior to this that were lost). So what set her apart from Bella? After all, Olive overlapped her mother's territory and in time came to dominate the core area Bella had once claimed. Was it simply individual differences in mothering skills? We know from watching other leopards that some of them are more careful and wary, more cautious about moving their cubs in the first few weeks and months, a critical time when cubs can easily be killed. Some make better decisions under pressure from lions, hyenas, baboons and aggressive buffaloes, or perhaps are better at avoiding trouble in the first place.

Olive was rigorous about keeping her cubs hidden during the first two to three months, preferring to tuck them away among the roots and earth caves at the base of the giant figs bordering the Talek River. When she did move with them she was vigilant in checking ahead before setting off and in being mindful of the nearest escape route if challenged. She was clever, crafty and wise. We watched as she raised her twin daughters Binti and Ayah, who were as different in temperament as any two cats could be: Ayah nervous and retiring, content to stay in the shadows, while Binti was outgoing, playful and a joy to watch.

A year later Olive gave birth again. One cub survived – a mischievous young male called Kali who became so bold that on one occasion he even jumped on to the bonnet of a safari wagon! He would saunter alongside the vehicles and peer up at the human occupants, then hiss out a warning if someone moved suddenly or spoke loudly. Next came a litter of two males, Paja and Nkaiyoni, who both gave us hours of wonderful game-viewing. They could sometimes be found with their mother and her next litter, feeding from a kill that Olive had made or attempting to play with their two younger siblings. Olive stage-managed this with great authority – just as she had when Kali and his older sisters came together, in the same way that Half-Tail had sometimes tolerated contact between her year-old daughter Beauty and the younger Mang'aa and Taratibu. One of the new arrivals survived – a little female called Bahati, who has the bluest green eyes that sparkle like precious stones in the fading light.

The profusion of prey in Olive's range reduced the pressure on her to continue to find food for her growing offspring – they were better able to fend for themselves than they would have been in a less well-provided area – and meant that she could produce another litter more quickly than average without seemingly compromising the survival chances of her previous litter. Compressing the birth interval in this way increased the number of offspring she could raise in her lifetime. As we write, Olive is thirteen years old and accompanied by another young daughter, Saba, who is almost independent; apart from a broken lower canine and a distinctive nick in her left ear she looks in robust health. Through a combination of caution and experience – and an abundance of natural prey – Olive has proved more than a match for the lions and hyenas.

Sitting in our vehicle up on the rim of Leopard Gorge waiting for Zawadi to appear felt like theatre. It was as if we had come to witness some memorable epic, and in our minds we had. This was the ultimate game-watching experience: a mother leopard with a young cub. In the most graphic and painterly manner Leopard Gorge has always represented a truly wild place – somewhere so mysterious to the human mind that in the dead of night it belongs to another, more ancient world. The Gorge is so well concealed from the surrounding countryside that it doesn't reveal its existence until you are almost on top of it. It is as if an artist had summoned you to a viewing and only when he was sure that the whole world's eyes were on him would he whisk away the cloth to reveal his masterpiece.

There was a poignancy to watching Zawadi, now visibly weary and gradually losing condition, that allowed us the joy of reflection. She reminded us of all the times we had been privileged to share a window into her world. Not only was she a beautiful creature and sublime predator – the quintessential cat – she represented the wonder of nature. At times it seemed as if it were all she could do to stay awake, in marked contrast to her four-month-old cub Malaika, who exploded in a frenzy of pent-up energy whenever her mother returned to the Gorge. Angie and I both knew that it would take a miracle for Zawadi to live long enough to raise her daughter and indeed, after we had spent a memorable few days with our two leopards, they disappeared. They were seen one more time by game rangers along Fig Tree Ridge, but shortly after that Malaika vanished, with hyenas the most likely culprits. Over the next few months we continued to enquire about Zawadi, but it soon became apparent that she too had finally disappeared.

Zawadi was in her seventeenth year and had raised possibly six cubs to independence (two males and four females) from ten litters when she finally died. The only wild female leopard known to have lived longer than this was eighteen and a half years old and resident at Londolozi Private Game Reserve, bordering the Kruger National Park in South Africa.

Nature knows no pity and watching wild creatures such as these from birth to death creates a sense of reverence for all life. The wonder is that as one life story comes to an end there is always a new one beginning. Today there is another young female staking a claim to Leopard Gorge, bringing joy and amazement to those fortunate enough to see her. Another Chui or Half-Tail in the making perhaps, maybe even another Zawadi. Some people say it is her daughter, born in October 2008. But that is another story.

Authors' and Photographers' Note

The Leopard's Tale is based on personal observations and the information generously provided to me by rangers, drivers, couriers and camp managers, which often enabled me to know what was happening in two or three different locations at the same time. Events occurring during the night could sometimes be deduced from daytime evidence, though remained a question of speculation on my part. In recounting the two major incidents involving leopards and vehicles I have endeavoured to be as accurate as possible, relying on accounts of some of the people involved.

The excellent leopard studies conducted by Patrick Hamilton in Kenya and Brian Bertram and George Schaller in Tanzania have shed considerable light on certain aspects of leopard behaviour. The approachability of the Mara leopards in the early 1980s provided me with a unique opportunity to observe the development of these cats during their first year of life. Though I could not be certain of the age of Chui's cubs, I hope my estimates are within a month of the correct figure. There were many times each day when the cubs suckled, played or did nothing at all – aspects of their behaviour that could not be referred to on each page of text, but that should not be overshadowed by the more dramatic moments (which were usually all too brief!).

I never intended to be a photographer. My passion was always watching wild animals – particularly when it came to the big cats, and even more particularly when it came to leopards. Initially I was taking photographs as a way of providing myself with a source of reference for my pen-and-ink drawings; later I was just taking snapshots of interesting behaviour and when I was working with Chui and her cubs I was far more concerned with recording their lives in words than with trying to get ever closer for a better photograph. To have manoeuvred the vehicle continually for photographic reasons would have disturbed the leopards and in the end probably yielded less information and fewer pictures. The use of telephoto lenses helped partially to solve the conflict of interests. When the leopards hunted I followed their progress through binoculars. To have tried to establish a suitable photographic position would undoubtedly have had an adverse effect on their efforts.

I can count virtually on the fingers of one hand the usable leopard pictures that I managed to accumulate between 1976 and 1982. Unfortunately the action-filled incidents involving the leopards with baboons, hyenas and lions invariably occurred in extremely poor light, when it was raining, at dawn or dusk, or at distances that made photography impossible – but then that is the way with leopards. Ironically a 'good' leopard photograph is often something of a misrepresentation: a leopard caught in the open or revealed on a leafless branch in perfect light may look marvellous through the viewfinder, but does it give a true impression of the leopard's world? I suspect that the trunkful of reject slides that I collected over the years may be closer to the truth – a world full of shadows and partially obscured images.

Meeting Angie enabled me to grow as a photographer. She has loved photography since she was a child and challenged me to see in a more imaginative way.

Over the years our good friends Mitsuaki Iwago and Yann Arthus-Bertrand have also encouraged us to be more adventurous. But my greatest inspiration when it came to watching predators and understanding light was Hugo van Lawick. While I was playing it safe in the Mara, photographing with the sun over my shoulder, Hugo was in the Serengeti and in Ngorongoro Crater in Tanzania, using sidelight and backlight to create atmosphere and emotion, something that Iwago took to another level. I remember looking at Hugo's leopard shots and wishing I could just *see* what he had managed to photograph, let alone capture the moment on film.

No surprise, then, that Angie embraced digital photography years before I did. She processes our images and organises our workflow – an unenviable task – but we have forged a true partnership in life and as photographers. We encourage each other, constantly talking about what we are seeing, priming each other as to the next best move, with Angie using the big lenses while I cover the wider view. Photography has become a way of life for us both, the way we see the world and share it with others.

When I travelled overland through Africa in 1974 I agonised over what camera to buy, settling on the Canon EF Shutter Priority body – it was built like a tank and needed to be, the way I treated it. But that left me virtually penniless when I went to buy the 80–250mm zoom lens I needed to record my adventures. That first zoom lens proved pretty average as far as sharpness and colour balance were concerned. Worse still, it didn't sync automatically with my camera – needless to say it wasn't a Canon lens. When I got to Nairobi, my travels almost completed, I found to my horror that the lens had remained stopped down to the minimum aperture, allowing virtually no light to reach the film. There were a handful of successful shots taken in the Sahara where daylight was abundant, but the rest were blank. Ouch! Solution: test any new equipment before you set out on the safari of a lifetime, read the camera manual and carry it with you.

Top tip? Invest in the best lenses you can afford. Sell the car if you have to; just find the money for that Canon EF 500mm or 600mm f/4 Series 11 image-stabilised telephoto lens if you want to be a wildlife photographer. But before you do that, spend a year with a Canon Powershot 1GX or G15 looped on your belt so you can learn to see the shot and react fast enough to capture it. Familiarise yourself with the camera settings. Know what speeds to set to stop the action or to blur it in a more creative manner. Shoot with the camera low to the ground for impact or hold it over your head to give you a bird's-eye view of your subject. Use the slow-sync flash to best advantage – and explore the light. That way you'll capture moments others will have missed as they struggle to get their cameras out of their rucksacks. Think ahead. Start visualising the shots you want to take – look around you and see the possibilities; don't just react to what is in front of you. For wildlife, spend time studying your subject: learn its behaviour until you're able to predict where to be before 'the decisive moment' happens.

We use Canon EOS-ID X, 1D Mk IV and 5D Mk 111 camera bodies. The EOS-ID X and 1D Mk IV offer faster burst rates – up to ten to fourteen frames a second – which are crucial for wildlife action photography. They also have the latest autofocus technology, making it easier to track moving subjects. Our favourite Canon lenses are the EF 8–15mm f/4L Fisheye, EF 16–35mm f/2.8L 11 USM, EF 24–105mm f/4L IS USM, EF 70–200mm f/2.8L IS 11, EF 200mm f/2L IS USM, EF 500mm f/4L IS 11 and the EF 800mm f/ 5.6L IS USM. Crucially all the new telephoto lenses are sharper, significantly lighter, have the latest IS systems and are generally more user-friendly than anything that has gone before. We eagerly await Canon's new EF 200–400mm f/4L IS USM with built-in x1.4 Extender – the ultimate wildlife and travel lens.

Remember to buy skylight or UV filters to protect the front elements of your lenses (don't skimp on the expense, as this could affect the image quality of your lens) and a polarising filter to increase saturation and reduce unwanted reflections for landscapes. Angie uses a graduated filter to help balance the exposure of foreground and background, something that can also be achieved by employing high dynamic range. We sometimes use fill flash, but generally prefer to work with natural light. Digital photography has made a huge difference in this respect, as you can bump up your ISO setting to make your camera more sensitive to light. Downside? It may make the image 'noisier' – the equivalent of grain with film – something that Canon is working hard to eliminate.

Buy the best CompactFlash memory cards on which to capture your images. We are part of the SanDisk Extreme Team, and SanDisk products lead the field in terms of reliability and download speed. They produce 8GB, 16GB and 32GB cards ideal for capturing still and video images with your cameras, and their Extreme Pro range, featuring 64GB and 128GB cards, ensures the quickest burst modes and finest HD video capture.

And if you want the best chance of finding big cats and enjoying the Mara's amazing diversity of birdlife, invest in a good pair of binoculars. Swarovski are our choice here – they are outstanding optically, focus close up, feel great in the hand and are lightweight. Pick of the range for big-cat work is the EL Swarovision 10x32. And for economy *and* sharpness try the CL 8x30 or 10x30 models.

The pen and ink drawings in the book are a reminder to me that selling my artwork provided me with a good living in those early days. I soon started working with printers in Kenya to produce limited editions. The income enabled me to buy my first Toyota Landcruiser and invest in Canon camera equipment and Kodachrome 64 film. In time Angie and I worked together on the drawings and have written and illustrated twenty-six books to date, including a number of titles in the award-winning children's collection, *Collins Big Cat*, and our recently revised *Jonathan and Angela Scott's Safari Guides to East African Animals* and *Birds*.

Jonathan and Angela Scott
Nairobi, Kenya
February 2013

Acknowledgements

MANY PEOPLE have been most generous with their time and assistance, providing hospitality and information in the course of preparing this new edition of *The Leopard's Tale*. Their generosity goes back many years and in this respect we would particularly like to thank: our children Alia and David, who have enriched our lives beyond words and who continue to share many wonderful times with us in the Mara; Carole Wyman, for her many acts of kindness to our family; Jock Anderson of East African Wildlife Safaris, a dear friend who first gave Jonathan the chance to live in the Mara at Mara River Camp; Jeff and Jorie Kent of Abercrombie and Kent, who owned Kichwa Tembo where Jonathan lived from 1982 to 1992; the Grammaticus family at Governors' Camp, for their long-standing support and for providing us with a permanent base in the Mara, and Patrick Beresford and his staff at the workshop for keeping our vehicles on the road; Jonathan's good friend Boris Tisminieszky, for pointing him in the right direction when he first came to Kenya; the Block family, who encouraged Jonathan to pursue his love of illustration and wildlife; the memory of Colonel T. S. Conner, who provided Jonathan with a base in Nairobi for many years. And to Jonathan's sister Caroline, brother Clive and his wife Judith, niece Julie and her husband Tony, nephew Mark and his wife Navita, and to Angie's brother David and his wife Mishi, Bill and Bridget Biddell, Clive and Sarah Webster and all Angie's cousins at Hampton Estate in Surrey – our heartfelt thanks for all you do for us.

Special thanks to the Senior Game Wardens in the Mara, who have been generous and supportive of our work over many years, especially James Sindiyo, Stephen Minis and Michael Koikai from Narok County Council, and David Seur, Brian Heath and Jonny Baxendale from the Mara Triangle. Brian Heath and Stephano Chelli made it possible for us to spend time in the Mara North Conservancy, a breath-taking stretch of country beyond the reserve boundary, where Chui, her mother the Mara Buffalo Female and Half-Tail and Zawadi lived. Our thanks also to Warden Benson Ketere, Conservation Manager Marc Goss and Game Rangers Robert Yiaile, Duncan Noosaron, Dennis Tinka, Evans Kamoria and Joshua Odupoi for their help and hospitality.

Over the years we have had the good fortune to be able to call on the expertise of one of the world's most knowledgeable big cat specialists, Dr Luke Hunter, President of the *Panthera* Fund. Luke has always been immensely generous with his time and advice. For this new edition he shared his writing on the leopard for *Mammals of Africa*, which at the time was eagerly awaited but had not yet been published. He also provided us with a copy of a paper he and his colleagues had compiled, collating information on forty-four breeding females observed over thirty-two years at Londolozi Private Game Reserve, bordering the Kruger National Park in South Africa. Details can be found in the Bibliography.

We would particularly like to thank Adrian Phillips of Bradt Travel Guides, who believed that an updated edition of this book – and *The Marsh Lions* before it – would appeal to a new generation of readers thirty years after they first appeared. Caroline Taggart, who also worked on the original publication, was as masterly as ever in her editing and organisational skills, and Brian Jackman cast an eagle eye over the original text thirty years ago, providing much needed encouragement to Jonathan as a fledgling author. Our agent Jonny Pegg gave invaluable guidance; Lee Dalton at NHPA/ Photoshot was generous with his time whenever we needed to access our wildlife images, as was Katie Simmonds, who has helped transform the Canon Ambassadors Programme; and José Puy willingly shared with us his encyclopedic knowledge of the Mara's big cats. Over the years it would have been impossible to keep track of the lives of the cats we were following without the support of the drivers and guides at Governors' Camp, Mara

River Camp, Mara Buffalo Camp, Rekero, Mara Intrepids, Kicheche and Kichwa Tembo. In particular naturalist guides Paul Kirui, Ian Johnson, Warren Samuels, Jackson Ole Looseyia, Stephen Mutua, Simon Sitienei, Samuel Kiplangat, Isack Langat, Moses Manduku, Solomon Kenduiywo, Samuel Ruto, Japhet Kivango and the photographers Federico Veronesi and Michel Denis-Huot were generous in providing us with information on events that we were unable to witness first hand.

Finally, the world owes a huge debt to countries such as Kenya, where so many wild animals still roam free. Providing sanctuary for wildlife when local people are struggling simply to meet their basic needs is a formidable challenge. The continued existence of places like the Masai Mara and the adjoining Wildlife Conservancies in today's world is nothing short of a miracle. But it comes at a price, which is why all of us must play our part in helping to ensure their future in whatever way we can.

Bibliography

I WAS FORTUNATE in being able to draw on the wealth of information currently available on the behaviour and ecology of African animals. Though I have not cited individual references in the text I found the works of the following scientists and authors invaluable in preparing *The Leopard's Tale* – all of whom remain blameless for any inaccuracies or simplifications that I may have made in interpreting their work.

Adamson, J. (1980) *Queen of Shaba: The Story of an African Leopard* (Collins, London)

Altmann, S. A. and Altmann, J. (1970) *Baboon Ecology* (Univ. of Chicago Press, Chicago)

Balme, G. *et al.* (2012) *Reproductive success of female leopards* Panthera pardus*: the importance of top-down processes* (Mammal Society/Blackwell Publishing)

Bertram, B. C. R. (1978) *Pride of Lions* (J. M. Dent, London)

Burney, D. A. (1980) *The effect of human activities on cheetahs (*Acinonyx jubatus Shreber*) in the Mara region of Kenya.* M.Sc. thesis, Univ. of Nairobi

Eaton, R. L. (1976) *The status and conservation of the leopard in sub-Saharan Africa.* Carnivora Research Institute, Univ. of Washington and Safari Club International

Ewer, R. F. (1973) *The Carnivores* (Weidenfeld and Nicolson, London)

Guggisberg, C. A. W. (1975) *Wild Cats of the World* (David and Charles, Newton Abbot)

Haltenorth, T. and Diller, H. (1980) *A Field Guide to the Mammals of Africa including Madagascar* (Collins, London)

Hamilton, P. H. (1976) *The movements of leopards in Tsavo National Park, Kenya, as determined by radio-tracking.* M.Sc. thesis, Univ. of Nairobi

Hamilton, P. H. (1981) *The Leopard* Panthera pardus *and The Cheetah*

Acinonyx jubatus *in Kenya: ecology, status, conservation, management.* Report for the U.S. Fish and Wildlife Service, the African Wildlife Leadership Foundation and the Government of Kenya

Kingdon, J. (1977) *East African Mammals. An Atlas of Evolution in Africa. Vol. III A. (Carnivores).* (Academic Press Inc, London)

Kingdon, J. *et al.* (2013) *Mammals of Africa* (Vols 1–6). Vol 5*: Leopard* by Hunter, L., et al.

Kruuk, H. (1972) *The Spotted Hyena: a study of predation and social behaviour* (Univ. of Chicago Press, Chicago)

Leyhausen, P. (1979) *Cat Behaviour: the predatory and social behaviour of domestic and wild cats* (Garland STPM, New York)

Moss, C. (1976) *Portraits in the Wild* (Hamish Hamilton, London)

Myers, N. (1976) *Status of the leopard and cheetah in Africa.* The World's Cats, Vol.3(1): 53-69

Myers, N. (1976) *The leopard* Panthera pardus *in Africa.* IUCN Monograph No. 5. Morges

Reader, J. and Croze, H. (1977) *Pyramids of Life* (Collins, London)

Schaller, G. B. (1967) *The Deer and the Tiger: a study of wildlife in India* (Univ. of Chicago Press, Chicago)

Schaller, G. B. (1972) *The Serengeti Lion: a study of predator-prey relations* (Univ. of Chicago Press, Chicago)

Sinclair, A. R. E. and Norton-Griffiths, M. (eds.) (1979) *Serengeti: Dynamics of an Ecosystem* (Univ. of Chicago Press, Chicago)

Singh, A. (1982) *Prince of Cats* (Jonathan Cape, London)

Smithers, R. H. N. (1983) *The Mammals of the Southern African Subregion* (Univ. of Pretoria, Pretoria)

Tabor, R. (1983) *The Wildlife of the Domestic Cat* (Arrow Books)

Turnbull-Kemp, P. (1967) *The Leopard* (Howard Timmins, Cape Town)

Wilson, E. O. (1975) *Sociobiology: the new synthesis* (Harvard Univ. Press, Cambridge, Massachusetts)